THE LIVING WORD COMMENTARY

Editor
Everett Ferguson

The Letters of Paul to
The Ephesians, the Colossians,
and Philemon

The Letters of Paul to the Ephesians, the Colossians, and Philemon

Michael R. Weed

πᾶσα γραφὴ
θεόπνευστος

SWEET PUBLISHING COMPANY

Austin, Texas

LIBRARY OF CONGRESS CATALOG CARD NUMBER: 79-134688

STANDARD BOOK NUMBER: 8344-0055-3

PRINTED IN U.S.A.

Acknowledgment

This commentary is based on the text of the Revised Standard Version of the Bible, copyrighted 1946 and 1952 by the Division of Christian Education, National Council of Churches, and used by permission.

Writers in *The Living Word Commentary* series have been given freedom to develop their own understanding of the biblical text. As long as a fair statement is given to alternative interpretations, each writer has been permitted to state his own conclusions. Beyond the general editorial policies, the editors have sought no artificial uniformity, and differences are allowed free expression. A writer is responsible for his contribution alone, and the views expressed are not necessarily the views of the editors or publisher.

Contents

Foreword

EPHESIANS, Philippians, Colossians, and Philemon have traditionally been grouped together as the Prison Epistles of Paul, because in each Paul indicates that he is in prison (Eph. 4:1; Phil. 1:12ff.; Col. 4:3; Phile. 1, 13). The prevalent view has identified this imprisonment with the one at Rome described in Acts 28:16ff. (see below the Introduction to Philemon and for Philippians, Volume 12, pp. 18ff.). Of these letters, Ephesians, Colossians, and Philemon are especially closely related in content and circumstances and so are brought together in one volume in this series.

Several features indicate that Colossians and Philemon were written together. Onesimus, the slave whom Paul is returning to his master Philemon, is mentioned as accompanying both letters (Col. 4:9; Phile. 10-12). Archippus receives messages in both letters (Col. 4:17; Phile. 2). The same Pauline associates send greetings in both (Col. 4:10-14; Phile. 23, 24).

Colossians and Ephesians are linked by the same messenger, Tychicus, who is given the same assignment (Col. 4:7f.; Eph. 6:21f.). But it is particularly the similarity of the contents, so that Ephesians and Colossians have been regarded as companion if not twin epistles, which links these two letters together and makes a parallel study desirable. Such study, however, soon reveals significantly different nuances in the treatment of the same subjects. Hence, not all have accepted the traditional view of common authorship and date for these letters. Therefore, a separate discussion to introductory questions for each of the letters must be given.

Philemon is placed first in this volume, because the sending back of Onesimus, accompanied by Tychicus, apparently provided the occasion for Paul to address himself to errors threatening the church at Colossae, as reported to him by Epaphras (Col. 4:7ff.; 1:8). Paul intercedes with

Philemon on behalf of the slave Onesimus, who has now become a Christian convert.

Colossians follows, because Philemon was probably a member of that church (Col. 4:9). Colossians was likely written before Ephesians. It better precedes Ephesians for study purposes because it is addressed to a specific problem confronting Colossae and the other churches in the Lycus River valley of Asia Minor. Paul develops the proper understanding of the nature of Christ and of his place in the universe and in the scheme of salvation as the answer to the false teaching which was threatening the church.

Ephesians is placed last, because the situation described in Colossians probably provides the explanation for the purpose and destination of Ephesians. Therefore, the commentary on Ephesians assumes the material in Colossians. Ephesians is a more general letter possibly intended to be read in several churches. It works out the implications of the Colossian heresy for the doctrine of the church. With Colossians in the background, Ephesians develops a positive view of the divinely ordained history of salvation, with an emphasis on the church within that history. Whereas Colossians stresses the Christ, the head of the church, Ephesians stresses the church, the body of Christ.

The Letter of Paul to Philemon

Introduction

PHILEMON HAS generally been accepted as genuinely Pauline. The letter is especially treasured because of its picture of Paul as he pleads the case of a delinquent slave before his master. It was originally intended to be read to the church (see vss. 2, 3) and by virtue of its acceptance into the canon is acknowledged as a document of the church.

THE OCCASION

Paul was in prison at the time of writing (see vss. 1, 9, 10, 22, 23). He had converted Onesimus (vs. 10), a runaway slave. The letter is addressed to the slave's master, Philemon, who is also a friend and convert of Paul and a resident of Colossae or nearby Laodicea (vss. 1, 16, 19). Onesimus may have met the apostle by chance, or he may have intentionally sought the apostle's assistance. It is also uncertain whether one may fairly describe the slave as "runaway." Perhaps he had abandoned Philemon's service while engaged on some special mission on his master's behalf. What is certain is that the apostle converted and kept the slave for some time, finally sending him back to his master accompanied by Tychicus and the apostle's letter (see Col. 4:7-9).

The letter's brevity and tact create some obscurity regarding the request Paul makes of Philemon. On the surface, it seems as if the apostle asks Philemon to give Onesimus a fair and forgiving reception. Yet the implications of this are far-reaching. While Paul does not plead for Onesimus' freedom, he requests far more in appealing for Philemon to receive Onesimus as a brother (vs. 16). Even this, however, may not be the entire substance of the apostle's request. It has been suggested that Paul subtly asks Philemon to return the slave so that he might continue helping the apostle's mission efforts (see comments on vss. 10, 13, 14, 18, 20, 21).

PLACE AND DATE OF WRITING

Rome has long been accepted as the place from which the imprisoned apostle wrote Philemon, Colossians and Ephesians, although two essential objections to Rome as the place of writing stand out. First, the distance of Rome from Colossae raises the question whether a runaway slave would have made such a lengthy journey (over one thousand miles). Second, the apostle's intention of visiting Philemon has raised some question. In light of the apostle's known intention of going on to Spain from Rome (see Rom. 15:28), a two thousand mile detour to Colossae seems inconceivable. A further argument is made by those maintaining that the apostle requests Onesimus' return: Paul hardly would have sent the slave on the distant journey back to Colossae only to be returned.

In light of the foregoing and other objections, Caesarea and Ephesus have both been suggested as alternatives to the traditional view. Caesarea meets the requirements insofar as a period of imprisonment is concerned (see Acts 24:27). And Caesarea is somewhat nearer Colossae than Rome and thus more accessible to a runaway slave. Nonetheless, the Caesarean hypothesis is not generally accepted. Paul's Caesarean imprisonment would hardly have led to an optimistic expectation of release (vs. 22), and a runaway slave would have been more conspicuous in Caesarea than in Rome's teeming masses. Further, the thought expressed in the three letters (especially Colossians and Ephesians) is more readily understood as developing lines of thought in Paul's earlier letters than vice versa.

Ephesus has also been suggested as the city from which the apostle penned the letters. An early tradition ascribes an Ephesian imprisonment to the apostle, and such an experience may be suggested in Paul's own letters (cf. 2 Cor. 11:23). It is argued that an Ephesian origin avoids the conflict between the apostle's intended visit to Philemon and his announced plans of going to Spain that attends the traditional Roman origin. Likewise, it is argued that the proximity of Ephesus to Colossae makes it preferable as the destination of the fleeing Onesimus. If Ephesus is adopted as the letter's point of origin, a date of approximately A.D. 52 to 54 may be suggested.

In spite of these and related arguments, by no means have the majority of scholars surrendered the Roman imprisonment as the time of Paul's authorship. It may be argued that Rome is a more likely destination for Onesimus' flight precisely because of its great distance, a journey the slave might have financed with purloined funds (vss. 18, 19). Again, it is necessary to remember that Onesimus' status as a runaway slave is questionable. He may have abandoned Philemon's service some distance from Colossae while engaged in some mission for his master. Likewise, the seeming contradiction of the apostle's intended visit to Spain and his stated intent of visiting Philemon need not cause undue anxiety. Paul may have altered previous plans in light of the dangerous heresy which was threatening Colossae and the churches of the area (cf. Col. 2:4, 8, 16; 2 Tim. 1:15). If Rome is accepted as the place of writing, a date of A.D. 60 to 62 may be adopted.

PAUL AND SLAVERY

Although Philemon has long been viewed as a "non-theological" example of Paul's personal correspondence, it provides more than a glimpse into the apostle's diplomacy, sensitivity, and even humor (vss. 11, 20). Philemon is of great theological significance since it illustrates the impact of the Christian message upon existing social standards.

Philemon introduces the reader to a climate in which

slavery would become increasingly intolerable. It would be difficult to exaggerate the strain placed on existing social patterns when masters and slaves ate together at the Lord's Table or when slaves presided in public worship, returning to daily life as their masters' personal property without any rights whatsoever (see Col. 3:22ff.). While at first altering the status of the slave, this situation would have become increasingly strained for all concerned, psychologically, socially and theologically (see Col. 3:11; Gal. 3:28; 1 Cor. 12:13; John 17:21). The early church could make only temporary peace with a world filled with slavery and injustice while preaching a gospel of freedom and equality. Thus it is not surprising that one of the earliest expressions of Christian benevolence is the use of funds to purchase the freedom of slaves (*I Clement* 55:2; Hermas, *Mandates* VIII:10; Ignatius, *To Polycarp* 4).

OUTLINE

I. INTRODUCTION, 1-3
II. THANKSGIVING, 4-7
III. THE APOSTLE'S REQUEST, 8-20
IV. CONCLUSION, 21-25

SELECTED BIBLIOGRAPHY

BRUCE, F. F. "St. Paul in Rome: The Epistle to Philemon," *Bulletin of the John Rylands Library.* Vol. 48, No. 1, 1965.

KNOX, JOHN. *Philemon Among the Letters of Paul.* Chicago: University of Chicago Press, 1935.

———. "The Epistle to Philemon," *The Interpreter's Bible,* edited by George A. Buttrick, *et al.* Vol. 11. New York: Abingdon Press, 1955.

SCOTT, E. F. *The Epistles to the Colossians, to Philemon, and to the Ephesians.* Moffatt New Testament Commentary. London: Hodder and Stoughton, 1930.

THOMPSON, G. H. P. *The Letters of Paul to the Ephesians, to Colossians and to Philemon.* Cambridge Bible Commentary on the New English Bible. Cambridge: The University Press, 1967.

Commentary

INTRODUCTION, 1-3

[1] Paul's reference to himself as a **prisoner** may be symbolic (see comments on Col. 4:10; cf. Rom. 1:1; 6:22; 1 Cor. 7:22; Phil. 1:1; Gal. 1:10); yet Paul also believes his imprisonment is a result of his efforts for Christ (see vs. 3; Phil. 1:12, 13; 2 Cor. 11:23ff.; 2 Tim. 2:9; Acts 28:20). Moreover, he is not unaware of the tactical advantage his self-designation as a **prisoner for Christ Jesus** gives to the request he is about to make of Philemon (see vss. 9, 13; cf. Col. 4:18). The delicate nature of the matter explains Paul's omission of the title "apostle": he wants to avoid even the appearance of force or compulsion (see vs. 14). **Timothy** (see Col. 1:1) is probably known to the recipient and may be acting as Paul's secretary in writing the letter (vs. 19).

The addressee is **Philemon,** known solely through this short letter. He is apparently a convert of Paul (though possibly through Epaphras; see comment on vs. 19), known to the apostle (and Timothy) from the time of the earlier ministry in Ephesus (see Acts 19:10). The designation of Philemon as **fellow worker** (see vs. 24; Col. 4:11; Rom. 16:3) may refer either to his service as the apostle's associate at some earlier time or to his present service in the Colossian church. It may be assumed that Philemon is wealthy, possibly a merchant who owns slaves and a house used by the church. His home is probably in Colossae, where he is among the leaders of the church (Col. 4:17).

[2] **Apphia our sister,** also otherwise unmentioned in the New Testament, is generally assumed to be the wife of Philemon, though there can be no certainty (and she may as well be his sister). **Archippus** (see Col. 4:17) is desig-

13

¹ Paul, a prisoner for Christ Jesus, and Timothy our brother,

To Philemon our beloved fellow worker ² and Apphia our sister and Archippus our fellow soldier, and the church in your house:

³ Grace to you and peace from God our Father and the Lord Jesus Christ.

---

nated fellow soldier (cf. Phil. 2:25), undoubtedly indicating his role in proclaiming the gospel.

Long thought to be the son of Philemon and Apphia, Archippus was given prominence in a theory proposed by John Knox in 1935 (see Bibliography). Knox argued that the leader of the house church addressed may be Archippus and that he, not Philemon, is the master of Onesimus and the actual addressee. Knox theorized that Philemon is named first not only because he is known to Paul (whereas Archippus is not) but also because Philemon may be acting as the absent Epaphras' successor (see Col. 1:7; 4:12) and as a leader in the church of the entire area. According to this theory, Paul seeks Philemon's aid in influencing Archippus to honor his request concerning Onesimus. Though interesting, Knox's hypothesis is questionable, and the evidence by no means demands his solution.

And the church in your house points to the practice of using homes of individual Christians as meeting places for worship (see Col. 4:15; Rom. 16:5; 1 Cor. 16:19). This particular statement raises a question regarding exactly who owns the house in question. The RSV obscures the difficulty which the text presents, namely, that the term your is in the singular, thus referring to some one and not necessarily to Philemon's "family" as long maintained. The reference may well be to the house of Archippus (the last proper name before the pronoun) and Christians meeting there; this role would not be incompatible with the singular attention Archippus receives in Colossians (4:17).

[3] As is always his custom, the apostle sends his special form of Christian greetings: Grace to you and peace from God our Father and the Lord Jesus Christ (see comments on Eph. 1:2; Col. 1:2; Phil. 1:2).

⁴ I thank my God always when I remember you in my prayers, ⁵ because I hear of your love and of the faith which you have toward the Lord Jesus and all the saints,

---

THANKSGIVING, 4-7

Paul begins with a thanksgiving with which he customarily opens his correspondence. The thanksgiving is intended to establish a relationship between Paul and his reader that will best facilitate a gracious reception of the letter. For example, Paul's reference to Philemon's **love** is the foundation of the request that he makes in verse 9, which is "for love's sake." Likewise, his mention of **sharing** (vs. 6) sets the stage for the request based on Philemon's "partnership" with the apostle (vs. 17).

[4, 5] Philemon is assured that although he has not seen Paul for some time, he is remembered in the apostle's prayers and is a source of constant comfort in an otherwise difficult situation. More subtly, Paul informs Philemon that neither Epaphras nor his slave, Onesimus, has borne unfavorable tales about him that might in any way reflect upon his good reputation.

Although Paul names Timothy as coauthor, the letter bases its appeal on the personal relations between Paul and its recipients. Paul informs Philemon that he remembers him in his own personal prayers with thanksgiving (**I thank my God**; cf. Col. 1:3). The word **remember** (*mneian*) occurs in virtually all of Paul's epistolary thanksgivings and may be a term drawn from the language of public worship, which included intercessory prayer (see Col. 4:18). If this is the case, the apostle reminds Philemon that he continues to pray in his behalf. **Always** may be taken to express the frequency of Paul's giving thanks (ASV, NEB) or may be indicative of the frequency with which Paul mentions Philemon in prayer (KJV, Jerusalem Bible).

I hear specifies the cause of his thanksgiving as Paul refers to the reports he has received from Epaphras and Onesimus which tell of Philemon's **love** and **faith toward the Lord Jesus and all the saints.** This last statement, however, raises some questions. Though the words are simple

15

⁶ and I pray that the sharing of your faith may promote
the knowledge of all the good that is ours in Christ.

---

enough, the structure is not. One may understand love and
faith as directed toward both the Lord Jesus and all the
saints. Or, one might take only faith as specified in its
direction. It is possible, however, to read love with saints
and faith with the Lord (see Eph. 1:15; Col. 1:4). This
type of structure would not be unusual for the apostle and
provides the clearer meaning (Gal. 4:4, 5). Love (*agapē*)
is, of course, singularly important in the apostle's understanding of the individual Christian's life style and vital
for the proper atmosphere in the Christian community,
which is constituted through love as a single harmonious
body of Christ (see Col. 3:14; Eph. 4:2; 5:2).

[6] And I pray that (an interpretive addition implying
the continuation of the prayer previously begun) introduces
a difficult verse. Sharing (*koinōnia,* "participation," "fellowship") is used by Paul to indicate the Christian's "sharing" with Christ (1 Cor. 1:9; 10:16; Phil. 3:10), with the
Holy Spirit (2 Cor. 13:14; Phil. 2:1), with fellow Christians
(Rom. 15:27) and in specific Christian tasks (see Phil. 1:5;
4:14). Frequently the word is used by Paul to mean "contribution" of money or the like (cf. Rom. 12:13; 15:26, 27;
2 Cor. 8:4; 9:13; Gal. 6:6; Phil. 4:15). Among possible interpretations, the following should be noted: (a) Paul is
commending Philemon's "sharing" or generosity, itself the
outworking of his faith in Christ; (b) Paul commends
Philemon's sharing or fellowship with Christ through faith
which is behind his generosity and "love toward the saints";
(c) or, Paul may be commending Philemon's faith because
it is the faith shared by the church at Colossae. The first of
these suggestions seems to fit best with the apparent goal
that Philemon may promote the knowledge of all the good
that is ours in Christ. Knowledge (*epignōsis*) might be
translated "perception" but involves something more than
intellectual mastery of abstract truth. Used by itself, the
word tends to indicate a personal relationship with Christ
(see Col. 1:9); but here it is defined by the good (*agathou*),
which most likely indicates some specific deed or action to

⁷ For I have derived much joy and comfort from your love, my brother, because the hearts of the saints have been refreshed through you.

⁸ Accordingly, though I am bold enough in Christ to command you to do what is required, ⁹ yet for love's sake I prefer to appeal to you—I, Paul, an ambassador * and now a prisoner also for Christ Jesus—

* Or *an old man*

---

be performed (see Jerusalem Bible, "all good things we are able to do . . ."; vs. 14; Rom. 14:16). Paul is commending Philemon for his generosity (the use of his house, etc.), which enables his fellow Christians to perceive the good which belongs to the community of those in Christ (see comments on Eph. 3:18, 19).

[7] Paul returns to give fuller attention to the motive for his thanksgiving (vs. 4), namely, Philemon's ministry among the Colossian Christians. The RSV's hearts aptly translates the Greek word *splagchna* (used three times in the letter; see vss. 12, 20), literally meaning "viscera" or "entrails" (see Acts 1:18) but figuratively designating the "seat of emotion" or "affection" (see Phil. 1:8; 2:1; Col. 3:12). Refreshed (*anapauō*) means "to cause to cease," "to give someone rest" or "to refresh someone" (see vs. 20). The common use of the word, as here, refers to the "inner man" (see 1 Cor. 16:18). The word is used of the effects of Jesus' ministry (Matt. 11:28).

THE APOSTLE'S REQUEST, 8-20

[8, 9] Accordingly refers to the exhibitions of Philemon's love just referred to and upon which Paul now expressly bases his appeal. Paul's disclaimer of invoking his apostleship has the effect of reminding Philemon of the writer's authority (bold enough in Christ). Rather than use the authority he rightly exercises, Paul wants to entreat (appeal), not order, Philemon (cf. 1 Thess. 2:6, 7). For love's sake indicates the ground of the apostle's appeal. One may understand this reference in several ways (e.g., Paul's love for Onesimus and Philemon, Philemon's love for Paul, etc.), but it is more probable that Paul has in

17

¹⁰ I appeal to you for my child, Onesimus, whose father I have become in my imprisonment.

---

mind the more general love permeating and unifying the entire Christian community (see Col. 3:14). Philemon's demonstration of his participation in this love encourages Paul to shape his request as an appeal and not a command.

Paul again calls his imprisonment to his reader's mind, using the titles **ambassador** and **prisoner** (see vs. 1). As the RSV footnote indicates, the word *presbutēs*, found in the better manuscripts, generally would mean "old man." Yet on at least one occasion this word is found to carry the connotation of "ambassador" or "emissary" (see 2 Macc. 11:34), which would more commonly be conveyed by adding a single letter to form the word *presbeutēs* (cf. 2 Cor. 5:20; Isa. 52:7). It may be that the two words were interchangeable in Paul's time. Additionally, the parallel statement in Ephesians 6:20 and the apostle's evident understanding that his imprisonment is a result of his service for Christ ("ambassadorship"; see vss. 1, 13) may be taken as a cumulative argument in favor of the RSV's **ambassador.** Nonetheless, Paul would probably have been in his sixties and well qualified for the appellation "old man."

[10] With the preceding verses as preparation, the apostle now makes his request. **Onesimus** (which means "profitable"), the delinquent slave of Philemon, is mentioned for the first time (see Col. 4:9). Having converted Onesimus while in prison, Paul refers to him (see vs. 16) in filial terms (see 1 Cor. 4:15; cf. Gal. 4:19). It is possible that the name "Onesimus" is the slave's new "Christian name" given to him at the time of his conversion; but this is uncertain (see vs. 11). The apostle's situation and consequent feelings of sorrow and nonproductivity may in some measure account for his special feeling for Onesimus, a convert and source of encouragement in this period of confinement (see 2 Cor. 1:8ff.). Paul's word **for** has been taken as indicating that he actually desires the slave's return, not merely appealing "on his behalf" but actually "for" him. Both interpretations are possible in Greek as in English.

[11] (Formerly he was useless to you, but now he is indeed useful [b] to you and to me.) [12] I am sending him back to you, sending my very heart. [13] I would have been glad to keep him with me, in order that he might serve me on your behalf during my imprisonment for the gospel; [14] but I preferred to do nothing without your consent in order that your goodness might not be by compulsion but of your own free will.

[b] The name Onesimus means *useful* or (compare verse 20) *beneficial*

---

[11] Paul now makes the first of several statements with double meanings. Making a play on Onesimus' name, "useful" or "profitable," Paul says to Philemon that whereas his slave was once "useless," in having run away, now he is indeed useful to you and to me.

[12, 13] The apostle stresses the value that Onesimus has been to him, describing this with the word heart (*splagchna*; see vss. 7, 20). Paul is aware that the return of Onesimus appears as a sacrifice on his part and is, in a sense, portraying himself as doing Philemon a favor. Paul may imply that Onesimus has really been doing what Philemon would naturally have wanted him to do. The apostle is also quick to emphasize that Onesimus' service has been in no way simply for his own personal benefit but actually in the line of duty to the gospel for which Paul is imprisoned and in whose service Philemon is also engaged (see vss. 1, 17, 20).

[14] Paul's expressed desire to do nothing without your consent probably refers to his keeping Onesimus. Paul could have kept the slave without Philemon's approval. Yet, such an act could be understood as compulsion and not a free exercise of Philemon's own will (cf. 2 Cor. 9:7; 1 Peter 5:2). Paul wants to leave the way open for Philemon to have an opportunity to illustrate the truth of his good reputation without his feeling "forced." But Paul is not only concerned to avoid pressuring Philemon; he wants to avoid even the appearance that he has forced him. An act giving the appearance of compulsion might damage Philemon's reputation, especially in a troubled church such as that in Colossae.

¹⁵ Perhaps this is why he was parted from you for a while, that you might have him back for ever, ¹⁶ no longer as a slave but more than a slave, as a beloved brother, especially to me but how much more to you, both in the flesh and in the Lord.

---

[15] Paul suggests to Philemon that Onesimus' departure and the subsequent hardship on his master may have been by the will of God: **was parted** may reflect this, indicating that Onesimus did not really separate himself, but that he "was parted" (presumably by God; cf. vs. 22 and Gen. 45:5). It is easy to understand how the apostle seeks to discern the purposes of God in the events leading to Onesimus' conversion. It is instructive, however, to note that Paul is reluctant to assert his interpretation and is equally hesitant to prescribe the precise course of action that Philemon should take.

For a while ("for an hour"; cf. 2 Cor. 7:8; Gal. 2:5) glosses over the slave's offense and the duration of his absence. Seemingly, the apostle feels that Philemon's loss has been but momentary, more than compensated by the result. Paul's word **have him back** (*apechēs*) may embody the idea of restitution, i.e., to receive back what has formerly been in his possession. Or, it may carry an additional meaning of now "having more completely than before." **For ever** (*aiōnion*) does not imply that the relationship between Philemon and Onesimus will endure into the Christian future beyond the grave. Rather, Paul is stating that now Onesimus has returned "for good" (NEB); Paul here uses the same terminology found in the Septuagint with reference to the slave-master relationship ("for life"; see Ex. 21:6).

[16] Philemon is called on to recognize and actualize Onesimus' new life in his manner of acceptance by receiving his slave **as a beloved brother**. Onesimus' status is granted by virtue of his incorporation into Christ. Significantly, Paul does not urge Philemon to receive Onesimus as a "free man," as some Hellenists would have in cases of close friendship or as a reward for meritorious service rendered by a slave. Paul rather uses the term **brother**, which was generally reserved for racial and religious comradeship,

¹⁷ **So if you consider me your partner, receive him as you would receive me.**

---

or, among the Jews, designated the truly devout (see Acts 22:5; 28:21). Yet this term comes to serve as the equivalent for "Christian" (see Rom. 8:29; 1 Cor. 5:11).

Paul alludes to his own relationship with Onesimus (**especially to me**), emphasizing that Onesimus will be of even greater value to his former master now that he is a brother. Possibly Paul hints that Onesimus should be received as if he were the writer's own brother (17b). If Paul was the one who converted Philemon (see vs. 19), he may be thinking of a relationship between the two to whom he has personally given "Christian birth." Yet, it would be difficult to reconcile this concept with Paul's designation of himself also as "brother." More probably Paul is referring to the common incorporation of both Philemon and Onesimus into the body of Christ. By virtue of their new birth, they are in a new relationship to one another. **In the flesh and in the Lord** expresses the magnitude of the new relationship. Paul may be saying that Philemon will now find his relations with Onesimus altered not only in the specifically Christian sphere (**in the Lord**) but also in everyday affairs (**in the flesh**). However, if the distinction that the apostle has in mind is of such a nature, the result is actually a limitation of the relationship **in the Lord,** as if one's religious relations could be separated from everyday affairs (see NEB). More likely, the apostle here designates levels of understanding (see 2 Cor. 5:16; 10:3) and in no way endorses a division between "religious" and "secular" affairs.

[17] Paul's word **partner** (*koinōnon*), a frequently used word in his letters, can mean commercial enterprises or legal sharing. Thus it is possible for the apostle's appeal to be understood as based strictly on secular considerations of the friendship between the apostle and Philemon (see vs. 18). Or one may see here another play on words, as Paul uses a term that is familiar to the wealthy merchant in his professional life. Although these considerations may not be totally disallowed, the apostle probably has in mind a specific Christian use of the word **partner** (NEB, "partner

¹⁸ If he has wronged you at all, or owes you anything, charge that to my account. ¹⁹ I, Paul, write this with my own hand, I will repay it—to say nothing of your owing me even your own self.

---

in the faith"; cf. 1 Cor. 1:9; Phil. 1:5). Paul here alludes to Philemon's incorporation into Christ and his participation with Paul in the Christian cause ("fellow worker" vs. 1). Paul's exhortation that Philemon **receive** (cf. Rom. 14:1, 3; 15:7 "welcome") Onesimus in the same manner that he himself would be received may be intended to punctuate the value that the apostle places on the slave as well as the elevation of the new relationship between Philemon and Onesimus (cf. Matt. 25:34ff.). It is possible, however, for one to interpret this as meaning that in the event the theological import of Onesimus' conversion fails to insure his acceptance, Paul also appeals to Philemon's regard for him as a friend.

[18] Paul expresses his willingness to make restitution personally for any debts incurred by the slave. It would seem that Onesimus has, in fact, committed some act inappropriate to his situation as a slave. Whether or not Onesimus has actually robbed his master (as is often assumed) is uncertain. The temporary loss of his labor may have meant some financial loss to Philemon. If Onesimus actually took enough money to finance a trip to Rome, his debt may have amounted to a substantial sum. Paul's word **wronged** occurs in Colossians in the context of his remarks regarding slaves, possibly indicating that those remarks are occasioned by Onesimus' case (see Col. 3:25). The apostle refers to his **account**, again using the language of commerce. It is unclear, however, whether the meaning is figurative or indicates some actual arrangement between Paul and Philemon. Those who believe that the letter is a subtle request for Onesimus' return to Paul find here a hint of this fact. It was customary for the new owner of a transferred slave to accept whatever debts were involved.

[19] Paul's "signature," **I Paul write this with my own hand,** does not indicate whether it is at this point that he takes the pen or has actually written the entire letter. In contrast to similar notes in Paul's letters where the more

[20] Yes, brother, I want some benefit from you in the Lord.
Refresh my heart in Christ.

---

probable concern is that of authenticity or authority (1 Cor.
16:21; 2 Thess. 3:17; Col. 4:18), the reference here tends
to be more in the nature of an I.O.U. The word used here
may designate a type of legal bond, validated by the signature (see Col. 2:14). Yet the apostle's overt expression of
willingness to pay Philemon is somewhat diminished by
the not too subtle reminder of Philemon's own "indebted-
ness": **you owe me your own self.** Paul probably refers to
his responsibility, direct or indirect, for Philemon's own
conversion (see Col. 1:7, 29), though one might argue that
he has in mind some otherwise unknown previous service
(see vss. 1, 17). In any case, Paul does here introduce an
element of "spiritual coercion."

[20] Paul now entreats Philemon as **brother** (see vs. 16;
for **Yes** see the Greek of Phil. 4:3), appealing to the relationship that they enjoy by virtue of their both being in
Christ. Paul's phrases **in the Lord** and **in Christ** may embody slightly different nuances; but generally speaking, the
terms are used interchangeably and the difference here may
be taken as stylistic (see 1 Cor. 7:22; cf. Rom. 14:8f.). **In
the Lord** may be understood as saying, in effect, "as a
Christian" (NEB). In Paul's word **benefit** another possible
double meaning is encountered (see vss. 11, 17, 18). The
word Paul uses, *onaimēn,* is the verbal form of "Onesimus"
("benefit," "useful," "profit"). Those who argue that Paul
is requesting the return of Onesimus hold that the benefit
(*onaimēn*) the apostle actually has in mind is precisely
Onesimus (*onēsimos*).

The word **I** (*egō*) might be understood as asserting that
Paul's concern is not limited to anxiety over Onesimus but
includes himself, the "I" possibly intended as emphatic
(i.e., "I and not Onesimus, want . . ."). Yet the following
phrase probably indicates that the apostle still has Onesimus' welfare foremost in his mind. **Refresh my heart** doubtlessly echoes verse 7 and charges Philemon to live up to his
reputation and now to minister to Paul as he has to others.
Paul asks Philemon to refresh his **heart** (*splagchna;* see
comment on vs. 7) just as he has others (vs. 7). Yet one

23

²¹ Confident of your obedience, I write to you, knowing that you will do even more than I say. ²² At the same time, prepare a guest room for me, for I am hoping through your prayers to be granted to you.

---

also recalls that Onesimus has himself been designated the "heart" (*splagchna*) of the apostle (vs. 12). Thus the apostle requests that Onesimus be a full recipient of the same Christian benefits that Philemon has willingly shown others of the Colossian church, in Christ indicating that the ground of the relationship and the basis of the appeal are theological (see vs. 6).

Conclusion, 21-25

[21] **Confident of your obedience** may contain a further reminder of the good report Paul has received about Philemon. His word **confident** may be translated by either "persuaded" or "convinced" (see Phil. 1:25; 2:24). **Obedience** (*hupakoē*) is predominantly used in reference to compliance with God's commands but also designates the slave's obedience to his master (see Col. 3:22). It is impossible to be certain what nuance the apostle here intends. Perhaps the verse subtly indicates the apostle's authority. One cannot be certain other than that the apostle desires the compliance of Philemon with the request of the letter. The phrase **knowing that you will do even more than I say** has been taken as a final expression of Paul's desire for Onesimus to be returned to him, although it may only refer to the apostle's conviction that Onesimus will be received with even greater Christian charity than he has requested.

[22] Paul's statement, **prepare a guest room for me**, raises questions. Does the apostle literally mean that he has indication he will shortly be released? And, if so, has he changed his plans to go on to Spain (Rom. 15:24)? A trip from Rome to Colossae would involve a journey of several hundred miles, including crossing a considerable amount of water. Such an alteration of the apostle's plans is not inconceivable and might be explained either by the heresy threatening the churches of the Lycus Valley or by the

²³ Epaphras, my fellow prisoner in Christ Jesus, sends greetings to you, ²⁴ and so do Mark, Aristarchus, Demas, and Luke, my fellow workers.

---

apostle's increase in years. Yet, the statement may also give credence to the conjectured Ephesian imprisonment as the time of writing (see Introduction).

It is also possible, however, that Paul is speaking figuratively to his old friend. Rather than optimistically expecting his release, Paul may be indicating that he recognizes his release will only be achieved through an act of God. In addition, it is difficult to understand why (unless Philemon is the "letter to Laodicea"; see Col. 4:16) the apostle would neglect mentioning such an important matter in the Colossian letter (assuming the two letters are written at the same time). Paul's word **granted** (*charisthēsomai;* cf. Acts. 3:14; 25:11) may indicate the working either of God (see vs. 15; cf. Phil 2:24) or of court officials. The statement recognizes and expresses thanks for the prayers of Philemon (and the church at Colossae).

[23, 24] Paul now lists others in his entourage who also send greetings to Philemon. The correspondence of these names with those at the close of the Colossian letter is one of the reasons the two letters are thought to have been written at the same time (see Col. 4:10ff.). Epaphras is mentioned first because he is a Colossian and the apostle's chief emissary for the entire area (see Col. 1:7; 4:12). Paul's designation of him as **fellow prisoner** indicates either a literal incarceration with the apostle or some special service he provides for the imprisoned writer. (See comment on Col. 4:10, where the term is used for Aristarchus.) Both **John Mark** (cf. Acts 12:12; 13:4; 15:37), the cousin of Barnabas, and **Aristarchus**, the Macedonian, are Jewish Christians, whereas **Demas** and **Luke**, the physician, are both Gentiles (see comment on Col. 4:11). All are apparently known to Philemon. Jesus Justus, mentioned in Colossians, is perhaps omitted because he is a Roman and unknown to Philemon. All these companions of the apostle are identified as **fellow workers** (see Col. 4:11), indicating that the apostle does not feel as if his ministry has come to a complete halt by his confinement.

[25] The grace of the Lord Jesus Christ be with your spirit.

---

[25] Paul's benediction uses the plural, your (*humōn;* see vs. 2), possibly remembering Apphia and Archippus (cf. Gal. 6:18; 2 Tim. 4:22). It is equally possible, however, that Paul has in mind the church at Philemon's house (see comment on vss. 2, 4, 5) or even the entire group of Colossian Christians.

The phrase **be with your spirit** is a curious one, with the word **your** in the plural and **spirit** in the singular. Possibly the apostle indicates his sense of the composite unity which the several individuals have in Christ (see Col. 2:2; 3:15; Eph. 4:3ff.; cf. 1 Cor. 3:16, 17; 10:17; 12:12ff.).

II

The Letter of Paul to the Colossians

Introduction

COLOSSAE, a city of Asia Minor, was located on the western border of Phrygia astride the Lycus River. Nearby were the cities of Hierapolis ("Sacred City") and the more prominent Laodicea; eighty miles west was Ephesus. The Lycus Valley itself forms a pass in the Cadmus Mountains, strategically locating Colossae on an overland trade route between eastern and western Asia Minor. Colossae was at one time a flourishing commercial community transporting and trading in wool, textiles, and a type of dye unique to the area. But by the first century the importance of the city had waned.

Religious influences in the area were diverse. Neighboring Hierapolis proudly possessed a famous shrine to the goddess Cybele. Egyptian and Eastern religions, the mystery religions, and philosophies of the Stoics, Epicureans and others were influential. Significantly, there was considerable Jewish influence in the area, an important point for understanding the nature of the Colossian heresy. The Jewish historian Josephus (*Antiquities* XII, iii, 147-152) reports that two thousand Jews were settled in the area under an edict of Antiochus III (2nd century B.C.). These Jewish residents were imported not from Palestine but from Mesopotamia and Babylon. Additional evidence suggests the existence of a large Jewish population in the area by the first century; calculations made on the basis of taxes sent to Jerusalem indicate that there were approximately eleven thousand adult Jewish males in the district of Laodicea a century prior to Paul.

THE CHURCH AT COLOSSAE

Like the churches at Hierapolis and Laodicea, the Colossian church was probably established by Epaphras (himself a Colossian; 1:7; 4:12, 13) or some other member of Paul's entourage working under his direction during his three-year stay at Ephesus (Acts 19:10; cf. 1 Cor. 16:19). Though the apostle had not personally visited the churches of the area (2:1), he nonetheless felt a close kinship with their struggles, because of both his indirect role in their conversion and the graveness of the threat presented by the heresy (described below).

The size and makeup of the church is difficult to determine. The Colossian church included at least two "house churches" (see 4:15 and 4:9 with Phile. 2). As would be expected in a church probably established by a Gentile evangelist (Epaphras), the names of the members mentioned indicate that the church consisted largely of Gentiles (see also 1:21, 27; 2:13). This supposition may be reinforced by the letter's lack of Old Testament references. Nonetheless, the church was not free from strong Jewish influences: the heresy which threatened it most probably consisted largely of a speculative or nonconformist Jewish phenomenon which had made inroads among local Gentiles.

In contrast to such churches as Rome and Ephesus, the church at Colossae played no major role in the subsequent history of the church. The city itself was virtually destroyed by an earthquake shortly after Paul's letter was written. The importance of the letter resides in two factors: first, the Colossian heresy was apparently a local manifestation of a rather widespread religious outlook of the time. Paul's opposition to it proved important for other churches facing the threat posed by similar tendencies, especially in the second century when this religious climate developed into the elaborate systems of Gnosticism. Second, Paul's statement of the cosmic significance of Christ is one of the most exalted and important Christological statements in the New Testament.

AUTHENTICITY

The Pauline authorship of Colossians was first seriously questioned by the famed "Tübingen School" in 1838 on the basis that it was obviously dependent on Ephesians, which was thought to be non-Pauline. Although modern scholarship has recognized the extremes of many of the presuppositions of such views, many scholars still question the apostolic authorship of the letter. The main reasons given for denying Pauline authorship of the letter are the type of heresy opposed at Colossae, the unique vocabulary, and the theology of the letter.

The type of heresy present at Colossae was long believed to represent a second-century phenomenon. While many scholars still maintain this, the argument is now less formidable. There is increasing recognition that the roots of the elaborate systems of second-century Gnosticism are at least partially imbedded in Judaism prior to the time of Christ. The Dead Sea Scrolls have unveiled developments within Judaism confirming suspicions that it contained a speculative element which would well account for the existence of the type of phenomenon which the writer of Colossians opposes.

With regard to the peculiarities of style and vocabulary, it is pointless to deny the fact that the letter does present difficulty. However, to account for these difficulties, it is not necessary either to deny Pauline authorship or to assert that an original Pauline letter has been overlaid by later interests of the church in argument with second-century Gnosticism. A large number of the estimated thirty-four words not found elsewhere in the New Testament are located in 1:9-25 and in 2:8-23. The first section is highly liturgical and contains a pre-Pauline hymn (see "Christ Hymn" below) while the second section is engaged in a refutation of the heretical concerns. It may be argued that the apostle uses the technical terms of his opposition, giving them new interpretation and content with regard to Christ, and the peculiarities of vocabulary could be seen as arising from the unique circumstance in which the apostle finds himself and the specific problems to which his attention is called.

Likewise, the style of the letter shows some variation from Paul's previous letters. For example, the writer uses long sentences (1:9-20) and many synonyms (e.g., 1:9, 22). Nonetheless, similar variations of style may be seen in Paul's earlier letters, although the letter does contain certain stylistic peculiarities that are found only in Paul. But arguments on the basis of style are inconclusive and may be attributed to the context of the letter as well as the flexibility of the apostle's style.

Many of the arguments against Pauline authorship of Colossians center around the theology of the letter. Some maintain that the letter has unique emphases which constitute radical departures from Paul's theology. The question is whether this poses irreconcilable departures from the thought of Paul's earlier letters. For example, it is argued that the active role ascribed to the pre-existent Christ in Colossians differs from the simple assertion of pre-existence seen elsewhere (e.g., Phil. 2:5ff.) and that the use of terms from Jewish Wisdom literature represents a transition from Paul's earlier emphases. Yet, it may be argued that the Colossian heresy provided him an occasion more fully to formulate ideas which he had previously only touched on, and the use of many terms of Wisdom speculation may be the result of the influence of such thought on the heresy itself.

The Heresy

Paul's letter is written to oppose some type of false teaching which is threatening the Colossian church (2:4, 8ff.). The apostle specifies some of the tendencies of the heresy in verses 2:8-23: it considers itself a "philosophy" (2:8) with access to ancient "wisdom" and "knowledge" (2:3). Its doctrines are regarded as secret "mysteries" only available to the few elite "mature ones" (1:27, 28). The heresy teaches the observance of ritual feasts and festivals (2:16) and ascetic practices (2:20ff.), possibly with a goal of producing ecstatic experiences such as visions (2:18).

Additionally, the false teachers are urging angel worship (2:18). Although Paul does not provide a complete picture of the heretical teaching, there are parallels between it and better attested groups of the approximate period and strong affinities with the elaborate systems of second-century Gnosticism which seriously threatened the church.

There are also parallels between the Colossian heresy and Jewish developments evidenced in the Essenes and the Qumran Community (disclosed in the 1947 discovery of the Dead Sea Scrolls). These and other sources (e.g., Philo of Alexandria, intertestamental literature) indicate that in the centuries following the exile (586 B.C.) Judaism underwent a considerable amount of change as it was forced to adjust to the demands and pressures of new experiences. God increasingly came to be conceived of as far removed from the creation (cf. Ps. 80:14). Consequently, much attention was given to the manner in which a transcendent God relates himself to the creation and to angels as God's agents (e.g., 2 Macc. 3:24-28; 10:29, 30; 11:8). On the other hand, Wisdom, poetically personified in Proverbs (chapter 8), came to be regarded in certain Jewish circles as an emanation of God, the agency of his action and presence in the world (Wisd. of Sol. *circa* 100-50 B.C.).

In addition to this, Judaism apparently began to entertain certain philosophical questions arising out of its experience of exile and its continued contact with other religious and philosophical thought. Consequently, Jews in certain circles showed an openness to such Greek ideas as the immortality of the soul in place of future bodily resurrection. Perhaps influenced by Persian thought, Judaism grew more favorable to a cosmic dualism wherein supernatural forces of evil control the creation and war with the forces of God.

Thus it is increasingly evident that first-century Judaism was a widely variegated entity which in some areas was quite fluid, capable of different types of expression and influenced to varying degrees by its surroundings (cf. Acts 19:13). What is known about Colossae would indicate that it was an ideal setting for the development of a type of speculative Judaism. Its considerable Jewish population, settled from Mesopotamia and Babylon (thus perhaps already influenced by non-Jewish concepts), together with the diverse religious emphases of the Hellenistic world, provided an atmosphere conducive to an interplay between Jews and non-Jews.

The Colossian heresy evidences a curious mixture of both Jewish and Hellenistic religious and philosophical ideas. It seems to have been built around a dualism removing God from the world, envisioning man as alienated from God and under subjection to the onslaughts of various good and evil spiritual powers (including angels). These beings were probably arranged in a hierarchy and identified with various stars and planets believed to control the fate of men just as they were thought to determine the changing of the seasons. "Salvation" in such a system was probably divorced from morality and portrayed more in the form of "escape" from the world. It was achieved through the possession of special "wisdom" and "knowledge" and by the enactment of special rites. Information was communicated through visions and other ecstatic experiences in which the individual communicated with various members of the celestial hierarchy who in turn acted as protectors and mediators on his behalf. The Jewish hypostatized Wisdom may well have been allotted a prominent place in this hierarchy, a fact at least partially accounting for the apostle's heavy use of Wisdom terminology in the letter.

Although it is not known what secret truths were believed to be communicated, they probably included such things as secret names of various influential members of the supernatural host, as well as sayings and rites through which they might be appeased and communicated with. The adherents of the system were probably quite sectarian, dividing into different categories or spiritual ranks of greater and lesser "mature ones" (see comments on 1:28) through which the individual advanced en route to "salvation."

Because of his suffering and death (and the apostle's imprisonment), Christ was probably envisioned as one of the lesser luminaries in the hierarchy of celestial beings controlling the universe. The heretics argued that men needed additional liberation from the more powerful astral forces controlling their destiny. Thus redemption available through Christ was portrayed as incomplete and therefore inadequate (cf. 1:9-14, 22; 2:3; 3:1). Consequently, the heretics worshiped angels and other more significant heavenly powers in addition to Christ (see comments on 3:17). And like the importance of redemption in Christ, the significance of Christian baptism was also minimized. Christian baptism likely became one of the lesser among many rites and experiences (including circumcision, fasts, trances and visions) through which the initiate advanced to the higher stages of "spiritual maturity."

Such a system actually brought two radically opposed outlooks into conflict. Christianity, like more orthodox Judaism, conceived of the creation as an originally perfect entity spoiled by man's sin. Redemption was primarily the forgiveness of sins (1:14) and the deliverance of the creation which would happen in history at some future date to be awaited by those faithful to God. The heretical system, however, understood salvation as escape from history and creation. Whereas Judaism and Christianity, envisioning man's problem to be related to sin and guilt, concerned themselves with morality, many of the Hellenistic religions made little or no connection between morality and religion. If the world and matter were evil (or under the power of evil forces) the desires of the flesh could either be stifled (rigid asceticism) or allowed free rein (antinomianism). Obviously such an outlook and the system embodying it posed a serious threat to the Christian movement of the first century.

Paul's response to the heresy is based on the "Christ Hymn" of verses 1:15-20. Paul describes Christ in the terminology of Jewish Wisdom literature, identifying him with the Wisdom of their speculations and ascribing to him functions attributed to Wisdom. The letter is in the form of an elaboration making clear the significance of this identification.

The Christ Hymn

Analysis reveals Colossians 1:15-20 to contain stylistic and syntactical traits closely paralleling those found in sections of the New Testament believed to embody fragments of early Christian hymns. On the basis of its poetic style, Colossians 1:15-20 is usually regarded as "hymnic." Thus it is widely held that Paul has here, as elsewhere in his letters (e.g., Phil. 2:6-11; 1 Tim. 3:16; 2 Tim. 2:11; Titus 3:4-7; Eph. 5:14 and possibly Rom. 6:8-11), incorporated a hymn or a hymn fragment into his letter.

The unique nature of the section is more clearly seen if it is arranged in two strophes: the first (vss. 15-18a) exalts Christ's superiority over the creation, and the second (vss. 18b-20) shows his primacy in God's redemptive plan.[1]

Strophe A

15 Who is (Greek relative pronoun, RSV "He is") the image of the invisible God, the first-born of all creation;

16 For in him all things were created, in heaven and on earth,
Visible and invisible,
Whether thrones or dominions
Or principalities or authorities—
All things were created through him and for him.

17 He is before all things,
And in him all things hold together.

18 He is the head of the body, the church;

Strophe B

Who is (Greek relative pronoun, RSV "He is") the beginning, the first-born from the dead,
That in everything he might be pre-eminent.

19 For in him all the fulness of God was pleased to dwell,

20 And through him to reconcile to himself all things,
Whether on earth or in heaven,
Making peace by the blood of his cross.

The parallels are even more apparent when placed beside one another:

A1 *Who is* the image of the invisible God, *the first-born* of all creation

A2 *For in him all* things were created, in heaven and on earth

A6 *All things* were created through him and *for him*

B1 *Who is* the beginning, *the first-born* from the dead

B3 *For in him all* the fulness of God was pleased to dwell

B4 And through him to reconcile *all things to him*

[1] This arrangement is adapted from A. M. Hunter's translation of E. Norden's analysis of these verses. Cf. A. M. Hunter, *Paul and His Predecessors* (Philadelphia: The Westminster Press, 1961), pp. 124, 125.

Outline

Beyond the judgment of the passage as hymnic, however, several alternatives are available. Paul himself may have composed the hymn, or he may have adapted an early Christian hymn (possibly baptismal) already in existence (e.g., as in Phil. 2:6-11). Or he may have borrowed and adapted a hymn originally directed to the hypostatized Wisdom of Jewish Wisdom speculation, possibly used by the heretics themselves who were heavily influenced by Jewish thought (see "The Heresy" above). This latter supposition is based on the fact that many of the attributes which the hymn ascribes to Christ closely parallel those describing Wisdom in Jewish Wisdom literature (e.g., Ecclesiasticus 24; Wisd. of Sol. 7). Details are noted in the exposition, along with points where Paul has gone beyond current Wisdom speculation.

OUTLINE

SELECTED BIBLIOGRAPHY

ABBOTT, T. K. *The Epistles to the Ephesians and to the Colossians.* International Critical Commentary. Edinburgh: T. & T. Clark, 1897.

INTRODUCTION TO COLOSSIANS

BEARE, FRANCIS W. "The Epistle to the Colossians," *The Interpreter's Bible*, edited by George A. Buttrick, *et al.* Vol. 11. New York: Abingdon Press, 1955.

BRUCE, F. F. "St. Paul in Rome: The Epistle to the Colossians," *Bulletin of the John Rylands Library*. Vol. 48, No. 2, Spring, 1966.

DAVIES, W. D. *Paul and Rabbinic Judaism*. New York: Harper and Row, 1948.

DODD, C. H. "Colossians," *The Abingdon Bible Commentary*. New York: Abingdon Press, 1929.

HUNTER, A. M. *Paul and His Predecessors*. Philadelphia: The Westminster Press, 1961.

KNOX, W. L. *St. Paul and the Church of the Gentiles*. Cambridge, 1939.

KÜMMEL, W. G. *Introduction to the New Testament*. New York: Abingdon Press, 1966.

LIGHTFOOT, J. B. *Saint Paul's Epistles to the Colossians and to Philemon*. Grand Rapids: Zondervan Reprint Edition, 1959 (originally 1879).

MOULE, C. F. D. *The Epistles to the Colossians and to Philemon*. The Cambridge Greek Testament Commentary. Cambridge: The University Press, 1958.

MUNCK, JOHANNES. *Paul and the Salvation of Mankind*. Richmond: John Knox Press, 1959.

ROBINSON, JAMES M. "A Formal Analysis of Colossians 1:15-20," *Journal of Biblical Literature*. Vol. 76 (December, 1957), pp. 270-87.

SCHWEIZER, EDUARD. "The Church as the Missionary Body of Christ," *New Testament Studies*. Vol. 8 (October, 1961), pp. 1-11.

WILSON, R. M. *Gnosis and the New Testament*. Philadelphia: Fortress Press, 1968.

See further the Bibliography to Philemon.

Commentary

INTRODUCTION, 1:1-14

Salutation, 1:1, 2

[1] PAUL OPENS HIS LETTER in the distinctive style which sets Christian correspondence off from secular counterparts of the time. The identity of the writer is elaborated by the designation **an apostle of Christ Jesus by the will of God** (cf. Eph. 1:1, 2). Known to his readers only by reputation, Paul clarifies his right to intervene in their affairs by identifying himself as **an apostle of Christ Jesus**. While *apostolos* is used to designate the Twelve (Mark 3:14; Luke 6:13), it cannot be assumed that this qualification is always in the minds of the writers employing the term in the New Testament (see Rom. 16:7; Acts 14:14; Rev. 2:2; 2 Cor. 8:23).

Timothy (*timotheos*, "one who honors God"), son of a Jewish Christian mother and a Gentile father, had accompanied Paul since his visit at Lystra (Acts 16:1f.) and served in the apostle's entourage in varying capacities (see 1 Cor. 16:10; 1 Thess. 3:1-5). The apostle holds Timothy in high esteem (see 1 Thess. 3:6; Phil. 2:19f.), and he may have converted the younger man himself (1 Cor. 4:17). The inclusion of Timothy in the opening greeting is not unusual in Paul's letters (cf. 1, 2 Thessalonians, 2 Corinthians, Philippians and Philemon), and it possibly indicates Timothy's function as the apostle's amanuensis (see 4:18).

[2] Paul's designation of the recipients of his letter foreshadows the line of argument he follows in addressing the particular problems besetting the church at Colossae. The word **saints** (*hagiois*) might possibly be taken as an adjective parallel with **faithful,** thus reading "holy and faithful

¹ Paul, an apostle of Christ Jesus by the will of God, and Timothy our brother,
² To the saints and faithful brethren in Christ at Colossae:
Grace to you and peace from God our Father.
³ We always thank God, the Father of our Lord Jesus Christ, when we pray for you,

---

brethren." The word is, however, used as a substantive by Paul elsewhere (cf. 1:4; Rom. 1:7; 12:13; 15:25, 26; Eph. 1:1) and it is so understood by the RSV and the majority of translations. Though perhaps the word is a technical term for "Christian" by the time of Paul's letter, it derives its meaning from the Hebrew _kadosh_ and primarily indicates (when referring to the people of God, cf. Ex. 19:5f.) dedication and commitment to God rather than excellence of character (which no doubt develops from such dedication). Preaching is the event by which Paul's readers have become "holy" (cf. 1 Thess. 1:5; 2 Thess. 2:13f.).

In Christ, more than any other phrase, is representative of the theology of the letter. Here, Paul uses the term to define the preceding clause. Those steadfastly remaining in Christ through loyal devotion to him stand in a relationship with one another similar to that of **brethren. Grace to you and peace from God our Father.** Paul's salutation combines both Greek and Jewish custom, elevating the greeting almost to the form of a prayer. Paul is also announcing a present reality already obtained by those in Christ. **Grace** (_charis_) indicates the favor or unmerited love of God (Gen. 6:8) which has been demonstrated and experienced in Christ (Rom. 5:15f.; Phil. 1:7). The Christian's experience of God's love shown in Christ also issues in the experience of **peace** (_eirēnē_) or harmony (see 3:15, cf. Phil. 4:6, 7).

Thanksgiving and Prayer, 1:3-14

[3] The apostle asserts that the Colossians are always in his prayers. Whether one reads **always** (_pantote_) with **we thank** (RSV; cf. 1 Cor. 1:4) or with **we pray** (_proseuchomenoi,_ "praying" KJV; cf. Eph. 1:16) is of little significance for the meaning of the verse. It is important, however, in

⁴ **because we have heard of your faith in Christ Jesus and of the love which you have for all the saints, ⁵ because of the hope laid up for you in heaven. Of this you have heard before in the word of the truth, the gospel**

---

light of the subsequent line of Paul's arguments, to note the close relationship between God and Jesus, designated as the **Lord** (*kurios*).

[4] The ground of Paul's thanksgiving is twofold. Paul has not seen the Colossians personally but has been informed by Epaphras (vs. 8) of their steadfastness (**faith,** see vs. 2 above) **in Christ** and of their **love for all the saints** (see 2:1, 2; 3:14; Phile. 5; Eph. 1:15).

[5] The triad of faith, love and **hope** frequently occurs at this position in the prayers of Paul's letters (e.g., 1 Thess. 1:3; cf. 2 Thess. 1:3f.; 1 Cor. 13:13). Yet the first part of the verse occasions some question. Is **hope** (*elpis*) to be joined with **faith** and **love** as a third cause for thanksgiving? Or is it to be understood as the ground of the previous two? The latter seems to be the case inasmuch as Paul and other New Testament writers speak of the Christian's future "inheritance" as an incentive for present perseverance (cf. 1:12; 3:24; Phil. 3:8-16; Heb. 6:17-20). **Hope** describes both a future goal and the present life-style it produces (1:23, 27; Eph. 1:18; 2:12; Rom. 15:13; cf. 1 Peter 1:21; 3:15). The precise nature of the reward, however, and the selflessness requisite for its reception render the reward motive a Christian impossibility. In verse 5 Paul emphasizes the security of the Christian hope in describing it as **laid up** (*apokeimenēn,* possibly "reserved") **for you in heaven.**

But Paul is also anxious to point out that the Christian hope is grounded precisely in the message which the Colossians **have heard before** (from Epaphras, see 1:7, 23; 2:6). This previous message which the Colossians have received is **the word of the truth, the gospel** (Eph. 1:13f.). Although the apostle's use of **before** possibly means before the present letter, many scholars feel that Paul makes an oblique reference to the recent heretical teachings, in effect saying "the true gospel you heard before you heard false teachings" (see 2:4, 8).

[6] which has come to you, as indeed in the whole world it is bearing fruit and growing—so among yourselves, from the day you heard and understood the grace of God in truth, [7] as you learned it from Epaphras our beloved fellow servant. He is a faithful minister of Christ on our [a] behalf [8] and has made known to us your love in the Spirit.

[a] Other ancient authorities read *your*

---

[6] Again Paul emphasizes that the message which the Colossians received was no inferior or truncated gospel. It is the same message preached everywhere in the whole world and is everywhere showing its truth by bearing fruit and growing (cf. Rom. 1:13; 1 Thess. 1:8f.). The apostle appeals to the standard of universality to oppose the Colossian heresy, which is by implication local and inferior (cf. 1:23, 28).

The term **bearing fruit** (*karpophoroumenon*) is found only here and in verse 10 in Paul's letters. Irenaeus, writing in the second century, indicates that at that time the expression was a regular technical term among Gnostics (cf. *Against Heresies* I. i. 3; iv. 4; viii. 5; xiv. 5). It may be conjectured that some of the false teachers in Colossae had been urging Colossian Christians to "grow" and "bear fruit" in the sense of advancing in the attainment of abstract knowledge and wisdom. By contrast, Paul argues that true "fruit bearing" and "growth" are found in the Christian message which demonstrates its power by bearing fruit in the lives of Christians "in every good work" (vs. 10 below).

[7, 8] Verses 7 and 8 provide information regarding events prior to and leading up to the writing of Paul's letter. For the first time, Paul mentions Epaphras by name (see 4:12). Verse 7 makes it plain that Epaphras was the one who founded the church in Colossae, probably evangelizing the entire area. Paul indicates that he holds Epaphras in high esteem, calling him **fellow servant** and **faithful minister** (cf. 4:7 on both terms).

A question arises regarding whether one should read **our behalf** (ASV, RSV, NEB) or "your behalf" (KJV). The difference in the Greek is slight (*hēmōn*, "our," *humōn*, "your") and constituted a frequent problem for scribes (cf. 1:12; 1 Cor. 3:2; Gal. 4:28). If one accepts the original read-

⁹ And so, from the day we heard of it, we have not ceased to pray for you, asking that you may be filled with the knowledge of his will in all spiritual wisdom and understanding, ¹⁰ to lead a life worthy of the Lord, fully pleasing to him, bearing fruit in every good work and increasing in the knowledge of God.

---

ing as **your,** it would be possible to understand Epaphras as a representative of the Colossian church (similar to Phil. 2:25; 4:18; Phile. 13). Or Paul might be referring to Epaphras' preaching to the Colossians as his service on their behalf. On the other hand, if one accepts the reading **our,** several insights are gained. Paul indicates that Epaphras has evangelized Colossae and the Lycus Valley under his direction (possibly during his stay in Ephesus; see Acts 19:10). This also explains the apostle's authority in a church he has never seen. Further, Paul in effect says that the message received from Epaphras bears his seal of approval and its hearers stand in no need for additional or new teachings (see 1:5). Paul also assures his readers that Epaphras has not simply informed him of their bad traits and weaknesses. Rather, **he has made known to us your love in the Spirit.**

In spite of the RSV's capitalization of "Spirit" (*pneumati*), the absence of the article makes it uncertain whether the apostle here refers specifically to the Holy Spirit or is using "spirit" in a more general sense (as in vss. 9; 2:5; cf. Eph. 1:3; 6:12; Rom. 1:11; 7:14). If the reference is to the Holy Spirit, it is the only one in the letter.

[9] Paul now continues in intercessory prayer because of the information gained from Epaphras (KJV "for this cause," cf. Eph. 1:15-17). In praying that the Colossians **be filled with the knowledge of his will,** he touches the center of the dangerous heretical tendency which is threatening the Colossian church. The word **filled** (*plērōthēte*) may carry the meaning of "completion" or "maturity" (cf. 1:25; 4:12; Eph. 3:19), indicating that Christians have access to adequate knowledge for maturity in the Christian message. Paul's word **knowledge** (*epignōsis*) is found in the opening prayers of all the "prison letters" (cf. Eph. 1:17) and is generally reserved for knowledge of God (though not exclusively, see Rom. 3:20).

[11] May you be strengthened with all power, according to his glorious might, for all endurance and patience with joy,

---

The filling of the Christian with the knowledge of God's will is carried out in his having **spiritual wisdom and understanding**. Here again Paul contrasts Christian knowledge which gives spiritual wisdom with the apparent wisdom of the false teachers in Colossae (see 2:8, 23; cf. 1 Cor. 1, 2 for contrasts between human and spiritual wisdom). While the emphasis falls on **spiritual** in contrast to the false counterparts, the words **wisdom** (*sophia*) and **understanding** (*sunesis*) are important (cf. Eph. 1:9). They are familiar to Paul's readers and may well be part of the vocabulary of the heretical teachers. By **wisdom,** Paul means mental excellence; by **understanding** he means the critical judgment to distinguish between truth and falsehood.

[10] Paul heightens the contrast between Christian knowledge and the abstract, speculative doctrines of his opponents by linking Christian knowledge with conduct. Christian "knowledge" leads to a life-style enabling one **to lead a life worthy of the Lord** (see comments on Eph. 4:1; cf. 1 Thess. 1:12; 2 Thess. 1:5; Phil. 1:27), a life which testifies to the truth of the Christian message by virtue of its **bearing fruit in every good work** (see 1:6; Phil. 1:11; cf. Eph. 2:10). **Increasing** indicates that there is a progression or growth in the Christian life, while **the knowledge of God** may be understood as indicating the avenue through which Christian growth comes (see Eph. 4:13).

[11] Paul further elaborates the process referred to in the previous verse (cf. Eph. 1:18). The Christian is continually being **strengthened** (present participle) by God so that he might bear himself in steadfastness facing the vicissitudes of life. Whereas the previous verse focused on outward conduct, Paul here emphasizes qualities of character with which God supplies the Christian. In general, **endurance** (*hupomonēn*) indicates that attitude of mind which does not succumb to cowardice or the onslaughts of despondency. Elsewhere it is allied with the hope which gives it confidence (1 Thess. 1:3). **Patience** (*makrothumian*) designates an attitude of self-restraint, an unwillingness to engage in hasty retaliation or revenge (see 3:12; cf. 1 Cor. 13:4; Gal. 5:22).

¹² giving thanks to the Father, who has qualified us ᵇ to share in the inheritance of the saints in light.

ᵇ Other ancient authorities read *you*

The RSV reading provides rather clear meaning in referring to God's **glorious might** (cf. 1:29; 2:12; Eph. 1:19; 3:16; 6:10). Yet it is also possible to understand the apostle as saying that Christians are strengthened by "the might of his glory" (ASV). Though *doxa* (glory) is used in various ways in the New Testament (see 1 Cor. 11:7; 15:40f.; 2 Cor. 6:8), the use of the term is essentially shaped by its use in the Septuagint translation of the Old Testament where it translates the Hebrew *kabod* (and several related words), a term closely associated with the mode of God's being as it is revealed in his mighty revelatory acts and is often associated with visual imagery (e.g., Ex. 24:17; 34:29ff.; cf. Ezek. 1:4ff.; Acts 7:2). Likewise, in the New Testament the term is closely associated with "light" (1 Cor. 15:40, 41; 2 Cor. 3:7-18, "splendor" RSV; 4:4; Rev. 21:23; cf. Luke 9:29-31) and "power" (Rom. 6:4; 1 Cor. 15:43; Eph. 3:16; Phil. 3:21; 2 Thess. 1:9; Matt. 24:30). Thus *doxa* is appropriate to use regarding the revelatory acts of Jesus' death (John 13:31) and resurrection (Rom. 6:4). Yet, the New Testament writers further assert that Jesus actually shares in the *doxa* of God (e.g., John 1:14; 2 Cor. 4:4, 6; Heb. 1:3), himself the "Lord of *doxa*" (1 Cor. 2:8).

[12] Thanksgiving to God forms a natural response to the believer's experience of having a new nature (mind, moral stature, and good works). Paul's reference to God as **the Father** without qualifying words is slightly unusual though not unique (see Rom. 6:4; Eph. 2:18; 3:14). The believer knows God through what he has done through Christ: that is, he **qualified us to share in the inheritance of the saints in light.** This entire clause utilizes the Old Testament concept of God's qualifying his people for the promised land (see Josh. 14:9). Here, of course, the concept has been altered to refer to a heavenly (vs. 5), not earthly, goal (see Phil. 3:20).

Qualified (*hikanōsanti*) indicates that God has made Christians adequate to that which is necessary in order for them to share in the future of those chosen. Against the

¹³ He has delivered us from the dominion of darkness and transferred us to the kingdom of his beloved Son,

---

Colossian heretics' charges that Christians lack further knowledge or redemption (see Introduction), the apostle emphasizes the finality of what God has already done for the Christian—a tendency that runs throughout the letter. Part of the occasion for the Christian's thanksgiving stems from the fact that such qualification is a gift from God, not an attainment. The Christian may only be called "worthy" (vs. 10) in a limited sense; his qualification has been allotted by God, not won by human action. The Christian has a share or portion in the lot set aside by God for the saints in light.

[13] Not only has God "qualified us" (vs. 12), he has also delivered and transferred us. Deliverance (*errusato*) is particularly connected with the Old Testament concept of God's rescue of his people from various situations of adversity (Egypt, Assyria, Babylon). Here, however, the concept has been turned into a spiritual metaphor. Christians have been delivered from the dominion of darkness, the realm of moral and intellectual "darkness" accruing from man's self-alienation from God (see 1:21; Rom. 1:21; Eph. 4:17, 18; 5:8, 11; 6:12; 1 Peter 2:9). There is no reason to understand "darkness" as referring to Satan (but compare Acts 26:18 and Eph. 2:2; 6:12).

Using a word calling to his readers' minds the mass deportations of various peoples by oriental potentates (similar to Nazi deportations of Jews), the apostle states that Christians have already been transferred (*metestēsen*) from the realm of darkness. By implication, Christians are now in the realm of light (compare with the use of light as strictly future in verse 12). They are no longer subject to the forces ruling this world (see 2:8, 15, 20; 3:2) but have, at the time of their baptism (see 2:12, 20; 3:1; cf. Eph. 5:14), been removed to the kingdom of God's beloved Son. The continual stress on the significance and finality of Christian baptism that one finds throughout the letter probably indicates that the heresy diminished its significance (see 2:11, 12, 20; 3:1, 5 below). In contrast to the teachings of the Colossian heretics, the Christian does not stand in a subservient relation-

¹⁴ in whom we have redemption, the forgiveness of sins.

ship to various inferior intermediary forces and beings (see 1:16; 2:18; cf. Heb. chs. 1-2). Rather, Paul here speaks of the Christian as having been moved or transferred to the realm of the one described as superior to all powers, namely God's beloved Son (a description possibly derived from current Jewish messianic speculation regarding Psalm 2).

[14] The apostle continues his emphasis on the complete efficacy of God's acts on behalf of man, saying, **we have redemption**. Paul here uses the term **redemption** (*apolutrōsis*) in a general sense of "rescued" or "emancipated" and not with the more specific connotation of ransomed or sacrificed (KJV "through his blood" is probably a scribal error influenced by Eph. 1:7). Even more significant, however, is the fact that the apostle speaks of redemption as a present possession (cf. Rom. 8:23; Eph. 4:30). More precisely, the Christian's experience of redemption is defined as the **forgiveness** (*aphesin*, "release," "cancellation") **of sins** (see 2:13). This further note is probably due to a false understanding of redemption espoused by the Colossian heretics. *Apolutrōsis* is known to have become a popular term in later Gnosticism, which divorced it from the moral realm and equated it with immortality and special secret doctrines (see vs. 9) and rituals. Perhaps **redemption** was a term used by the heretics to designate an escape from the body or an escape through the heavenly spheres; hence Paul's specification. As he does repeatedly in the letter, Paul emphasizes that the problem of man and the universe has moral roots, being grounded in the problem of sin. Therefore, the present redemption has a moral character, **the forgiveness of sins** (see 3:5ff.).

THE PRE-EMINENCE OF CHRIST, 1:15-23

In a hymn exalting Christ as both creator and savior of the cosmos (see Introduction), the apostle develops the core of his argument against the Colossian heresy (vss. 15-20). The words strike the reader familiar with Paul's other letters as somewhat unusual. In composing or adapting the hymn (see Introduction), the apostle consciously

¹⁵ **He is the image of the invisible God, the first-born of all creation;**

---

addresses his words to the concerns of Hellenistic man who understood himself as resident of a world alienated from God and under the influence of myriad spiritual forces controlling human life. Christ is thus presented not just in terms of individual salvation; he is here exalted as Lord of the cosmos.

The hymn, possibly intended by the apostle to be used in the worship of the Colossian church (see 3:16), forms the basis of his subsequent arguments throughout the letter. In opposition to the heretics' diminishment of Christ's significance by counting him among a multiplicity of divine mediators, Paul asserts Christ's superiority by attributing to him all the roles and functions distributed among the heresy's hierarchy of celestial beings. With regard to the creation: Christ is pre-existent; he is God's agent in creating the cosmos, including all sentient beings in heaven and on earth; he is presently sustaining the entire creation; he is also the goal of the entire creation. Parallel to Christ's relationship to the creation, he is also the agent of God's redemption of the entire cosmos and equally pre-eminent in the new creation; he is the agent of God's reconciliation of all things, including the heavenly beings; he is the source of the life of the new creation, his body; he is also the ultimate goal of all God's redemptive activity.

Christ and the Universe, 1:15-17

[15] Paul begins his description of Christ by identifying him as the image, visible by inference, of the invisible God. Image (*eikōn*) occurs twenty times in the New Testament (eight times in Paul's letters, e.g., 2 Cor. 4:4). Literally, the word means a "representation" or a "reflection"; yet it also carries a metaphorical meaning more akin to "mental image" or "likeness." The term was used to describe the personal characteristics of individuals in official documents. The term is also ascribed to rulers (especially in Egypt), who are understood to be living images of the gods. The passage can also be related to Christ and Adam (see Gen. 1:27), the implication being that Christ is what Adam was in-

tended to be. In other words, Christ manifests not only God, but as the true image of God, he shows true manhood. Certainly the Adam-Christ typology has far-reaching significance for Paul (Rom. 5:12-21; 1 Cor. 15:22, 45-49) and is implicit in certain contexts (Phil. 2:5-11; Gal. 3:28). Still another possibility stems from the development of the Logos (Reason) speculation in Alexandrian Judaism. Prior to Paul's time, the Logos, God's creative reason and power, had been described by Philo as the *eikōn* of God. However, the most probable source for Paul's description of Christ as the *eikōn* of God is the Jewish Wisdom literature of the Old Testament and intertestamental thought. Paul ascribes to Christ certain functions that one finds ascribed to the hypostatized Wisdom in the Wisdom writings (see especially Job 28, Ps. 33, Prov. 8, Ecclesiasticus 24, Wisd. of Sol. 7:24-27; 9:1, 2).

The possibility of a conceptual link with the Wisdom literature is strengthened by the occurrence of several words in this section of the letter also used in the Jewish Wisdom Literature to describe Wisdom (for example, *eikōn*, Wisd. of Sol. 7:26; *archē* vs. 18, Prov. 8:22; also Paul's words "renewing," "treasures," "riches," "hide" in 2:2, 3 and 3:10 are found in Wisd. of Sol. 7:14, 27). Thus Paul is drawing on a complex of ideas and terms developed in Jewish Wisdom speculation rather than on some other source such as the mystery religions or Greek philosophy (see 1 Cor. 1:24, 30; 2 Cor. 4:4).

Christ's mediatorial function is implied by Paul's reference to Christ as the **first-born of all creation.** The word **first-born** (*prōtotokos;* used eight times in the New Testament, elsewhere by Paul in vs. 18; Rom. 8:29) is used in the Old Testament in describing Israel's special relationship as God's heir (Ex. 4:22; Jer. 31:9). The term came to be used as a messianic title (Ps. 89:27) indicating the Messiah as God's heir and is used in the New Testament as a messianic title (Heb. 1:6). The apostle's designation, however, may be understood as a reference to Wisdom, existing before the creation of the world (Ecclesiasticus 1:4; 24:9). From Proverbs 8:22, "The Lord created me at the beginning of his work," Jewish rabbinical thought had taken the word "beginning" (*rēshîth,* Gen. 1:1) as a desig-

[16] for in him all things were created, in heaven and on earth, visible and invisible, whether thrones or dominions or principalities or authorities—all things were created through him and for him.

---

nation for Wisdom. Speculation on Genesis 1:1, "In the beginning God created the world . . . ," proceeded on the basis of the identification of wisdom with "beginning." The preposition "in" (Hebrew *be*) was also capable of meaning "by" or "into," so a creative function was ascribed to Wisdom by rendering Genesis 1:1, "By Wisdom God created . . ." *Prōtotokos* (as the words "beginning" and "head," vs. 18) was a possible translation of the Hebrew word behind "beginning." If this connection does in fact underlie the use of the term first-born (here and in verse 18) in the hymn, Paul is ascribing to Christ the creative role (more explicitly stated in the following verse) ascribed to Wisdom by rabbinic speculation and probably influential on the heretical thought at Colossae (cf. Rom. 8:29f.; Heb. 1:1-6). The expression **all creation** thus designates the inclusiveness of Christ as the agent of God in creating all that has been brought into existence.

[16] Paul further elaborates the significance of his designation of Christ as "image" and "first-born." For (*hoti*) might better be translated "so that," indicating the close connection between the preceding statement and that which follows. **In him** may be influenced either by Philo's speculations which spoke of the Logos as the place where the divine thoughts resided, or by Stoic speculations conceiving of the Logos as a divine essence permeating all things. More likely, as already indicated by his employment of Wisdom terminology (e.g., "image" and "first-born"), Paul here consciously describes Christ in terms of the creative functions attributed to the hypostatized Wisdom of Rabbinical Judaism (see Prov. 8:22-31; Wisd. of Sol. 7:22; 8:5, 6; 9:2, 9). Thus, in opposition to the heavy Jewish flavor of the Colossian heresy (see Introduction), Christ is here portrayed as the agent of creation ("by" him) and equated with God's creative Wisdom. **All things were created** is a reference to the act of creation (see 1 Cor. 8:6; John 1:3; 1 John 4:9, 10). The RSV's **all things** refers to the

entire created order, the universe. There is no hint here of the Stoic concept of a self-sustaining reality. Paul conceives of the universe as an orderly, cohering unity that owes its existence to something other than itself, namely, to a creator.

To avoid misunderstanding, Paul adds that the creation was **in, through** and **for** Christ. He first uses the Jewish concept of the **heavens and the earth** (see Gen. 1:1; 2:1) and then the Greek concept of **visible and invisible** (cf. 2 Cor. 4:18). Obviously these expressions are not exactly parallel in that visible may be "in heaven" (moon and stars) and vice versa. Paul makes the unmistakable point that everything is created in Christ; at the same time he implicitly but effectively repudiates the dualism that may have undergirded the heretical teaching in Colossae (see vss. 20, 22; 2:20ff.).

With this basis for his statements, the apostle moves with more force against the angel worship present in the Colossian heresy (cf. 2:15, 18, 20). Grouped among the things created in Christ, Paul lists **thrones, dominions, principalities** and **authorities.** These words are probably technical terms used by the Colossian heretics to designate supernatural powers. They possibly represent a hierarchy of celestial beings such as those characterizing the elaborate systems of Gnosticism in the following century (where there were as many as three hundred sixty-five such beings in one system). Thus Paul refutes the assertions of the heretics who probably attribute some creative roles to the various angelic beings who were also envisioned as presently "sustaining" and controlling the universe. Christ is the sole agent of the creation, creating the very beings which the heretics worship (2:18) and himself presently undergirding the universe. Since such beings are clearly inferior to the one through whom they were created and in whom they now exist, there is no justification for regarding them as additional mediators.

The apostle continues to use prepositions to express the all-encompassing superiority of Christ. He has designated Christ as the agency of the creation, God's creative Wisdom ("in him," *en autō*). Now Paul states that Christ is also the goal or destiny of all things (cf. Eph. 1:10; 3:9, 10), the

¹⁷ He is before all things, and in him all things hold together.

---

universe being **created through him and for him.** Thus Christ is both the agency of the creation and the ultimate goal of the creation (see Rom. 8:19; 1 Cor. 8:6; 15:28; Rev. 22:13; John 1:3, 10; Heb. 1:2). This latter statement, that the creation is for Christ and finds its ultimate meaning and purpose in him, probably carries Paul beyond the functions ascribed to Wisdom by rabbinical Judaism and introduces a new note to the heretics who were influenced by such concepts. Additionally, this statement sets Christianity apart from religious views (such as probably influenced the heresy) which conceived of salvation as "escape" from the world and the ongoing of history. Paul asserts that the whole cosmos moves in history toward a final goal in Christ.

[17] Paul's emphatic use of the pronoun **he** (see Eph. 2:14; 4:10, 11; 1 John 2:2; Rev. 19:15) more literally means "He it is who is. . . ." That is, Christ and no other power is pre-existent and pre-eminent in the cosmos (see John 8:58). It is uncertain, however, whether one should read "is" or "exists." The use of the present tense (instead of "was," see John 1:1) may emphasize a qualitative difference between Christ's existence and that of the created universe. This is, of course, implicit throughout the argument here and not dependent on this point. The phrase **before all things** (*pro pantōn*) asserts Christ's pre-existence. Although it is possible that the preposition **before** (*pro*) signifies priority in the sense of superiority (cf. James 5:12), the apostle's intent here is to reassert the identification of Christ with the pre-existent and creative Wisdom of God (cf. Prov. 8:22-31). Nonetheless, Christ's pre-existence and the creative role previously attributed to him connote superiority over that which is created.

All things (*ta panta;* "the all") encompasses the universe (including the angelic functionaries of the previous verse). Paul has just indicated that Christ is the agent and ultimate goal of creation. He now continues to develop more clearly a point suggested by the concluding words of the previous verse regarding the present relationship of Christ to the universe (see vs. 16). Namely, it is in Christ that **all things**

¹⁸ He is the head of the body, the church; he is the beginning, the first-born from the dead, that in everything he
might be preëminent.

---

hold together (ASV "consist"). Wisdom too had been said
to permeate all things and hold them together (Wisd. of
Sol. 1:7; 7:24). The term **hold together** (*sunestēken;* found
only here and 2 Peter 3:5) means "to cohere" or "to hold
together in an orderly fashion." In effect, Paul designates
Christ as the principle of cohesion which presently upholds
the universe and gives it order and design. The universe is
continually being sustained by Christ as the one who causes
it to be "cosmos and not chaos" (cf. Heb. 1:3).

Christ and the Church, 1:18-20

[18] Having shown the relationship of Christ to the
universe, Paul now turns to the relationship of Christ to the
church, the new creation (see 3:10; cf. Gal. 6:15). Paul now
asserts the precedence of Christ in the church, not only
demonstrating the superiority and authority of Christ over
the church but also stressing the importance of the church.
The Colossian heretics had minimized the church in their
doctrines, which had had a divisive effect (cf. 2:19; 3:15).

Paul again uses the emphatic pronoun, saying in effect,
"And he it is, precisely he who is over the cosmos, who is
the head of the church." In previous letters Paul has spoken
of the church as the **body** (*sōma;* see 1 Cor. 10:16, 17; 12:12,
27; Rom. 12:5) but has not spoken of Christ as its **head**
(*kephalē*) as he does both in Colossians and Ephesians (see
2:19; Eph. 1:22, 23; 4:15; 5:23). In the early letters **body**
is used as a metaphor; here there is an essential relationship.
The basis for this development is already in Romans 12:5,
"we are one body in Christ."

The word **head** (*kephalē*) literally refers to that part of
the physical body; or metaphorically, it may indicate "rule"
or "authority" (as the mind rules over the body). Additional
light is cast on Paul's use of both **head** and **beginning** in
this verse by the usage they have in the Septuagint, where
both words are used to translate the Hebrew word *rosh*
("head," "first," or "chief because of priority in being").
When there is a difference it is generally that *archē* ("be-

ginning," RSV) translates the feminine *rêshith* with the connotation of "first" or "source." The close relation between these two words in the Greek Old Testament has led to the suggestion that Paul's use of *kephalē* designates the literal closeness between the head and body while *archē* carries a connotation from its Old Testament usage and means "source" (Rev. 3:14). Such an explanation recognizes a parallel between the designation of Christ as the source of the universe in the first half of the hymn and the source of the life of the church in the second half.

Paul's designation of the church (*ekklēsia*) as the *body* (*sōmatos*) has far-reaching implications. In contrast to the heresy, which probably had a severe individualistic tendency, Christians are portrayed as members of the same body. Paul's statement cannot be taken simply as a metaphor. Rather, he asserts that the church is an organism in which the individual members actually form vital parts (cf. Eph. 4:16). Christians are not isolated individuals in Christ who are only incidentally related to each other. To be in Christ is to be at the same time incorporated into his body, the church.

Of equal importance in opposing the heresy is the indication of Christ's power and authority. That Christ is able to incorporate into himself all who follow him testifies to his power to protect and empower his followers in the new life (see 3:1-4). The relationship between Christ and the church forms the premise for a number of Paul's further statements. As the members of the body are in Christ, it may also be said that Christ is in them (see 1:27; cf. 3:3). To honor something other than the source of life, the head, is to cut oneself off from the body which it permeates with its life (see 2:19; cf. 3:11).

Paul's understanding of Christ's centrality in the church and in God's cosmos-embracing plan stems from the resurrection. The source of the designations with which he has referred to Christ center in this event. Christ is the first-born from the dead (Acts 26:23; Rom. 14:9; Rev. 1:5). Again, the repetition of first-born (*prōtotokos*) heightens the parallel between Christ's relationship to the universe and to the church. Paul also refers to the preaching which the Colossians first received from Epaphras, undoubtedly centering

¹⁹ **For in him all the fulness of God was pleased to dwell,** ²⁰ **and through him to reconcile to himself all things, whether on earth or in heaven, making peace by the blood of his cross.**

---

on the resurrection (see 1 Cor. 15:3ff.). The parallel is not exact, however, for the resurrection not only has significance in the church but also demonstrates the authority and significance of Christ in the entire universe (see Eph. 1:22; Phil. 2.9-11; 1 Peter 3:21, 22; Rev. 1:5). Nonetheless, the resurrection is the unique event which creates the church, giving it confidence and hope (see 1 Cor. 6:4; 15:20; cf. 1 Peter 1:3).

The ultimate goal of God's purpose in Christ is **that in everything he might be pre-eminent.** Paul continues to destroy any possible understanding of Christ's role in God's plan which would allow room for other mediators. God's act in Christ moves to the goal of making him the focus of all of God's purposes for the entire universe (see 1:26).

[19] The RSV somewhat masks the difficulty of the verse. The word "God" does not appear in the Greek. **Fulness** is the subject of the verb unless, as it has been suggested, **was pleased** (*eudokēsen*) is a Jewish idiom for "the will of God." Yet, there is no evidence to support such an idiomatic use of the word (cf. Rom. 15:26, 27; 1 Thess. 2:8; 3:1; 2 Thess. 2:12). It is probably better to take **fulness** (*plērōma*) as equivalent to "God in his fulness" and the subject of the verb. That is, one may understand *plērōma* to refer to the totality of the divine attributes (NEB, "the complete being of God"; Jerusalem Bible, "all perfection") which are not separated among numerous supernatural beings but are displayed in Christ (see 2:9, 10; cf. Eph. 1:22, 23 where the church is included in the fulness).

To dwell (*katoikēsai*) occurs again in 2:9 with "fulness" and possibly indicates a permanent dwelling, though the word does not necessarily have to bear this meaning with all New Testament writers (cf. Acts 2:5; 7:4).

[20] Paul's word **reconcile** (*apokatallaxia*) is not his customary word for expressing this concept and may be intended to emphasize that what is involved is the restoring of an originally harmonious relationship which has been

lost (cf. Rom. 5:10, 11; 11:15; 1 Cor. 7:11; 2 Cor. 5:18, 19).
The word that the apostle here uses is twice used in close
connection with **peace** (vs. 20 and Eph. 2:16), and on all
three occasions of its use in the New Testament it is associated with Christ (see 1:22; Eph. 2:16). Such a conception
carries a rebuttal to any dualism in Colossae, insisting that
there is no inherent alienation between God and the created
world. The biblical teaching is that although man may live
in a world under evil influences, the world itself is not evil
but an originally good thing despoiled by man's sin. This
concern may explain the cosmic application of the concept
of reconciliation. The context implies that the whole universe, not just man, is the subject of reconciliation (see
Rom. ch. 8). The creation, originally created in, for, and
unto Christ, is in its entirety to be restored through him
(RSV, "to himself," cf. Eph. 1:10). It should be noted that
though elsewhere God is both subject and object of the
verb (2 Cor. 5:19f.; Rom. 5:10), the apostle here refers to
Christ as both the agency of reconciliation (see vs. 16) and
the one to whom all things are reconciled. The reconciling
work of Christ is all-inclusive, embracing all things whether
on earth or in heaven. Christ is the agent of all the divine
reconciling, just as he is the sole agent of the creation of
the universe. (Again it should be noted that these roles are
those ascribed to hypostatized Wisdom in Judaism; cf.
Wisd. of Sol. chs. 10, 11.)

The statement that God, through Christ, has made peace
is to be understood in the context of a first-century outlook
of a universe inhabited by partially hostile supernatural
forces which war among themselves and pose a constant
threat to vulnerable man. In particular, Paul's statement is
directed against the Colossian heresy which, undergirded
by this world-view, urges the observance of special rites
and rituals to protect its adherents from such powers and
the fear that such an outlook occasions. **Peace** here thus
has a cosmic dimension in addition to the more usually
understood implications (such a dimension is not without
some basis in Paul's previous letters; see Rom. 8; cf. Isa.
11:6-9). Through Christ, God, the creator of all such powers, has put an end to all the warring forces at work in the
universe and is engaged in bringing all things into peace

²¹ And you, who once were estranged and hostile in mind, doing evil deeds,

---

under the rule of his beloved Son (see vs. 13 above; 2:15; 3:14, 15; but cf. Eph. 6:12).

In addition to asserting that God makes peace through Christ, Paul also states that the focal point of this act is located in the ignominious death of Christ on the cross: **by the blood of his cross.** The mention of Christ's blood undoubtedly contains a sacrificial significance (see Rom. 3:25; 5:9; 1 Cor. 10:16; 11:27; Eph. 1:7; 2:13) but may also include an additional counter to the dualism underlying the Colossian heresy (see vs. 16 above; cf. John 19:34; 1 John 1:7; 5:6, 8). The reference also calls to mind the apostle's use of the scandal of the cross in opposition to those seeking "wisdom" at Corinth (see 1 Cor. 1:18ff.). Similar problems are apparently posed by the heretics at Colossae who have set themselves up as spiritual or intellectual elite. The great cosmic event in God's purpose is centered in the death of the man Jesus of Nazareth on the cross. The apostle here refers to an event in recent history, an act and not some abstract philosophical principle. God has acted on man's behalf in Christ. By identifying Wisdom with the man Jesus and centering God's redemption in Jesus' death on the cross (cf. 1:22; 2:14, 15), Paul has moved beyond anything in Wisdom speculation and given new meaning to the familiar terms.

Application to the Readers, 1:21-23

[21] Prior to their reception of the gospel, the Colossians were **estranged and hostile in mind.** Here Paul is speaking to Gentiles, though elsewhere he takes this same tone regarding all men, Jews included (see Eph. 2:3). The word **estranged** (*apēllotriōmenous*) bears the connotation of "excluded" or "separated" (see Eph. 2:12; 4:18, RSV "alienation"). Man, not God, bears the responsibility for this condition. The Gentiles themselves had achieved this state. The resulting situation involves the total man. By virtue of their being alienated from God, men become **hostile** (*echthrous*, NEB, "enemies") towards both God and their fellow man (cf. Eph. 2:16). The word Paul uses for **mind** (*tē dianoia*) was common in Greek literature and had come

²² he has now reconciled in his body of flesh by his death, in order to present you holy and blameless and irreproach-able before him,

---

into the Jewish religious vocabulary through its use in the Septuagint where it is translated "heart." It embodies the total disposition of a person, including the intellect but also the emotions (see Eph. 4:18; Heb. 8:10; 10:16; 1 Peter 1:13; 2 Peter 3:1; 1 John 5:20). Thus Paul refers to the pre-Christian mode of life that the Colossians had previously experienced, a way of life characterized by an outlook hostile to God and expressing itself in evil deeds.

[22] Having reminded his readers of their prior condition, Paul now reminds them of what has been achieved on their behalf by Christ: You he has now reconciled in his body of flesh by his death (2 Cor. 5:19). Paul intends a sharp contrast between verses 21 and 22 (NEB, "but now"), indicating that the former condition has been overcome by God. The Colossians have been reconciled (*apokatēllaxen*). They have not been partially reconciled, necessitating further reconciliation (see vss. 12, 13). Having previously mentioned the cross (vs. 20), Paul refers to Christ's body of flesh, distinguishing this reference to Christ's natural body from the earlier designation of the church as his body (vs. 18; Eph. 2:15, 16; cf. Col. 2:11 where a different concern is present).

Through Christ's death the Colossian Christians are presented (*parastēsai*, "placed before," "entrusted" or "commended"; cf. Eph. 5:27) to God. Paul's word here is a sacrificial one (as are two of the following words) and sets the tone of the whole statement. Through Christ's sacrifice, all those incorporated in him are in turn presented to God (see Rom. 12:1; Phil. 2:17). Thus Paul here points to the principle of self-identification of the Christian with Christ (see 2:12). In light of Paul's concern to emphasize the completeness of the reconciliation achieved through Christ and his earlier emphasis on that which God has done on behalf of the Christian, it seems best to understand this reference to the present state of the Christian rather than the future judgment (though such an interpretation is not impossible).

²³ provided that you continue in the faith, stable and stead-fast, not shifting from the hope of the gospel which you heard, which has been preached to every creature under heaven, and of which I, Paul, became a minister.

The Colossians are reminded that their present status before God and through Christ is **holy and blameless and irreproachable**. The word holy (*hagious*), in light of the sacrificial reference, here carries the connotation of something set aside and dedicated to God rather than assertations of worth (NEB, "dedicated men"; cf. 1:2; 3:12). Implications of worth are, however, carried in Paul's other words. **Blameless** (*amōmous*) is perhaps better translated "without blemish" (NEB, ASV, RSV so translate Jude 24; cf. Eph. 1:4), while **irreproachable** (*anegklētous;* cf. 1 Cor. 1:8, 1 Tim. 3:10; 6:14; Tit. 1:6, 7) may better carry the idea of being blameless (cf. Eph. 5:27). Paul's word **before** (*katenōpion*, "in sight of" or "in the presence of") is used in the New Testament only with regard to a relationship with God. Although the term may be used in reference to the future judgment (e.g., Jude 24), Paul expresses the future judgment differently (2 Cor. 5:10). Here, the term may be understood in concert with the letter's emphasis on the believers' present relationship with God through Christ (see Eph. 1:4; cf. Rom. 14:22; 1 Cor. 1:29; 4:2; Heb. 4:12f.).

[23] Paul cautions his readers that their promised in-heritance (**the hope of the gospel**) is jeopardized by the false teachers. The Colossians are encouraged to stand fast like a well-built building, not entertaining the strange doctrines espoused by the heretics. By so doing they will preserve their present status before God, a status depending upon their faith in the universal gospel.

The word **provided** (*ei ge;* cf. Gal. 3:4; Eph. 3:2) introduces the fact that the present status of verse 22 is conditional (see Heb. 3:14). The Colossians must **continue in the faith** (*epimenete;* the preposition *epi* perhaps adds emphasis to locality, i.e., "abide in"). **The faith** (cf. 1:4) probably designates the message which the Colossians had received from Epaphras (**the gospel which you heard**) see 1:5f., 11) and through which God's reconciling power is available to the believer (cf. 1:2; Eph. 1:19). The Colos-

²⁴ Now I rejoice in my sufferings for your sake, and in my flesh I complete what is lacking in Christ's afflictions for the sake of his body, that is, the church,

---

sians are exhorted to remain stable (*tethemeliōmenoi;* cf. Eph. 3:17, "grounded"; and 1 Cor. 7:37) and steadfast (*hedraioi;* see 1 Tim. 3:15), connoting the image of a building constructed on proper foundations (possibly echoing the parable of the housebuilder where *tethemeliōmenoi* is also found; see Matt. 7:24ff.). The hyperbole **every creature under heaven** (possibly "whole creation," NEB; cf. Mark 16:15) points to the universality of the Christian message and its wide circulation as a testimony to its truth (see 1:6; Rom. 1:8; 1 Thess. 1:8; 2 Cor. 2:14). The expression involves an implicit contrast between Christian preaching and the heretics' sectarian and secretive tendencies (cf. comment on 1:28). Paul asserts that it is through the Christian message that God reconciles all that is reconciled.

THE ROLE OF THE APOSTLE, 1:24—2:5

Suffering, 1:24

[24] Paul's term **now** significantly echoes the "now" of verse 22. It is in light of what God has now done in Christ (cf. vss. 21, 26) that Paul says, **I rejoice in my sufferings.** Here Paul states one of the paradoxes of the Christian faith: there is positive meaning and purpose invested in the sufferings endured by Christians (see 1 Peter 1:6; Rom. 5:2f.; Heb. 12:3-11). This statement is to be understood against the background of Jewish expectations of the "Messianic Woes" which immediately precede and announce the completion of God's purposes unfolding in history (cf. Ezek. 38; 39; Zech. 12:11; cf. 2 Esdras 2:1-14; 6:18-24). The Lord himself had indicated that developments prior to the parousia would include such distress (cf. Mark 13:7-13, 28-37; John 15:18-21; 16:1-4, 33). Suffering is a gift received from God (see Phil. 1:29) allowing Christians to share in the birth pains of the coming age which has now been inaugurated in the recent events of the cross and resurrection. Hence, Christians may **rejoice** as partakers in the events of the end time (1 Peter 1:8; 4:13).

Paul's reference to his **sufferings** (*pathēmasin;* see 2 Cor. 1:5, 6) no doubt here points to his situation as a prisoner (4:3). The apostle may be partly concerned to defend himself against charges that his imprisonment vindicates charges that redemption in Jesus is incomplete.

Though Paul may be concerned to refute the heretical charges, he is not advancing into totally new areas in his thought. His suffering is endured in the line of duty as an apostle (cf. Acts 20:23; 1 Cor. 4:9ff.; 2 Cor. 11; Eph. 3:1, 13; 2 Tim. 2:9). This suffering of hardships in evangelism **is for your sake,** benefiting not only the Colossians or Gentiles (both of which Paul may have particularly in mind here), but all who receive the gospel through such efforts (including Jews, cf. Eph. 3:13; Rom. 9:2, 3; 2 Tim. 2:10).

Paul further elaborates the value of his sufferings endured in the task of preaching with a difficult statement: **in my flesh I complete what is lacking in Christ's afflictions for the sake of his body, that is, the church.** Paul's word **complete** (*antanaplērō,* found only here in the New Testament) is of disputed meaning but may be taken to mean "fill up and complete." The expression is to be understood in relation to the apostle's use of related words with regard to the completion of his preaching ministry, itself a necessary stage in the completion of God's plan in history (see vss. 23, 25; Rom. 11:25; 15:19, 29; cf. Eph. 3:19; 4:13). Here, **afflictions** probably designates the suffering which the Christian proclamation necessitates (cf. 1 Thess. 1:6). It is, of course, through the proclamation that the church is built up to "completion" or "fulness" (cf. Eph. 4:13). Thus, until the gospel is preached to the whole world and the further stages of God's plan are actualized, the full amount of suffering which is to come before the parousia (and perhaps even hastens it—Matt. 24:6; Luke 21:24; Rev. 6:11) is still **lacking.**

Additionally, it should be noted that the word **affliction** (*thilpseōn*), though frequently found in the New Testament, is never used in reference to Christ's passion or sacrificial sufferings. From this, it is assumed that the sacerdotal or vicarious sufferings of Christ are not in the apostle's mind.

²⁵ of which **I** became a minister according to the divine office which was given to me for you, to make the word of God fully known, ²⁶ the mystery hidden for ages and generations ° but now made manifest to his saints.

° Or, *from angels and men*

Preaching the Mystery to Every Man, 1:25-29

[25] Paul presents himself to his readers as one speaking by both duty and right. Paul has been chosen by God (cf. Gal. 1:1; Eph. 3:2) to perform a special task, namely, **to make the word of God fully known** (cf. Rom. 15:19). Although the RSV ascribes the phrase **according to the divine office** to that which Paul has received, the verse may more suitably be translated otherwise. While the word **office** (*oikonomian*) may mean "stewardship" (1 Cor. 4:1; 9:17; 1 Peter 4:10) in the sense of one commissioned or entrusted with the management of a specific task or assignment, the word is also used by Paul to designate God's plan of salvation which is unfolding in history according to his administration and prearranged strategy (see Eph. 1:10; 3:2, 9). Thus the verse here may more suitably be translated to say that Paul has received his ministry of preaching according to the plan of God which is being brought to completion in history. Paul's preaching ministry, just as was his suffering (see vs. 24 above), is itself a vital part of God's plan which is working in history toward the goal of the reconciliation of all things. Paul's function in the plan of salvation is to make the word of God fully known (cf. Rom. 1:5; 1 Cor. 14:36; 2 Cor. 2:17; 4:2).

[26] Paul now momentarily digresses, advancing upon "the word of God" as a mystery (*mustērion*). Though the word had come into Jewish usage long before the apostle's time (see Dan. 2:28ff.), **mystery** is also part of a complex of terms associated with the esoteric rites and doctrines of the Hellenistic "mystery religions" which were given renewed currency by Gnosticism. The New Testament includes diverse uses of the word, but in general, when used in regard to God's revelation, it carries the idea of a divine secret now divulged. The term is frequently found in close association with words connoting announcement or publi-

²⁷ To them God chose to make known how great among the Gentiles are the riches of the glory of this mystery, which is Christ in you, the hope of glory.

---

cation (cf. 4:3; Rom. 16:25, 26; 1 Cor. 2:7; 14:2; Eph. 3:3, 9; 2 Thess. 2:7). In contrast to the secretive connotations of the Hellenistic "mysteries," the Christian mystery is one proclaimed or published. Moreover, because of its universal import (vss. 15-20), it is proclaimed to all men and not just limited to an elite few. In contrast to the usage in both Gnosticism and the mystery religions, the Christian use of the term is eschatological and historical. That is, the Christian mystery is integrally related to history, i.e., the cross and the future goal of all history.

Although Paul may be borrowing the terminology of the Colossian heresy, he sets it in a Christian context. Paradoxically, the Christian "mystery" is an "open secret." The mystery of God's purpose unfolding in history, although previously hidden (cf. 1 Cor. 2:7f.), is now, by contrast (see vs. 24), made manifest to his saints (see vs. 22 above; cf. Eph. 3:5). More precisely, in light of the preceding verse and the use of *mustērion* in Romans 11:25, the apostle here refers to the new stage in God's plan of salvation history, namely, the blessings of Christ now available to Gentiles. Ages (*aiōnōn*) and generations (*geneōn*) punctuates the fact that God's redemptive purposes have reached a new stage in history. Prior to what God has inaugurated in Christ, God's purposes were only partially understood at best (see Eph. 3:5, 9; cf. Matt. 13:17; 1 Cor. 2:7, 8; 1 Peter 1:12). Now no longer hidden, God's redemptive purpose is known to the saints, those called and sanctified through Christ (see comment on vs. 1 above).

[27] The greatness of God is most clearly seen for Paul precisely in regard to the inclusion of the Gentiles into the church. Riches (*ploutos*) is a term the apostle frequently uses in regard to the reign of God's grace now embracing even the Gentiles (see Rom. 11:12, 33). In Christ, the wealth of God's self-manifestation spills over the barriers of nationality and race into a universal demonstration of his greatness (see Rom. 9:24; 11:17, 33). Paul's statement the riches of the glory of this mystery may well refer to the

²⁸ Him we proclaim, warning every man and teaching every man in all wisdom, that we may present every man mature in Christ.

---

realization of the truth of the Christian message by virtue of the new life now lived by the Christian.

This mystery, which is Christ in you is obviously of paramount importance in understanding the verse. Although it is possible to refer **Christ in you** back to **riches,** the most obvious interpretation is that Paul here defines the **mystery.** The mystery Paul has in mind has been suggested to be the mystery of the "indwelling Christ," an interpretation that has much to commend it and could be understood as another way of phrasing the significance of being in Christ (1:18), i.e., to be in Christ is also to have Christ in you (see Eph. 3:16, 17; Rom. 8:10; 2 Cor. 13:5; Gal. 4:19). Yet, the mystery is really the divine plan, unfolding in history, which God has kept hidden until its revelation in Christ, a plan which unfolds with the inclusion of the Gentiles (cf. 2:2; Eph. 3:9; Rom. 9:23, 24; 11:17, 33). **Christ in you** may be better interpreted as "Christ among you," paralleling the "among the Gentiles" earlier in the verse. It is the presence of the Jewish Messiah proclaimed to the Gentiles that the apostle refers to here. This is the basis for the hope and confidence in the fulfilment of the future promise. For **glory** see comments on verse 11. In addition to the meanings noted there, the word was used to signify the future of Christ (cf. Luke 24:26; Mark 10:37) and also the Christian (see 3:4; Rom. 5:2). Thus **hope** and **glory** often belong together (as Rom. 8:18-25).

[28] In contrast to the "open secret" of Christian preaching, the heresy probably was communicating secret doctrines to a select few, trading on terms such as **wisdom** (*sophia*) and **mature** (*teleion*) which are known to have been religious terminology in Hellenistic religions prior to the time of Paul's writing and to have had broad use in later Gnosticism. Paul's mention of preaching and **warning** may indicate some connection in his mind between the two functions (see Acts 20:21). His mention of **every man** three times in succession is a pointed rejoinder to the local nature of the heresy and to its selectivism. By contrast, Christian

²⁹ For this I toil, striving with all the energy which he mightly inspires within me.

¹ For I want you to know how greatly I strive for you, and for those at Laodicea, and for all who have not seen my face, ² that their hearts may be encouraged as they are knit together in love, to have all the riches of assured understanding and the knowledge of God's mystery, of Christ,

---

preaching contains the "true wisdom" which brings all men to God by incorporating them into Christ (see 1:9; 2:3). Only it is able actually to make men mature ("complete" or "full," see 2:10; 4:12).

[29] Though Paul is in prison, his activities are not curtailed. He understands his role as one of continuing ministry, perhaps through the use of emissaries who carry out the work of evangelism under his supervision (see 1:7; 4:13). His efforts in this endeavor are not dependent upon himself but proceed through the power of God (see Phil. 2:12ff.; Gal. 2:20; 5:6; Eph. 1:19; 3:20; 1 Cor. 4:20; 15:10; Rom. 1:5). The word **toil** (*kopiō*), frequently used by Paul regarding his ministry, generally designates the labors of an athlete (cf. 1 Cor. 15:10; Gal. 4:11; Phil. 2:16). **Striving** (*agōnizomenos,* "contending," as in the games) may here be used in reference to the apostle's prayers on behalf of his converts (see 1:3; 4:12; Rom. 15:30, cf. 1 Tim. 4:10; 1 Thess. 2:2).

Concern for All Christians, 2:1-5

[1] The universal scope of the Christian message justifies the apostle's interest in the affairs of the churches of the Lycus Valley. It is actually on their behalf that his "strivings" (*agōna,* see 1:29) are undergone (see 1:24). Paul mentions **those at Laodicea,** with the exchange of letters in mind (see 4:16). Paul returns to the general scope of his ministry, stating that his efforts are **for all who have not seen my face,** a general reiteration of the apostle's responsibility toward "all men."

[2] Paul has just defined his goal as "presenting men mature in Christ" (see 1:28). He returns to his goal here again, stating that his desire is that his readers may have a complete grasp of Christ and that their **hearts may be**

³ **in whom are hid all the treasures of wisdom and knowledge.**

---

encouraged (*paraklēthōsin,* see 4:8; Eph. 6:22; 2 Thess.
2:17). The word **knit together** (*sumbibasthentes*) possibly
may be translated "instruct" (see 1 Cor. 2:16), thus reading
"instructed in love." Yet in light of the use of the word in
2:19 and Ephesians 4:16, the RSV reading is perhaps better.
The apostle understands **love** (*agapē*) as the cohesive ingredient of the church (see 3:14; Eph. 3:17b; 4:16; 5:2; cf.
1:5).

Again Paul echoes 1:9f. as he emphasizes the total adequacy of redemption in Christ. He desires the Colossians to
have **all the riches** of assurance (NEB, "wealth of conviction"; see 1 Thess. 1:5; Heb. 6:11) which is brought by
complete **understanding** (*suneseōs;* see 1:9) and **knowledge** (*epignōsis*) **of God's mystery, Christ.** The word used
here for knowledge, *epignōsis,* is a word which connotes
far more than mere intellectual mastery of concepts but, in
that the mystery is Christ, involves one's total being in a
personal relationship, a new life (see 3:16; cf. Phil. 3:8).

Paul's statement that the **mystery is Christ** is a difficult
reading, a fact illustrated by numerous textual variants for
this verse. Some scholars maintain that the word "Christ"
has been inserted at this point, arguing that the text makes
good sense without it. As the text stands one may interpret:
(a) "the mystery, the God of Christ" (cf. Eph. 1:17); (b)
"the mystery, the God Christ;" or, (c) take Christ in ap-
position to mystery as does the ASV, "the mystery of God,
even Christ" (cf. 1 Tim. 3:16). The last seems preferable.
It accords with the emphasis in Colossians on the centrality
of Christ, the fulfilment of God's plan once hidden but now
revealed.

[3] The apostle proceeds to define the mystery more
precisely; in Christ are hidden all of the **treasures of true
wisdom and knowledge.** As before, Paul is probably using
the vocabulary of the Colossian heretics. The word **hid**
(*apokruphoi*) is known to have later become a favorite
term of Gnosticism designating secret doctrines and may
have been in use in Colossae at this time, though this is not
the only possible source of the term; it may be understood

⁴ I say this in order that no one may delude you with beguiling speech. ⁵ For though I am absent in body, yet I am with you in spirit, rejoicing to see your good order and the firmness of your faith in Christ.

as derived from the teaching of Jesus (cf. Mark 4:22) or from intertestamental Jewish apocalyptic circles speculating on such passages as Isaiah 45:3.

Paul is saying that the secret teachings the heretics covet and prize so highly are incomparable to the true wisdom and knowledge one has in Christ (see 1:9, 10, 28; 3:16; cf. Rom. 11:33; 1 Cor. 12:8).

[4] Paul indicates that the heresy consists of deceit or false reasoning (delude, *paralogizētai;* cf. James 1:22). **Beguiling speech** (*pithanologia*) is perhaps better rendered "speculative reasoning" or "persuasive speech." This word was used by earlier philosophers without pejorative connotation as a reference to arguments lacking mathematical certainty (see 1 Cor. 2:4). It is possible, however, that among common people the term had come to mean something akin to the modern expression "fast talk." In effect, the apostle warns the Colossians against succumbing to the pseudo-reasoning and impressive language of the heretics who commend their teachings as a "philosophy" (see 2:8, 23).

[5] As he has elsewhere with other churches, the apostle asserts his closeness with the Colossian church in spite of his physical absence. There is no need to translate this as a reference to the Holy Spirit (see 1 Cor. 5:3). The apostle rejoices (*chairōn;* cf. Phil. 1:18; 4:4) and is able to see (*blepōn,* in the sense of contemplation) the strength of the Colossian church. He describes this strength as visible in their **good order** and **firmness**. Paul is here using two military metaphors, perhaps due to his close association with soldiers (see Phil. 1:13). **Good order** refers to the keeping of lines in order, while **firmness** (cf. 1 Peter 5:9; Acts 16:5) refers to the keeping of a "solid front" before the enemy. If the military use of these terms is not in the apostle's mind, the emphasis is more on the orderly nature of the Colossian church in face of the threat posed by the heresy (see 1 Cor. 14:40).

⁶ As therefore you received Christ Jesus the Lord, so live in him, ⁷ rooted and built up in him and established in the faith, just as you were taught, abounding in thanksgiving.

WARNINGS AGAINST HERESY, 2:6—3:4

Participation in the Victory of Christ, 2:6-15

[6] The Colossians' strength in face of adversity depends on their abiding in the truth of the gospel which they first received from Epaphras (1:7). The word **received** (*parelabete*) is frequently used regarding the gospel and refers to the reception of something transmitted (see 1 Cor. 15:1, 3; Gal. 1:9; Phil. 4:9; 1 Thess. 2:13; 4:1, 2; 2 Thess. 3:6). As Paul has just designated the mystery as Christ, here he describes the gospel as the reception of **Christ Jesus the Lord** (cf. Phil. 1:15, 17). This unusual designation (elsewhere only in Eph. 3:11; cf. 1 Tim. 1:12) raises some uncertainty as to the exact meaning. Paul here combines two early confessions, "Jesus is the Christ" (see Mark 8:29) and "Jesus is the Lord" (cf. Rom. 10:9; 1 Cor. 12:3), emphasizing cardinal points of the gospel which are under question in Colossae. The historical person Jesus, not some mystic principle or mythological prototype, is the Christ who now reigns as the universal Lord, subject to no other powers (see 1:16; 2:15, 20) and able to incorporate all his followers into himself as his own body (see 1:18).

[7] Paul advances on his injunction that the Colossians live in Christ, using two additional metaphors and also making an important shift in tenses. He speaks of the Colossians as having been **rooted** (*errizōmenoi*) in Christ. That is, in the past they have been planted or located in Christ (see Eph. 3:17; cf. Rom. 11:16; Matt. 13:6). Then, shifting both tense and metaphor, Paul states that they are being **built up in him** (cf. 1 Cor. 3:10; Eph. 2:20; 1 Peter 2:5). Paul here uses the present tense, not captured by the RSV, saying, in effect, that the Colossians are progressively being built up in Christ and continually being strengthened (**established;** cf. 1 Cor. 1:6; 2 Cor. 1:21; Heb. 13:9) by their faith. Paul emphasizes not that Christ is that upon which

⁸ See to it that no one makes a prey of you by philosophy and empty deceit, according to human tradition, according to the elemental spirits of the universe, and not
according to Christ.

---

the church is built but that he is the principle of cohesion
which holds the church together as it is built up **in him**
(see 1:17; 3:14; cf. Eph. 2:20). **In the faith** may be better
interpreted as instrumental, "by your faith," thus making
faith that by which the building and strengthening takes
place, or continuing the metaphor, "faith is the cement of
the building" (see ASV, NEB margins; cf. Heb. 13:9). **As
you were taught** again refers back to the original presenta-
tion of the gospel by Epaphras. The nature and magnitude
of life in Christ occasions the Christian's **thanksgiving** (see
1:12; 3:15, 17; 4:2).

[8] Paul's choice of tenses indicates the reality of the
threat of danger. The indefinite **no one** (*tis*) may indicate
that he has someone in mind but does not choose to dignify
the heretic by naming him (see Gal. 1:7). He elaborates
the fear expressed in verse 4, urging that the false teachers
not be permitted to make a prey of the Colossians. His word
is better translated "kidnap" or "carry off," bringing to mind
the type of attack made by a slave raider. In the back of
the apostle's mind is possibly the Colossians' status as free
citizens in the realm of light (see 1:13), a privilege jeopardized by the heresy which deprives its adherents of their
fortune, "capturing" them again in slavery (cf. 2 Tim. 3:6;
Gal. 5:1).

The apostle belittles the boasted wisdom of his opponents in Colossae, again using one of their own terms,
philosophy (*philosophias*). Although the term did become
associated with subtle reasoning and abstract, speculative
discussions, there is no indication that the word itself carries this connotation to the apostle. Rather than the RSV's
philosophy and empty deceit, the lack of the article with
the second phrase makes it more likely that it is to be understood as a characteristic of philosophy rather than a
separate entity (NEB, "hollow and delusive speculation";
cf. Eph. 5:6). That is, the apostle here refers not to philosophy in general but to that philosophy specifically charac-

terized by empty deceit, in contrast to Christian teaching which is "the word of truth" (1:5), "wisdom and knowledge" (2:3). In comparison to the incomparable value of Christian teaching, all such thought is foolish (see 1 Cor. 1:20).

The apostle labels the teaching of the heretics as **according to human tradition** in contrast to Christian teaching, which is a tradition not from men but from God (see 2:6; cf. 1 Cor. 11:2; 2 Thess. 3:6). Such teaching may have been either written or oral but was no doubt essentially secretive (in contrast to the Christian "open secret," 1:27), probably given in stages to initiates as they underwent the different rituals and claiming antiquity as its vindication. The remainder of the chapter gives some indication of the content of the teaching.

Paul's further designation of the heresy as being **according to the elemental spirits of the universe** (vs. 20; Gal. 4:3, 9) is a much disputed phrase. Different meanings of **elemental spirits** (*stoicheia*) create the difficulty. On the one hand, the word was used to designate parts in a series, coming to refer to letters of the alphabet. The word then came to refer to that which is "elementary" or "fundamental" (see Heb. 5:12). The word also designated the basic substances of the natural world, the "elements" (cf. 2 Peter 3:10, 12). The general meaning of the phrase within the confines of the above alternatives would seem to be something akin to "elementary" or "rudimentary" teachings of the natural world (cf. ASV; Jerusalem Bible). Certainly such an interpretation would carry a strong rejoinder to Paul's opponents who brag of a "superior wisdom" and probably diminish the importance of the physical world.

On the other hand, the word also came to be associated with the idea of "elemental beings." Speculative Jewish thought had ascribed various important roles to angels, including the mediating of the law to Moses (Gal. 3:19), and strongly asociated their work with the changing of seasons (see *Enoch* 82:10ff.; *Jubiliees* 2; cf. Ps. 104:4, KJV; Rev. 7:1, 2; 14:18). With this interpretation the apostle's reference to the **elemental spirits of the universe** would refer to those spirits believed to be operating behind the phenomena of the visible world and apparently the focus

⁹ For in him the whole fulness of deity dwells bodily,

---

of worship on the part of the Colossian heretics. The argument for this understanding of the text is certainly commended by the apparent Jewish cast of the heresy (see 1:16; 2:15ff.). Also, one cannot overlook the interest in angels and seasonal rituals manifested by the heresy. The context also seems to juxtapose the "elemental spirits" (*stoicheia*) with Christ, a contrast which seems more appropriate if one conceives of the former as some sort of personal beings. The difficulty of this interpretation is, of course, Paul's paralleling these beings to the traditions of men. Moreover, the word in the sense required is not documented before writings later than Paul. Whatever its content, such teaching is **not according to Christ**.

[9] Paul now makes explicit his dependence on the "Christ hymn" in his argument against the Colossian heresy as he echoes his earlier statement (see 1:19) but here places it in direct opposition to the heretical teaching. The subject of this statement is clearly **the fulness** (*to plērōma;* see 1:19), a term which may have been used by the Colossian heretics in regard to a hierarchy of supernatural powers (see 1:16). **Deity** (*tēs theotētos*) occurs only here in the New Testament and is generally regarded as referring to the totality of divine attributes and power (cf. *theiotēs*, Rom. 1:20). Paul asserts that the divine power is not scattered throughout an array of divine beings but permanently **dwells** in Christ. The word **bodily** (*sōmatikōs*) gives rise to a number of interpretations. It has been suggested as a reference to the church which the apostle has already called the body (1:18). It has been taken as the equivalent to "essentially" or "actually." Or, one may understand the apostle to be asserting that the fulness of God rests in a single individual rather than a plurality of spiritual beings. Although these interpretations embody true theological insights, the most likely interpretation is that Paul is referring to the Incarnation, adding **bodily** to point to the Incarnation as the time at which the fulness which was previously in Christ was manifested bodily (see Phil. 3:21). The present tense (**dwells**) occasions some difficulty in that the past tense would more clearly indicate the event of the incarna-

[10] and you have come to fulness of life in him, who is the head of all rule and authority. [11] In him also you were circumcised with a circumcision made without hands, by putting off the body of flesh in the circumcision of Christ;

---

tion (see John 1:14). However, the present tense may be understood to refer to the enduring significance of the incarnation.

[10] The practical significance of this Christological assertion for the church is now brought to bear. Probably using the false teachers' own term for the divine mediators which constituted the "fulness," Paul asserts that Christians, by virtue of being incorporated into him in whom all the fulness dwells, **have** (already) **come to fulness of life in him** (NEB, "brought to completion"). As before (cf. 1:9-13, 22, 28; Eph. 3:19), the apostle emphasizes the Christian's present experience of redemption, not allowing any idea of incompleteness to encourage Christians to seek anything supplemental or additional. Christ is **the head of all rule and authority** (cf. 1:18). Those who are incorporated into him should neither need nor fear any other "elemental spirits" (vs. 8).

[11] Paul now emphasizes the Christian's "fulness" by pointing to his relation with Christ. The apostle's use of the term **circumcision** is possibly occasioned by a number of factors. It has been supposed that the Colossian heretics were urging circumcision on Gentile Christians as had "judaizers" in Galatia (see Gal. 5:1ff.). It is difficult, however, to believe that the apostle would not have found such an error significant enough to merit more specific attention. Others have supposed that the heretical teachers, if indeed Jewish, were using their own circumcision as a sign of their authority before the Gentiles. Additionally, it has been conjectured that the heretics may have used the term with reference to their ascetic practices (vs. 16f. below). If the apostle is responding to any of these possibilities, he says in effect: "You, as Christians, have been 'circumcised' with the 'true circumcision' as you were baptized (vs. 12) into Christ" (see Phil. 3:3; Rom. 2:25-29; cf. Gal. 6:15). As a symbol of submission and obedience, circumcision had al-

¹² and you were buried with him in baptism, in which you were also raised with him through faith in the working of God, who raised him from the dead.

---

ready been "spiritualized" in the Old Testament and had come to point to a far greater concept than the mere physical act (cf. Lev. 26:41; Jer. 6:10). On the basis of the New Testament association of circumcision with the Holy Spirit (e.g., Eph. 1:13), it may be that the apostle has in mind the Spirit's work at baptism. At any rate, it is to the broader concept of "circumcision," to **a circumcision made without hands** (see Eph. 2:11; Rom. 2:28; Phil. 3:3) that the apostle refers.

The circumcision of Christ may have reference to what Christ performs on the one who submits to him or to what Christ underwent in his submission and obedience on the cross, viewed as a "true circumcision." Similarly Paul's statement, **putting off the body of flesh** (cf. 1 Peter 3:21), may be taken in reference to Christians or to Christ. On the one hand, the majority of translators understand Paul to be making a moral exhortation, referring to the Christian's divesting himself of his unredeemed or sensual nature (*sarx;* see 2:18; Rom. 6:6; 7:24; Phil. 3:21), symbolized by the taking off of clothing at baptism. On the other hand the phrase may also be taken as a reference to Christ's own surrender of his body to physical suffering and death in self-giving obedience—an obedience from which the individual Christian benefits by virtue of being incorporated into Christ at baptism (see 1:22; Rom. 7:4; 1 Peter 2:24; 4:1). One of the difficulties facing this latter interpretation is the lack of the pronoun one would expect were the phrase to have this as its meaning (i.e., "body of *his* flesh").

[12] In the act of **baptism** the believer participates (**with him**) in the circumcision of Christ. That is, the one baptized is incorporated into Christ and his self-giving death; he dies in baptism to the carnal and sensual nature which is stripped from him (the best commentary on the verse is Rom. 6:1-11; see also vss. 1:20; Gal. 5:24; cf. 2 Cor. 5:15). Paul also asserts that the one baptized has been raised with Christ. Here and in Ephesians (cf. Eph. 2:6) Paul speaks of the resurrection as a past event, emphasizing

¹³ And you, who were dead in trespasses and the uncircumcision of your flesh, God made alive together with him, having forgiven us all our trespasses,

---

the completeness of the Christian's benefits received in Christ (cf. Rom. 6:5; Phil. 3:11; but also 2 Cor. 5:17). This emphasis counteracts the heretical teaching that the Christian needs mediators in addition to Christ and that baptism is only one among many rites necessary for complete redemption. The apostle asserts the reality of the Christian's resurrection as an accomplished fact (see 1:12, 13).

The source of the Christian's new life is God. The agency of this new life is the Christian's **faith in the working of God.** God's **working** is the object of belief (the genitive after *pistis* usually expressing the object; e.g., Rom. 3:22, 26; Gal. 3:22; Eph. 3:12; Phil. 1:27; 3:9; 2 Thess. 2:13). More precisely, it is by the belief in the resurrection that the power of God's working is available to those who participated in that event through baptism (see Rom. 4:24; 6:8; 10:9; cf. Phil. 3:10).

[13] Paul addresses the Gentiles specifically (cf. 3:7, 8; Eph. 1:13; 2:1), using the literal fact of their **uncircumcision** (*akrobustia*, literally "foreskin") to symbolize the more far-reaching fact of their spiritual depravity (cf. Rom. 2:25ff.; Gal. 5:6; 6:15; Eph. 2:1, 5, 11, 12). It is because of their sins (**trespasses**; *paraptōmasin*, "false step"; cf. Eph. 1:7) that the Gentiles are alienated from God. Paul describes their condition as death—they were separated from God, the source of life itself. Nevertheless, God has overcome this barrier and has **made alive** the Gentiles with Christ. This process of making alive involves the removal of trespasses. There is no need to suppose that these terms represent separate acts of God. Insofar as a distinction might be made, baptism brings forgiveness of sins and the Holy Spirit gives new life. To speculate whether the life here referred to involves immortality or refers to the Christian's new moral life carries an alien understanding of life into the text. These entities are inseparable in the mind of the apostle. The new moral life of the Christian is a reflection of his new life. To imply that the realization of the Christian's resurrection is "merely" or "simply" the new moral

¹⁴ **having canceled the bond which stood against us with
its legal demands; this he set aside, nailing it to the cross.**

---

life fails to understand the interconnectedness between
morality and life (see Rom. 6:12ff.; Gal. 5:25). Paul includes himself among those forgiven, shifting from **you to
us.** This shift perhaps includes all Jews and not the apostle
alone.

[14] Continuing the same line, the apostle metaphorically pictures God as canceling (*exaleipsas;* "erasing" or
"blotting out"; cf. Acts 3:19; Rev. 3:5) the bond which
mankind has incurred (vs. 13). **Bond** (*cheirographon*) is a
Greek technical term for the acknowledgment of a debt,
an I.O.U. (see Phile. 19). Most scholars hold that the
apostle is referring primarily to the Mosaic law which was
"signed" by the assent of the Jewish people (see Deut.
27:14-26) but also to the Gentiles, whose consciences recognize an obligation to God which their actions deny (cf.
Rom. 2:15ff.). **Against us** therefore includes all men (cf.
Rom. 3:9).

The RSV's **legal demands** interprets a difficult word,
dogmasin, as referring to the ordinances of the law (see
Eph. 2:15). One must also consider the use of *dogmasin*
here in light of its use in verse 20 below. If the bond mentioned refers not just to Jews, then the ordinances or **legal
demands** are more general than the demands of the law
alone, including the rules and regulations which have been
recognized by all mankind (see vs. 20; Eph. 2:15). Also,
had Paul intended a reference to the law, he would have
been more inclined to use the word *nomos.*

This he set aside (literally, "he has taken out of the
way") contains a change in construction. Paul at this point
turns from using participles to a finite verb, replacing the
aorist with the perfect tense. These factors have led some
to suppose that the subject of the verb here shifts from God
to Christ, i.e., "God canceled . . . Christ set aside. . . ."
Yet this shift of subject is uncertain (regardless of what one
understands regarding the subject of vs. 15), and one may
account for the change in construction as an effort to specify
the canceling of the bond as the event of the death of
Christ. To separate the subjects here separates God's act

¹⁵ He disarmed the principalities and powers and made a public example of them, triumphing over them in him.*

ᵈ Or *in it* (that is, the cross)

---

of "canceling" from Christ's "setting aside." It is less difficult to understand God as the subject of the entire verse.

The expression **nailing it to the cross** is best understood as referring to the body of Christ which carried the guilt of mankind when he was crucified on the cross (see Heb. 10:10). Christ paid the debt for mankind by surrendering his body. Therefore, those incorporated into him are freed from the debt and now stand released from the bond (cf. Rom. 6:7; 7:6; Gal. 2:19; 1 Peter 2:24).

[15] Though it is clear that the cross of Christ is the central act of a great cosmic drama, the RSV obscures the difficulties of the verse. As elsewhere in the letter (see 1:20) it is possible that the subject has shifted from God to Christ, either here or in the previous verse. If God is taken as the subject of the verb, the RSV's **disarmed** is perhaps the best translation of the word (*apekdusamenos* occurs only here, 2:11 and 3:9 in the New Testament). If Christ is taken as the subject of the verb, several interpretations of the phrase **principalities and powers** are possible. Paul may be referring to Christ's "stripping himself" of his physical body (some manuscripts actually add the word, indicating the difficulty felt by the scribes) in keeping with the use of the word *apekdusamenos*, "putting off" in 2:11 (cf. 2 Cor. 5:3). Or Paul may indicate Christ's death as a stripping away of the alien powers—**principalities and powers**—to which man is enslaved. Or, combining these views, Christ's surrendering of his body on the cross may be seen as a divestment of the body, the avenue through which alien forces seduce man (cf. Heb. 4:15; 2 Cor. 5:4).

Another option is opened by the association of the Colossian heresy with Judaism and the tendency of Jewish speculation to associate angels in mediating the law (see Gal. 3:19). That is, **principalities and powers** represent the law but have a power over Gentiles as well (cf. Gal. 1:8; 3:19; 4:3, 9; 1 Cor. 8:5ff.). These forces are stripped from Christ in his death to the law (see 2:11 above) and, conse-

16 Therefore let no one pass judgment on you in questions of food and drink or with regard to a festival or a new moon or a sabbath.

---

quently, his death to the power of those beings mediating the law (cf. Rom. 8:2; 1 Cor. 15:56).

The word **triumphing** (*thriambeusas*) literally means leading (as a victorious general leads) a procession of defeated enemies, making a **public** (bold) **example** of them (but see 2 Cor. 2:14). Paul's metaphor is one of the resurrected Christ's leading the defeated powers in triumphant public procession (see Eph. 1:19ff.). If one takes the concluding pronoun to be "it" instead of **him** (a decision influenced by whether God or Christ is taken as the subject of the last main verb; RSV footnote and cf. NEB), the reference is back to the cross of the previous verse. In this case the metaphor would be even bolder; the cross reflects the paradoxical victory over the powers (see John 12:31ff.).

Freedom From the Restrictions of the Heresy, 2:16—3:4

In verses 16-20, some of the practices and beliefs of the Colossian heresy come to light more clearly. One notices the distinctive Jewish flavor of the heretical beliefs which are concerned with ritual food laws and observances of special holy days. These beliefs are probably undergirded by a strong asceticism involving a concept of the universe which denies the value of the material creation. At the center of the heresy is the concept of angelic mediators or supernatural forces which are to be placated through the observation of various taboos. One may also suppose that the heretical teachers traded heavily on superstition and fear of the unknown forces of "fate." In essence, Paul's argument is that all of these "powers" are irrelevant. Contrary to the claims of their purveyors, such beliefs do not issue from "enlightenment" or "wisdom" but rather from ignorance; if one really understands Christ, he will not be susceptible to the overtures of the heretical teachers.

[16] Paul's words again point to some definite person he prefers not to dignify by naming (as in vs. 8 above). His injunction to the Colossians to **let no one pass judgment**

[17] These are only a shadow of what is to come; but the substance belongs to Christ.

---

on you (cf. Rom. 2:1a; 14:3ff.; James 4:11, 12) introduces the areas of concern for those judging the Colossian Christians. **Food and drink** are frequently paired, food being subject to Jewish distinctions of foods as clean and unclean. The injunction of the heretics against drink, however, moves the heresy out of the confines of traditional Judaism which had only very limited restrictions against drink (see Lev. 10:9; 11:34, 36; Num. 6:3). The Essenes are known to have prescribed rigorous restrictions regarding both food and drink, rendering it unnecessary to locate the basis of this practice outside the bounds of Judaism. However, the fact that these restrictions do extend beyond traditional Jewish food laws may serve to indicate that the underlying concern is a dualism denigrating the physical world and issuing in strict ascetic regulations (see vs. 18). For Paul, such misunderstandings concerning the Christian message cannot be tolerated (cf. Rom. 14:17ff.; Mark 7:15ff.).

The heretical asceticism is also concerned with rituals, festivals, new moons, and sabbaths (see Gal. 4:10; 1 Chron. 23:31), perhaps in the belief that the supernatural powers stand behind the seasonal changes (see Gal. 4:8-11). **Festivals** (*heortēs*) may be taken to indicate annual feasts of the Jewish religious calendar (Lev. 23:4-44). **New moons** (*neomēnias*) is best taken to designate monthly ritual observances (Num. 10:10, 11ff.) with **sabbaths** specifying the weekly holy day on Saturday (Ex. 20:8ff.; Lev. 23:3). The Dead Sea Scrolls have the same three designations together as a listing of holy days (*War Scroll* II, 4).

[17] For Paul, all **these** rituals and legal observances are irrelevant (cf. Rom. 14:2-6; 1 Cor. 8:8; 10:23-26). Paul basically contrasts the Mosaic law and Christ, yet he may include the Gentile rituals and rites in his word **these** (see vs. 14). Though these things had value in the past, when they were originally ordained, such is no longer the case. Now, they are but a shadow (*skia*) in contrast to Christ (cf. Heb. 8:5; 10:1). As a shadow has no independent existence but ultimately depends upon that of which it is a shadow, so it is with the Mosaic law and Gentile rituals.

¹⁸ Let no one disqualify you, insisting on self-abasement and worship of angels, taking his stand on visions, puffed up without reason by his sensuous mind,

---

The shadow is also now superseded and rendered obsolete by virtue of the presence of the reality (see Gal. 3:25).

Though Paul's contrast between the shadow and the reality could be ended at this point, the word for reality, *sōma* (substance), has previously been vested with great significance, and it is hard not to think that the apostle may still have that meaning of the word in mind (see 1:24).

[18] Paul again cautions his readers not to allow the heretical teachers to judge them (vs. 16), this time using an athletic metaphor, "to judge against," or **disqualify** (*katabrabeuetō;* see 3:15; Phil. 3:14; cf. Gal. 5:7). Rather than implying that the Colossians will be disqualified by following the false teaching, the more probable meaning is that Paul's readers should not accord anyone the status of judge or umpire in the first place.

Insisting on may also be interpreted as "delighting in" and taken to refer to the manner of disqualification, i.e., let no one delight in disqualifying you. But the RSV's reading is probably preferable. The particular concerns which are specified by the apostle are somewhat unclear. **Self-abasement** (*tapeinophrosunē*) may mean "humility" (cf. KJV, ASV). Yet, the word is known to have been a technical term for fasting and should probably be taken in such a manner here (see vs. 23; cf. 3:12).

The mention of one **taking his stand on visions** is problematic. Literally **visions** (*ha heoraken*) means "things seen." Thus the KJV accepts a rather poorly attested variant which inserts the negative making the apostle criticize the heretic for accepting that which he has not seen. It is better, however, to read **visions** and reject the negative. There is no evidence that the verb *embateuōn* can have the meaning **taking his stand**. More probably the apostle is using a special term of the heresy. The grammar is difficult but Paul is here likely referring to an essential feature of initiations in the Hellenistic mysteries where great value was placed on what the initiate saw during rites designed to lead to such spiritual experiences (cf. 2 Cor.

[19] and not holding fast to the Head, from whom the whole body, nourished and knit together through its joints and ligaments, grows with a growth that is from God.

[20] If with Christ you died to the elemental spirits of the universe, why do you live as if you still belonged to the

---

12:1-4). Thus the statement may be rendered "entering (or being initiated) into things which he saw."

Contrary to claims of possessing "wisdom," "reason" and "knowledge" which the heretics make, Paul ironically asserts that they are actually "vainly" puffed up (*eikē phusioumenos;* NEB, "bursting with futile conceit"; cf. 1 Cor. 8:1). Yet, in light of the heretics' claim to "deeper knowledge" (see Rev. 2:24), without reason is perhaps a better translation. In spite of such claims, the heretic is actually depending upon his own materialistic or sensuous mind (literally, "mind of his flesh" or "his physical mind"; see vs. 11; cf. Eph. 4:23).

[19] The heart of the problem is that the heretical teacher does not hold fast (*kratōn;* cf. Mark 7:8; 2 Thess. 2:15, "stand fast") to Christ. The Head (*tēn kephalēn;* see 1:18; cf. Eph. 1:22; 4:15), Christ, is the source of the life and energy of the body, the church (1:18, 24). From Christ the church is nourished (*epichorēgoumenon,* "furnished," "equipped"; cf. Gal. 3:5) and knit together (*sumbibazomenon,* "united"; cf. 2:2). The use of the present participles should be noted; the apostle points to a continuing process that stems from the body's dependence on the head. The terms joints and ligaments have been interpreted as designating specific "offices" of the church, but the metaphor should not be pressed into allegory. Paul simply indicates that it is from the head that the life and energy of the body flows through the various parts of the body which themselves become channels for the life that the head supplies (see Eph. 4:16).

[20] Paul returns to his earlier statement on baptism (vs. 12). Baptism, apparently misunderstood by the Colossian Christians and minimized by the heresy, is not only a death with Christ (cf. Gal. 2:20; 2 Tim. 2:11) but also a release, a dying from or "to" something ("sin" Rom. 6:2; "self" 2 Cor. 5:14, 15; "the law" Rom. 7:6), in this case the

world? Why do you submit to regulations, [21] "Do not handle, Do not taste, Do not touch" [22] (referring to things which all perish as they are used), according to human precepts and doctrines? [23] These have indeed an appearance of wisdom in promoting rigor of devotion and self-abasement and severity to the body, but they are of no value in checking the indulgence of the flesh.[e]

[e] Or, *are of no value, serving only to indulge the flesh*

---

elemental spirits of the universe. As before, Paul's word here translated "elemental spirits" may mean either "materialism" (see vs. 22) or "powers in control of the cosmos" (see vs. 8 and discussion there), i.e., the "angels" (vs. 18).

Paul queries the Colossians why, after being released from the control of these forces, they still act as if in subjection to them. By submitting themselves, or being submitted to such **regulations** (*dogmatizesthe;* see vs. 14) as they are apparently doing, they deny the true meaning and significance of their baptism. Incorporated into Christ and his death, their lives should illustrate the meaning of their freedom from such restrictions as are listed in verse 21 (cf. Gal. 5:1, 13).

[21] Paul repeats the injunctions of the false teachers, indicating the meticulous nature of their ascetic regulations, which possibly indicates a development beyond the Mosaic law, perhaps even including sexual abstinence (though one would think the apostle would give more attention to such a doctrine; cf. 1 Tim. 4:3; 1 Cor. 7:1). **Handle** and **touch** probably designate intentional and unintentional contact with "unclean" items.

[22] Paul parenthetically remarks that these regulations are irrelevant because they deal with things that **perish as they are used** (see Gal. 6:8b; cf. 1 Cor. 6:12ff.). Ultimately, their source is the carnal materialistic minds of their teachers (see Titus 1:14). It is significant to note that Paul's statement may be echoing the words of Jesus (see Matt. 15:1-20; Mark 7:1-23; cf. Isa. 29:13), words which the Colossians may earlier have received.

[23] Though the general meaning is clear, the precise meaning of this statement is not. Regulations (vs. 8) may

¹ **If then you have been raised with Christ, seek the things that are above, where Christ is, seated at the right**

---

give the appearance of **wisdom** (*sophias;* cf. vs. 8), but this is only illusory. The **devotion, self-abasement** and **severity** to the body advocated by the heresy are falsely impressive. Paul's word **devotion** may mean "voluntary service" but also "self-imposed religion" (a nuance not captured by the RSV; cf. NEB, Jerusalem Bible, "self-imposed devotion"). **Self-abasement** (*tapeinophrosunē,* NEB, "self mortification") is itself a Christian virtue (see 3:12; cf. Phil. 2:3), but in this context can only mean a "false humility" (vs. 18). **Severity to the body** doubtless refers to the asceticism indicated in the regulations just mentioned (vs. 21).

The last half of the verse poses the greatest difficulty. One may read the concluding phrase as referring to a favorable goal but one which the heresy is unable to achieve, i.e., "the reasonable wants of the body" which asceticism cannot supply. Yet, there is no indication that *plēsmonēn* ("indulgence," RSV) refers to the natural or worthy wants of the body (this is the only occasion of the word in the New Testament). Paul, however, may be quoting from the heretics' own statement but turning it against them in the sense that the rigors they urge are of no value in checking the **indulgence of the flesh.** Or, taking the RSV alternate reading, such efforts may actually lead to the sensual and carnal concerns which they seek to avoid (as in Phil. 3:19).

[1] Baptism has two sides: it is a death and a rebirth, an end and a beginning. The apostle has been writing of the negative side of baptism ("If you died with Christ," vs. 20). Now he shifts to the positive side of baptism, **If then you have been raised with Christ** (see 2:12). **If** (*ei*) repeats the "if" of 2:20 and is not intended to cast doubt on the baptism mentioned. Rather, Paul says in effect, "If it is so that you have been raised with Christ (which he knows is in fact so), then it follows that. . . ." As he has previously done, the apostle uses the aorist tense to express the Christian's resurrection as a completed action in the past (again, he is concerned to emphasize the "fulness" of the Christian's reconciliation in face of charges that it is inferior, imperfect or incomplete). Paul urges his readers to effect the

hand of God. ² **Set your minds on things that are above, not on things that are on earth.** ³ **For you have died, and**

---

fact of their resurrection in their life style. The new life is now theirs, yet they are to actualize it—not in order to gain it but because they already have it. Or, paradoxically, they are exhorted to "become what they are" (see Gal. 5:25).

Paul metaphorically expresses this by saying, **seek the things that are above, where Christ is.** The emphasis of the verse is on the spiritual in contrast to the unspiritual. Paul, however, is careful not to allow any room for his readers to interpret this as a contrast between the spiritual and material. In contrast to the heretics, who think matter is evil, the Christian knows that matter is transient and perishable but not evil in itself. The opposite of "things above" is more akin to self-seeking sensuousness (see 3:5ff.). The apostle does not mean for his readers to ignore or flee the practical concerns of daily life (see 3:18ff.). **Seated at the right hand of God** expresses Christ's authority and unity with the Father, another rejoinder to those who have diminished Christ's role as mediator (cf. Ps. 110:1; Matt. 28:18; Eph. 1:20; Phil. 2:9f.; Heb. 7:3).

[2] Paul expands his previous statement, urging his readers, **set your minds on things that are above.** The expression **set your minds** (*phroneite*) is one Paul frequently uses and more specifically focuses on the "mind," or "point of view" that the Christian should have (see Phil. 2:5; 3:19; Rom. 8:5). His use of the present tense here again (as in "seek") indicates that Paul conceives of "seeking" and "setting the mind" as continuing aspects of the Christian's realizing or actualizing the resurrection in his life. Paul here is encouraging his readers to cultivate a different frame of mind than that of the natural men—and the heretics.

[3] Though Christians are dead to sin (see Rom. 6:11), Paul uses the past (aorist) tense because he is referring to baptism: **for you have died. Hid,** however, is in the perfect tense, indicating the enduring effect of this death. As the one being baptized goes under the water, he is hidden from sight, symbolizing his burial. This burial or hiding from the world is also a union or incorporation into Christ. It has been suggested that Paul here uses pagan concepts of the

your life is hid with Christ in God. ⁴ When Christ who is our life appears, then you also will appear with him in glory.

---

dead being "hidden in the earth." If such is in the background, Paul's point would be that Christians are, by contrast, in baptism "hidden in Christ." Possibly the apostle also has in mind the fact that the source of the Christian's life is not visible to the world which does not recognize Christ. Whereas Paul might have been expected to use "in," his choice of with (*sun*) here and in the following verse ("with him") points to the believer's hope. Those who die **with Christ** in baptism (2:20; Rom. 6:8) anxiously but confidently await their being "with him" in the coming eschaton (cf. 1 Thess. 4:14, 17f.; 5:10; Phil. 1:23; 2 Cor. 4:14f.; 5:6-10; 13:4).

[4] Though the Christian's life is now hidden with Christ, and in this sense hidden from the unregenerate world, such will not always be the case. Paul amplifies his previous idea that Christ is the source of the Christian's life by describing Christ as **Christ who is our life** (cf. Phil. 1:21; Gal. 2:20; 1 John 5:12). Paul expects the future unveiling of the ultimate reality of Christ's sovereignty over the universe and the subsequent realization of the Christian's true identity as God's sanctified (cf. Rom. 8:17, 19; 1 John 3:2).

In glory (*en doxē*) introduces the tension that characterizes the Christian's stance. On the one hand, the Christian is already the beneficiary of what God has done in Christ (see especially 1:12, 13, 22; 2:12, 13). But on the other hand, there is the incomplete aspect to Christian existence with reference to that which is not yet fully actualized. This tension is central to the Christian's whole outlook. He lives with the knowledge that the decisive victory has already been won by Christ, freeing him to live a life shaped ultimately by that fact. Yet he knows that alien forces still operate both within himself and at large. The final consummation of the victory already won lies still in the future when believers, "with Christ" in his death, will be with him in glory (see comments on 1:11, 27).

⁵ Put to death therefore what is earthly in you: immorality, impurity, passion, evil desire, and covetousness, which is idolatry.

THE CHRISTIAN LIFE, 3:5—4:6

The transition in Paul's letters from doctrine to ethics demonstrates that Christian ethics derive their substance from Christian theology. Paul argues that the distinctive shape of the Christian life should grow out of and be determined by the Christian message (see 1:9; Rom. 12:1, 2). Paul's emphasis on baptism is partly motivated by the fact that the Colossian heresy minimizes the significance of baptism, making it an initial rite to be followed by more important steps toward maturity or "wisdom" (see 1:9; 2:20; and 3:16 below). Some scholars maintain that prior to the composition of any of the known Christian writings, there was a recognized body of ethical teaching imparted to converts at the time of baptism (see 1 Thess. 2:13; 4:2; 2 Thess. 2:15; 3:6). Paul may here be echoing standardized ethical instruction previously given to the Colossians at baptism in an effort to emphasize the application to the ethical life of his statements about baptism, which was the moment when the believer appropriated what Christ did on the cross. Indeed, verses 5, 8ff., and 12 show that the baptismal imagery still dominates the discussion.

The Christian's Transformation, 3:5-17

[5] If taken literally, Paul here recommends the most rigid form of asceticism. However, in light of his renunciation of the asceticism represented by the Colossian heresy (2:21-23), this would seem unlikely. The RSV understands Paul's statement not in a literal sense but as a spiritual metaphor much like Matthew 5:29ff. That is, Paul urges the Colossians to eschew any immoral use of their members, i.e., that which is earthly in them. The specific vices mentioned move from the less comprehensive to the more comprehensive. This order is particularly paralleled in Ephesians 5:3; Galatians 5:19, 24 and 1 Thessalonians 4:5.

Immorality (*porneian*) is frequently used in the New

Testament (see Rom. 1:29; 1 Cor. 5:1; 6:13; 2 Cor. 12:21; Gal. 5:19; Eph. 5:3) and is more specific than the RSV indicates. The term actually denotes sexual debauchery. It is possible that the heresy was in some way contributing to an attitude which condoned or at least allowed practices of sexual immorality. Certainly, if it was undergirded with a strong dualism, it is possible that the less significant life in the body was allowed to "run its course" and satisfy its appetites at will. Paul follows with the more general word **impurity** (*akatharsian,* literally "refuse"; see 2 Cor. 12:21; Gal. 5:19; Eph. 4:19; 5:3; 1 Thess. 4:7; Rom. 1:24; 6:19). The word is used in the Old Testament to designate ritual or ceremonial impurity (Lev. 18:19; 20: 23; cf. Matt. 23:27) which separates one from God (Lev. 22:3). Paul refers to the alienation of man from God which characterizes the pre-Christian life (see Rom. 1:24; Eph. 4:19; 2 Cor. 6:17).

Passion and **evil desire** are two concepts closely related and appearing together elsewhere in vice lists (Gal. 5:24). On the two other occasions that Paul uses **passion** (*pathos*), he qualifies it with the genitive (Rom. 1:26; 1 Thess. 4:5) to indicate a specific kind of violent emotion or "passion."

Desire (*epithumian*), qualified by **evil** (*kakēn*) here and by other words elsewhere in the New Testament (see 1 Tim. 6:9; 2 Tim. 2:22; 4:3; 1 Peter 1:14; 2 Peter 2:10; Eph. 2:3; cf. 1 Cor. 10:6), should be understood to cover a broader spectrum than the previously mentioned **passion.** **Desire** designates that part of man which withstands obedience and denotes a general disposition in man which may be understood to constitute the root of individual acts of sin (see Rom. 7:7; James 1:14, 15).

Paul's reference to **covetousness which is idolatry** presents some difficulty (cf. Eph. 5:3). Stoic philosophers had conceived of covetousness as the source of all evil, and Paul may be borrowing from this insight. Yet it is equally possible that Paul's picture of avarice as a religion may be derived from Jesus' words as reported in Matthew 6:24: "You cannot serve God and gain." Here, as elsewhere (see 1 Cor. 6:9-11), one sees portrayed through these admonitions something of the prevailing social standards of the Hellenistic world in which the Christian movement made its way.

⁶ On account of these the wrath of God is coming.' ⁷ In
these you once walked, when you lived in them. ⁸ But now
put them all away: anger, wrath, malice, slander, and foul
talk from your mouth.

ᶠ Other ancient authorities add *upon the sons of disobedience*

---

[6] Paul cites the goal of the life of the flesh—the old
man—as the ultimate destruction which is coming at the
end of the age. Though grammatically one might understand **is coming** as a presently realized reality, the word is
often used in reference to the certainty of future events (see
Matt. 17:11; John 4:21; 14:3). This being the case, **wrath**
(*orgē*) refers to the future coming Day of Judgment. The
RSV rendering of *orgē* as **wrath** has been questioned on
the basis that Paul is not referring to some divine emotion
of vindictive anger. Paul rarely uses *orgē* in connection with
God. The word "disaster" might be more appropriate, meaning not God's emotional reaction to sin but rather the inevitable result brought about by sin. The additional phrase
"upon the sons of disobedience" is found in several manuscripts but is generally regarded as the effort of some scribe
more closely to parallel the verse with Ephesians 5:6.

[7] Paul again contrasts the present sphere of the Christian's life with the former sphere as characterized by its actions (see 1:13). The verse understands—perhaps demands
—a contrast to exist between the manner in which the Christian once walked in his former state and the present character of his life in Christ (see Eph. 2:2; 5:8; Rom. 1:28; Titus
3:3; 1 Peter 4:3f.). It has been suggested that Paul here uses
walk (*peripatein*) to indicate the character of life, whereas
lived in (*ezēte en*) emphasizes that the character of the
Christian's life should be conformed to his condition as one
who is in Christ (see 1:13; 2:19, 20; Gal. 5:25; Rom. 6:2-14).

[8] Paul now elaborates five more sins (cf. Eph. 4.31)
which are possibly all sins of the mouth if **from your mouth**
be linked with the verb **put away** (*apothesthe*). The verb
itself is significant in that it literally means "to put off" as in
the removal of a garment and, in light of the context, it is
probable that the apostle envisions these sins as part of

⁹ Do not lie to one another, seeing that you have put off the old nature with its practices ¹⁰ and have put on the new nature, which is being renewed in knowledge after the image of its creator.

---

the old garment taken off prior to the act of baptism itself.

It is difficult to maintain a clear distinction between anger and wrath, although Stoic thinkers had distinguished the former as a continuing or sustained state while the latter was thought of as a more momentary outburst. Yet it is not certain that Paul has the Stoic distinction in mind. **Malice,** or deliberate intention to do harm, is questionable as an appropriate rendering of *kakian,* which may indicate a more general form of evil. Though the word may mean "trouble" or "evil," when having ethical import it may denote a particular act of evil (see Acts 8:22) or the evil which men tend to do to one another resulting from their separation from God (see Rom. 1:28f.; Titus 3:3; Eph. 4:31f.). **Slander** translates *blasphēmia* which may refer to the slanderous speaking against God or simply slanderous speech about anyone (see Rom. 3:8; 14:16; 1 Cor. 10:30; Eph. 4:31; Titus 3:2). **Foul talk** (*aischrologian*) includes filthy speech as well as abusive speech in a more general sense (see Eph. 5:4).

[9, 10] Paul's words recall the baptism of his hearers and the symbolic meaning of the candidate's disrobing as a "divestiture" of the old nature (**you have put off,** *apekdusamenoi*) followed by the "investiture" ("putting on"; *endusamenoi*) of a new nature. Paul thus emphasizes the all-importance of baptism. The Christian, incorporated into the new humanity—into Christ—at baptism, is not urged by Paul to become a new creation by virtue of moral conduct. Rather, as Paul has previously argued, the Christian is exhorted to conform or change his life to embody fully his condition as a new creation. The Christian life is succinctly summed up in Paul's statement that Christians **have put on the new nature, which is being renewed in knowledge after the image of its creator.** The Christian is a new creation (2 Cor. 5:17). Paul points back to baptism as the time at which this change in condition was achieved, by God, not by man. Yet, the Christian is **being renewed** (*anakainoume-*

¹¹ Here there cannot be Greek and Jew, circumcised and uncircumcised, barbarian, Scythian, slave, free man, but Christ is all, and in all.

---

non; cf. 2 Cor. 4:16), or progressively actualizing the new humanity in his life.

In contrast to the false "knowledge" given by the Colossian heretics, (see 1:9; 2:3), Paul speaks of the knowledge (*epignōsin*) that comes through the growing conformity of the Christian life with the **image of its creator.** Such knowledge is not merely intellectual but depends upon the inward renewal of one's nature progressively realized in the shaping of his total life (see 2 Cor. 3:18; 4:16). The phrase **image of its creator** raises some questions. The statement refers to Genesis 1:26. But does **creator** refer to God or to Christ? And, if **creator** must refer to God, does **image** (*eikona*) also refer to God (as in Genesis 1:26) or to Christ as the image to which the new man is conformed? The parallel statement in Ephesians 4:24 would indicate that both words refer to God. Yet in light of the unique problem presented by the Colossian heresy, and especially in view of Paul's statements in 1:15, 16, 19 (cf. 2 Cor. 4:4), it is hard to resist the interpretation that **image** (if not also the creator) here refers to Christ (see 1 Cor. 11:7; 2 Cor. 3:18; 4:4; Heb. 1:3; also John 12:45; 14:9).

[11] Taking on the new nature in baptism is at the same time being incorporated into the new creation. The church, as the visible body of Christ, is the actualization of the new creation. Paul here states an emphasis that he elsewhere makes in a baptismal context (cf. 1 Cor. 12:13; Gal. 3:27, 28), namely that the Christian cannot bear the characteristics of the old nature. Such characteristics include not only the previously mentioned vices of the "egoist" but also discriminatory distinctions on the basis of race, culture or social status.

Paul's argument here applies to the circumstances presented by the particular problems of the Colossian church. On the one hand, the distinctions made by Judaism between the Jews and the rest of the world's inhabitants (*hellēn*, RSV Greek) is criticized with some emphasis (**circumcised and uncircumcised**). On the other hand, Paul

¹² Put on then, as God's chosen ones, holy and beloved, compassion, kindness, lowliness, meekness, and patience, ¹³ forbearing one another and, if one has a complaint against another, forgiving each other; as the Lord has forgiven you, so you also must forgive. ¹⁴ And above all these put on love, which binds everything together in perfect harmony.

---

also criticizes the distinctions made by the Graeco-Romans between themselves (*hellēn*) and the rest of the world's inhabitants as **barbarian** (*barbaros*). **Barbarian** refers to one who speaks in an inarticulate, stammering, unintelligible language (the word itself possibly being onomatopoeic). **Scythian** simply designates the lowest type of barbarian (despised by both Jews and Graeco-Romans). The final reference to **slave** and **free man** is probably occasioned by the situation regarding Onesimus and Philemon which is very much on Paul's mind at this time (see 3:22; 4:9). All such distinctions are alien to the very essence of the Christian gospel. **Christ is all and in all.** The only thing that matters is Christ; all else is abolished (see Gal. 3:28; 1 Cor. 12:13; Rom. 10:12; 13:14; Eph. 4:24; John 17:21).

[12-14] The life of the new man and that of the church, as the expression of the new creation, are to be characterized by traits summed up by the all-inclusive bond of **love** (*agapē*). The apostle still couches his ethical instruction in the language of baptism. Having taken off the garments of the "old man," the Christian is encouraged to put on (*endusasthe*) the apparel of the new man. **Compassion** translates an expression more literally "entrails of pity" or "heartfelt compassion" (cf. Luke 1:78; Phil. 2:1; see comments on Phile. 7). Of the following words, only one, **lowliness**, is not listed among the fruit of the Spirit in Galatians 5:22f. **Kindness** (*chrēstotēs*) is commonly used in the Septuagint to describe a characteristic of God (see Pss. 106:1; 107:1; 136; Rom. 2:4) beyond moral holiness, namely, his kindness. **Lowliness** (*tapeinophrosunē*) may be used in both good and bad senses (see 2:18). Obviously carrying favorable connotations here, the word describes an attitude of humility or modesty (see 2:18, 23; Phil. 2:3; Eph. 4: 2; 1 Peter 5:5). **Meekness** is better translated by "gentleness" (NEB), which does not carry the connotation of weakness

or cowardice that **meekness** has to the modern reader. The word indicates a quality of self-control and strength which allows its possessor to avoid excessive concern for self (see 1 Cor. 4:21; 2 Cor. 10:1; Eph. 4:2; 2 Tim. 2:25; cf. Matt. 5:5; 11:29; 21:5). **Patience** (*makrothumia*) is an important characteristic of God (cf. Ex. 34:6; Micah 2:7; Matt. 18:23-35; Luke 18:7; Rom. 1:24; 9:22), shown in its fulness in Christ (see 1 Tim. 1:16; 2 Peter 3:9) and enjoined upon Christians who are incorporated into him (see 1:11; 1 Thess. 5:14). As the apostle has earlier stated, this longsuffering is only possible through the knowledge that the Christian has of God's redemptive purpose unfolding in history. Thus the Christian's longsuffering waiting for the "day of the Lord" and his patient stance toward his fellows take on redemptive significance. The phrase "in Christ" provides the undergirding here. As the body of Christ the church takes the stance of its Lord, bearing those characteristics which he bore both in its internal life (Phil. 2:1ff.; Rom. 15:1f.) and in its relation to the world (see 4:5; 1 Peter 2:21).

Thus the apostle states that Christians should be **forbearing** and **forgiving** (see Eph. 4:2). The word translated **complaint** (*momphēn*) refers to "errors of omission" such as unremitted debts. It has been conjectured that Paul may here have in mind the parable of the unforgiving servant (Matt. 18:23f.) if not the Lord's Prayer. The apostle also reminds the Colossians that as Christ forgave them, they should forgive each other and themselves as well.

Paul asserts that on top of all the figurative garments that the Christian is now to be clothed in, he is to **put on love.** Love (*agapē*), however, is more than just the outermost garment; it is one that holds all the others together (cf. Rom. 13:8, 10; Eph. 3:17; 4:15, 16; 5:2; Gal. 5:14; Phile. 9; 1 John 4:11; 1 Cor. 13). Also, while **all these** refers specifically to the characteristics mentioned in verse 12, some scholars feel that Paul is also asserting that love **binds** (*sundesmos*, cf. 2:19) **together** the community (to which he refers in vs. 13). The emphasis at this point, however, is probably on the all-importance of Christian love as that which gives cohesiveness to the virtues cited in verse 12. Yet in the back of the apostle's mind may be the identification of Christ as the principle of cosmic cohesion in 1:17.

¹⁵ And let the peace of Christ rule in your hearts, to which indeed you were called in the one body. And be thankful. ¹⁶ Let the word of Christ dwell in you richly, as you teach and admonish one another in all wisdom, and as you sing psalms and hymns and spiritual songs with thankfulness in your hearts to God.

---

[15] The Christian life is to be shaped by a cessation of the hostilities between the individual Christian and his fellows and a cessation of his inner conflicts as well. **Peace** (*eirēnē*) is the legacy of Christ to his disciples (John 14:27; 1 Cor. 7:15b; Phil. 4:7). The peace experienced by the individual Christian and made visible in the church is the result of the "cosmic" peace achieved by Christ and seen in his body, the church. The present realization of peace in the church is, in turn, only a foreshadowing of the universal actualization of reconciliation yet to come (see 1:20). Because they are **called in the one body** (*en heni sōmati*), Christians are to manifest the spirit of unity in their lives (cf. Eph. 2:16ff.; 4:3ff.; Rom. 12:5). Again, one sees the paradox of Christian behavior. Christians are called to actualize in their lives what they already are in Christ. Thus Paul calls on his readers to allow the peace of Christ to **rule** (*brabeuetō*) as the "umpire" or arbitrator rather than the heretics' rules and regulations (see 2:18). Here Paul may have in mind both the conflicts within the heart of a single individual and the inevitable differences of opinion that occur between Christians. The metaphor may involve not only the rule or reign of peace but also the ultimate goal as a reward (see 3:24, 25; cf. Phil. 3:14; 1 Cor. 9:24, 25; 2 Tim. 4:7; Heb. 3:1). The availability of peace to the individual Christian and the visible reign of peace in the corporate body is an occasion for Paul's **be thankful** (see 1:12; 2:7; 3:17; 4:2). The rule of peace is not an accomplishment of man; it is rooted firmly in what God has achieved for man through Christ (1:20).

[16] Christians are to be grounded in **the word of Christ** as the source and controlling factor in their lives. Only in this **word** is found **all wisdom**. There is neither need nor place for additional "wisdom" or mediators (cf. 1:9, 28; 2:3,

8, 18, 23). **The word of Christ** is the source and basis for Christian instruction and correction for mutual upbuilding. The unique use of **word of Christ**, found only here in Paul's letters, is conditioned by the letter's constant concern for the centrality of Christ. The expression may be taken to indicate specific ethical sayings "of Christ" which circulated among early Christians (e.g., Acts 20:35). More likely, however, Paul refers to the Christian proclamation "about Christ." In view of the context of the expression, Paul may more specifically have in mind the content of the singing in the church, such as the hymn of 1:15-20, which he intends to be used in the corporate worship of the church. It and other Christian hymns in the New Testament (cf. Eph. 5:14; Phil. 2:6-11; 1 Tim. 3:16; 2 Tim. 2:11-13) are always Christological and are used in ethical exhortation. Paul states that the Colossians are to allow the "word about Christ" to **dwell in** them **richly** (*plousiōs*, "abundantly," cf. 1 Tim. 6:17; 2 Peter 1:11), shaping the manner of instruction and admonition which issues from the thankful heart which the word produces.

In you (*en humin*) creates some difficulty as there is uncertainty whether to translate "in you," as individual Christians, or "among you," as the collective group (see NEB). Probably Paul has in mind the word controlling the individual Christian (see Ps. 37:31); but he sees this in the context of the community of believers which is created, sustained and bound together by the **word of Christ**. The phrase **in all wisdom** (*en pasē sophia*) may refer either to the contents of instruction or the style of such Christian activity (as in 4:5).

With regard to teaching and admonishing Paul specifically has in mind the use of **psalms and hymns and spiritual songs**. **Psalms** probably refer to the Psalms of David that the early church (like the synagogue) used in worship. **Hymns** are songs of praise composed by Christians (cf. 1 Cor. 14:26), whereas **songs** ("odes") is the more general term for a song. These words were used in this period without precise distinction. The qualification **spiritual** (*pneumatikais*) likely refers to the content of the songs (cf. 1:9; 1 Cor. 9:11), although it is not inconceivable that the word also implies that the manner of Christian hymnody

91

[17] And whatever you do, in word or deed, do everything in the name of the Lord Jesus, giving thanks to God the Father through him.

(in contrast to other prevalent types of boisterous celebration) issues from and corresponds to thankfulness in your hearts to God.

[17] The principle of correspondence between the outward act and the inner life-giving word should be evident in the total life of the Christian. In the name of Jesus echoes the baptismal formula (cf. Rom. 10:9, 13; 1 Cor. 1:2, 10, 31; Eph. 4:5; 5:20; 2 Thess. 1:12; 3:6; 2 Tim. 2:19; also 1 John 2:12; 3:23; 5:13) and ties this section back to the point of departure, namely the finality of Christian baptism and the all-encompassing sufficiency of Christ.

Household Duties, 3:18—4:1

Prior to the time of Paul, both Jewish and Hellenistic teachers (particularly Stoics) had employed ethical tables or lists in their teaching. Hellenistic Judaism, continually struggling with the need to teach morality to Gentile converts, adapted and made extensive use of such lists. Likewise, early Christian missionaries, facing similar problems, found that existing lists provided a ready-made tool for communicating ethical instruction to converts from diverse backgrounds. Thus one finds examples of such Christian adaptations at several places in the New Testament (Eph. 5:22—6:9; 1 Peter 2:18—3:7; Col. 3:18—4:1; also see Titus 2:1-10; 1 Tim. 2: 8-12; 6:1, 2).

The common structure and terminology of New Testament examples not only point to dependence on non-Christian forms (e.g., "to be subject," *hupotassesthai,* occurs in each occasion of an ethical list in the New Testament), but may also indicate a body of oral instruction of fairly fixed form existing among Christians prior to its finding a place in the various letters.

The fact, however, that Paul's ethical list here closely parallels non-Christian prototypes serves to highlight the differences as well as the similarities. Comparison reveals the significant point of distinction to be the motive rather

¹⁸ Wives, be subject to your husbands, as is fitting in the Lord.

---

than the content of Christian ethical behavior. The Christian motive is derived from the fact that the Christian is incorporated into Christ, who takes his followers into himself as his body (1:15-20; 2:5-7). The distinctively Christian element is shown by the recurring phrase "in the Lord." As members of his body, Christians are members of one another and stand in a unique relationship to each other; a relationship shattering and transcending all boundaries (see 3:11). The practical result of this new relationship "in Christ" is that, in a time before women's suffrage and when slaves had no legal rights, the apostle gives a table of duties which contrasts strongly with pagan and Jewish lists by enunciating the reciprocal nature of the relationships involved (e.g., the husband not only has rights, he also has duties and obligations to his wife, children, and even to his slaves). The significance of this contrast should not be minimized. Opponents of Christianity have been quick to criticize Paul for his seeming unconcern for the plight of the slave. Yet, while the apostle does not demand the immediate abolition of slavery with an outright attack on the institution itself, he expresses a principle which, when applied, could only lead to the elimination of slavery (see Phile. 16). Paul emphasizes the value of each person before God with no regard to social station (there is no partiality, vs. 25; see 3:11, cf. Gal. 3:28; James 2:1ff.). Furthermore, in the church all are equally privileged "in Christ."

[18] In stating the ideal conduct of wives, Paul does not necessarily imply that wives in Colossae had not been living up to their duty. The exhortation may, however, have been occasioned by the circumstance of some Christian wives abusing the liberty that the apostle preached. The Christian wife's behavior towards her husband, however, is not simply aimed at being fitting (*anēken*) or proper, as in pagan ethical lists. Rather, it is to be fitting in the Lord; this is the distinctive mark of Christian behavior. The Christian, incorporated into the body of Christ, has all of his relationships altered in the Lord. While Paul may not be imposing

[19] Husbands, love your wives, and do not be harsh with them. [20] Children, obey your parents in everything, for this pleases the Lord. [21] Fathers, do not provoke your children, lest they become discouraged.

---

a new shape on the existing practice (both pagan and Jewish) of the wife being subjected to the husband, he is shifting the motive for such subjection (see Eph. 5:24; 1 Peter 3:1-6; Titus 2:4, 5).

[19] In contrast to Jewish and pagan parallel ethical tables, which assign all rights to husbands and all duties to wives, Paul shows one of the distinctive features of the Christian ethic by calling on the husband to respond to his duties (see 1 Cor. 7:3, 4). Of foremost importance, Christian husbands are told to love (*agapē*) their wives and not to make them embittered or "cross" through impatience and nagging. In this closest of relationships, the all-encompassing Christian attitude of *agapē* is to be the ruling and controlling factor (see 3:14; Eph. 5:25).

[20] Likewise, the relationship between parent and child is a reciprocal one. Children are exhorted to be obedient to all of their parents' wishes, **for this pleases the Lord.** This phrase raises some difficulties grammatically and may be translated in a "conditional" sense akin to that of 1 Corinthians 7:39 and Philippians 2:19. Possibly Paul is commending that obedience that is pleasing only as judged by a Christian standard, or by those who are Christians. Thus, the corporate body is seen as the primary frame of reference for the Christian's behavior: an implication embodied in the phrase, which literally is "pleasing in the Lord," but not evident in the RSV's translation (see NEB, ASV; cf. Eph. 6:1).

[21] Again Paul sounds the reciprocal note. Not only are children to obey their parents, but the father is to avoid the type of treatment that produces discouragement (*athumō-sin,* "moroseness," "spiritlessness"). Perhaps Paul here has in mind fault-finding or "over-severity," but his obvious desire is that the father have respect for the child and not abuse or discourage him from proper growth (one may assume "in Christ" as modifying the meaning of "provoke"; cf. Eph.

²² Slaves, obey in everything those who are your earthly masters, not with eyeservice, as men-pleasers, but in single-ness of heart, fearing the Lord. ²³ Whatever your task, work

---

6:4; 2 Cor. 9:2 where Paul uses "provoke" in a favorable sense).

[22] In discussing the relationship between slaves and masters, Paul takes twice the space taken by his remarks regarding husbands and wives. One may possibly infer from these remarks something of the makeup of the Colossian church and problems posed for Christian slaves (see comments on Eph. 6:5ff.). In the forefront of the apostle's concerns, however, must be placed the return of Onesimus (see 4:9; Phile.).

The apostle exhorts slaves to **obey** their **earthly masters in everything** (see Eph. 6:5f.). Such obedience should not be with **eyeservice as men-pleasers**. Eyeservice (*opthal-modouliais*) may be a word which Paul himself has coined (it is not found in Greek literature prior to this time), meaning either "superficial work" or "with ulterior motive" (see 1 Chron. 29:17). Christians engage in their tasks not as **men-pleasers** but with **singleness of heart,** or "undivided loyalty." Thus Paul encourages a giving or committing of one's total self to whatever task he addresses, eschewing any fragmentation or compartmentalization of the Christian's duties which separate his obligations as a Christian from his business or vocational obligations (as a possible background for Paul's statements here, see Matt. 6:22 where some similar concerns and words are found).

Here again, the motive for Christian behavior is found to reside in Paul's phrase "in the Lord." Paul's pointed contrast of **earthly masters** with *the* "Master" is an emphasis weakened by the RSV's **the Lord** (see 4:1; Eph. 6:9). **Fearing the Lord** (cf. Acts 9:31; Eph. 5:21; 6:5; 1 Peter 2:17) finds its background in Judaism, where fear of God has a positive aspect in the awe produced by an apprehension of God's overwhelming majesty and compassion (cf. Ps. 111; Job 28:28; Prov. 1:7).

[23] Paul amplifies these statements, urging the slave to work at every task with the devotion and fidelity he would

heartily, as serving the Lord and not men, [24] knowing that from the Lord you will receive the inheritance as your re-

---

show to Christ (as serving the Lord). Paul thus undercuts any understanding of Christian freedom which would allow the slave to flag in his everyday work or to presume upon the goodwill of a Christian master (see Eph. 4:28; 6:5, 6). The gospel is seen as heightening, not lessening, the Christian's obligations. The apostle indicates not just that the Christian works "as if" serving the Lord but that such single-minded service is service to the Lord (cf. Rom. 12:11). This is especially true in light of the way in which the performance of daily tasks by the Christian (whether slave or master) reflects on the church and ultimately upon the Lord (cf. 4:5; 1 Peter 2:12f.).

[24] The "fear of the Lord" (vs. 22) is partly caused by the realization that it is from him that Christians will receive the inheritance as a reward (actually the text states a "recompense as an inheritance"). The Christian, particularly the slave, is not to seek ultimate satisfaction in his present situation (cf. Phil. 3:20; 4:11). Rather, the Christian looks to the future (cf. 1:5) and endures the present discomfort and even injustice. The term inheritance (*klēronomias*) must be understood against the Old Testament background of the "promised land" and "kingdom of God" (see 1:12; 1 Cor. 15:50; Gal. 5:21), but it is also clarified by Roman inheritance laws where, in contrast to both Jewish and Greek practice, the heir inherited not only benefits but also obligations and liabilities. What is striking is that the slave, virtually without rights in the first century, is an heir. Certainly Paul places great value on understanding the present hardships incurred by Christians as a participation in Christ's sufferings (see 1:24; Phil. 3:8, 10). The situation of the slave in the Roman Empire is particularly favorable to such an interpretation (see 1 Peter 2:18ff.). The expression Lord Christ is found only one other time in the New Testament, and that in a similar context contrasting earthly lords with the Lord (see Rom. 16:18). The apostle here secures the contrast, pointing to Christ as the focal point and source of all the Christian's behavior.

ward; you are serving the Lord Christ. ²⁵ For the wrongdoer will be paid back for the wrong he has done, and
there is no partiality.

¹ Masters, treat your slaves justly and fairly, knowing
that you also have a Master in heaven.

² Continue steadfastly in prayer, being watchful in it
with thanksgiving;

---

[25] The apostle continues, giving reason for the slave
to walk uprightly and not become obsessed with the in-
equities of life. The offender, whether slave or master, will
be repaid in kind (1 Thess. 4:6). The identification of the
"wrongdoer" (*adikōn*) cannot be confined either to the unscrupulous slave or the harsh master (see Eph. 6:8). Onesimus' offense may well have motivated the apostle to emphasize that such indiscretion on the part of a slave is not
permissible, yet the warning certainly includes the master
as well (see Phile. 18). Though Paul's warning is issued to
all, his reminder that there is no partiality (*prosōpolēmpsia;*
cf. Gal. 2:6; Rom. 2:11) is of significance for slaves who
would be inclined to assume a partiality on Christ's part
corresponding to that in everyday affairs which clearly fa-
vored the freeman and the wealthy.

[1] Yet, on the other hand, if slaves in Colossae had
mistakenly taken refuge in the gospel as a justification for
disobedience, Paul's warning moves in both directions (see
Eph. 6:8, 9). Masters are reminded that they also have a
Master in heaven. From this it follows that they are to show
the same fairness and equity which they would desire from
their master. But Paul moves beyond saying that the master
also has a Master. Indeed, the master and the slave have the
same master, an impartial judge in heaven who is master of
both (see Eph. 6:8, 9; cf. 2 Cor. 5:10; Rom. 2:6).

Necessity of Prayer, 4:2-4

[2] Paul urges the Colossians to continue steadfastly in
prayer (see Eph. 6:18ff.; Rom. 12:12), using a word that
may connote the idea of a siege or something akin to the
perseverance of Jacob in Genesis 32:26, "I will not let you
go unless you bless me." Nor can it be overlooked that Paul
has just emphasized that Christian prayer must be rendered

[3] and pray for us also, that God may open to us a door for the word, to declare the mystery of Christ, on account of

---

through the Lord Jesus. The idea of continuing steadfastly in prayer is also thus bound with a continual steadfastness to the one through whom the believer lives, works, and prays (see 1:22, 23; 2:6, 7; 3:17).

Being watchful goes back to Jesus (cf. Matt. 24:42f.; 25:13) and is a regular part of the instruction delivered to new converts (see e.g., 1 Thess. 5:6; cf. 1 Cor. 16:13). As an essential ingredient to the Christian outlook, watchfulness may be traced back to the earlier instruction given the Colossians by Epaphras, urging a spiritual alertness and readiness for the Lord's return, with the possible implication that prayer is a means by which the Christian protects himself from the enemies he faces.

Paul returns to thanksgiving (*eucharistia*) as a pervasive characteristic of the Christian life. From a realization of the all-encompassing magnitude of God's act in Christ, the Christian attains a mood of constant gratitude precisely because of the deliverance achieved through Christ. The supremacy and all-sufficiency of Christ (see 1:15-20) underlies these admonitions just as it does the instructions regarding conduct in the Christian home and in master-slave relations.

[3] Paul incorporates the Colossians into his ministry by requesting prayers both for himself and the others with him (see 1 Thess. 5:25; 2 Thess. 3:1; Rom. 15:30; Eph. 6:19). It is significant that he asks for the continuance of his word of preaching rather than relief from personal difficulty though he is in prison. Paul tells his readers to pray that he may have more opportunities to proclaim the gospel, using the metaphor of the open door to symbolize this (cf. Phil. 1:12-14; 1 Cor. 16:9; 2 Cor. 2:12; Rev. 3:8). Certainly he felt that already a door for the word had been opened even while he was in prison (see Phil. 1:12-14), and Paul must have been especially aware of the events surrounding Onesimus' conversion.

Again Paul qualifies his description of that which he proclaims as the mystery of Christ, the great "open secret" (see 1:26, 27). Here Paul refers to the message he preaches,

which I am in prison, ⁴ that I may make it clear, as I ought
to speak.
⁵ Conduct yourselves wisely toward outsiders, making
the most of the time.

---

the unfolding of God's plan revealed in Christ. While he
may have in mind the inclusion of the Gentiles as the prin-
cipal cause of his imprisonment (and there is truth in the
assertion, see Acts 21:28; 22:21, 22; 24:5, 6; 25: 6-8), it is
more likely that Paul's use of **the mystery of Christ** is here
inclusive of the entire scope of the universal purpose of
God's unveiled plan of salvation unfolding in history.

[4] This clause is dependent upon the previous one.
There are, however, at least two distinct ways of understanding Paul here. He may be stating that he desires his
readers' prayers that he may speak the gospel in all situations with all possible clarity. Or, he may be more particularly concerned with his coming defense before Roman
judges, at which time it is his desire **that I may make it
clear** (*phanerōsō*) to the judges "how I am bound to speak,"
this emphasis on the last phrase being not quite captured
by the RSV (see Eph. 6:19, 20; cf. Acts 28:17ff.). It is also
possible that Paul here emphasizes the necessity, in light of
the misunderstandings and perversions of the gospel he opposes in Colossae, for his clearly elaborating the full implications of the Christian gospel.

The Christian's Attitude Toward Non-Christians, 4:5, 6

[5] Paul shifts from his own situation to that of his readers, perhaps with some specific problem in mind beyond the
damaging effect of the heresy in the church. Using a common metaphor for one's conduct, Paul instructs his readers
to "walk in wisdom" (see 1:10; 2:6; 3:7; Eph. 2:2, 10; 4:1,
17; 5:2, 8, 15), with special concern for the impression that
they give to those who are outside of the church. Rather
than a simple exhortation to prudence (as in Eph. 5:15f.),
Paul may refer to specific Christian instruction previously
received by the Colossians or to Jesus Christ himself (see
1:9, 28; 2:3, 23). Yet it perhaps forces too much weight into
the word "wisdom" to interpret it as a technical term here
(cf. Matt. 10:16). Further, it should be noted that although

⁶ Let your speech always be gracious, seasoned with salt,
so that you may know how you ought to answer every one.
⁷ Tychicus will tell you all about my affairs; he is a beloved brother and faithful minister and fellow servant in

---

the New Testament literature is for the most part written
by, addressed to, and preserved by believers, its few references to outsiders reflect a positive attitude on the part of
Christians toward non-Christians (see Mark 4:11; 1 Cor.
5:12; 14:21, 22; 1 Thess. 3:12; 4:12; 1 Tim. 3:7; 1 Peter 2:12,
15; 3:1).

The precise manner of the conduct that the apostle is
commending to his readers is somewhat ill-defined in a difficult metaphor, making the most of the time. Two distinct
interpretations of the phrase are possible. The phrase may
refer to something like taking advantage of the available
time. Or *exagorazomenoi* (making the most of in the RSV)
may be understood to mean something more akin to "rescue" (see Gal. 3:13 where *exagorazō* means "redeem"). The
difficulty arising from the second interpretation is that it
seems unlikely that Paul would recommend the rescue of
time (*kairon*). Though it is probably incorrect to understand the apostle to be referring to an effort to "gain time,"
the metaphor probably reflects the early church's sense of
urgency, stemming from anticipation and expectation of the
Lord's return (see 4:2; 1 Thess. 5:1ff.; cf. Eph. 5:15f.).

[6] Of particular importance in the Christian's relationship with those outside the church is his speech, which is
indicative of his character and provides an avenue for influence. Paul reminds his readers that their speech should
always be gracious or "acceptable." The unique character
of Christian speech is then further defined: Christian speech
should be seasoned with salt. The metaphor is probably a
common one, here alluding to familiar words of Jesus (see
Matt. 5:13; Mark 9:50; Luke 14:34).

PERSONAL GREETINGS AND FAREWELL, 4:7-18

[7-9] These verses remind the reader of the life situation
surrounding the letter and, in particular, the importance of
word-of-mouth communication in the early church. Tychi-

the Lord. ⁸ I have sent him to you for this very purpose,
that you may know how we are and that he may encourage
your hearts, ⁹ and with him Onesimus, the faithful and beloved brother, who is one of yourselves. They will tell you
of everything that has taken place here.

---

cus, a native of Asia (possibly Ephesus), is one of Paul's
converts who accompanied the gift-bearing journey to Jerusalem (Acts 20:4). In calling Tychicus a **beloved brother**
(*agapētos adelphos*), Paul is using the general mode of
Christian address (cf. Rom. 1:13; 1 Cor. 1:10; Gal. 1:11;
Phil. 1:12; see also James 1:2; Heb. 3:1). The apostle can
also refer to Christians as "beloved" (*agapētoi;* see 1 Cor.
10:14; Rom. 1:7; 1 Peter 2:11; 1 John 2:7). More specifically,
Paul refers to Tychicus as a **faithful minister** (*pistos diakonos*), "faithful" here meaning "steadfast" or "trustworthy,"
and "minister" being used in a more general sense than
"deacon" (which is the usage in Rom. 16:1; Phil. 1:1; 1 Tim.
3:8, 12). The question is raised, however, whether Paul
refers to Tychicus' service to the churches or his service to
Paul. Certainly these alternatives are not mutually exclusive, but it would seem that Tychicus' primary service portrayed here and elsewhere is as an extension of the apostle's
ministry.

In calling Tychicus **fellow servant** (*sundoulos*), Paul
uses a word that he elsewhere uses only in 1:7 referring
to Epaphras and which is found only in Matthew 18:28, 29,
33 and Revelation 6:11; 19:10 in the rest of the New Testament. Paul desires to put Tychicus on an equal footing with
Epaphras in order to help secure the reception necessary
for his mission's success. **In the Lord** probably modifies all
three of Paul's terms describing Tychicus.

Tychicus, one of Paul's most trusted messengers (2 Tim.
4:12; Titus 3:12), is on this occasion entrusted with a difficult and complicated task. Not only is he bearing the letter
to the Ephesians (Eph. 6:21), he is also carrying the letter
to Laodicea (if this is to be distinguished from Ephesians)
and possibly the letter to Philemon as well. His mission in
Colossae is many-sided. Three times we are told that he is
to inform the Colossians about Paul's situation (7, 8 and 9),
but he is also to encourage them (vs. 8 "that he may en-

101

¹⁰ **Aristarchus my fellow prisoner greets you, and Mark the cousin of Barnabas (concerning whom you have received instructions—if he comes to you, receive him),**

---

courage your hearts") through his presence and the personal messages he brings (cf. Eph. 6:22). And, he may well bear additional messages sent by the Colossian, Epaphras (see 1:6, 7; 4:12).

Incumbent upon **Tychicus** is still another duty, possibly more delicate if less difficult. Traveling with him is a Colossian slave who has either run away or abandoned his master's service while engaging in some special mission but has subsequently been converted by the imprisoned apostle (see Phile. 10). **Onesimus** (a popular name for slaves, literally meaning "useful" or "profitable"; cf. Phile. 10, 11) is commended as **the faithful and beloved brother,** an object of love to be accepted as an equal in Christ on a par with Tychicus and Epaphras. Part of Tychicus' task is to insure that Onesimus receives a trusting and favorable reception by the Colossian church. The word **they** (vs. 9) indicates that Onesimus also has a share in Tychicus' mission and is calculated to accent Paul's trust in him. It should be noted, however, that Paul avoids any direct reference to Onesimus' reception, this being handled through another letter. The phrase **everything that has taken place here** refers primarily to Onesimus' conversion. It may also refer to developments leading to the apostle's apparent expectation of release, shown in the accompanying letter to Philemon (see Phile. 22).

[10] **Aristarchus** ("best ruler") is a Macedonian Jewish convert from Thessalonica and a member of the deputation to Jerusalem (cf. Acts 19:29; 20:4; 27:2). Tradition makes him a martyr in Rome under Nero. Being well-known to the Colossians from previous travels, he sends his greetings (Phile. 24).

Paul's word for **fellow prisoner** (*sunaichmalōtos*) means more literally "fellow captive," conveying the idea of those taken in warfare (cf. Phile. 23; Rom. 16:7). It has been suggested that Aristarchus' association with Paul may have aroused suspicion leading to his temporary imprisonment. Or, Paul may be referring to Aristarchus' having voluntarily

¹¹ and Jesus who is called Justus. These are the only men of the circumcision among my fellow workers for the kingdom of God, and they have been a comfort to me.

---

shared in his confinement—possibly in a type of rotating visitation shared by Paul's "fellow workers" (*sunergoi*). This suggestion might account for Paul's designation of Epaphras as "fellow prisoner" in Philemon 23. Others conjecture that Paul is using a "spiritual metaphor" (like "fellow slave" in vs. 7) meaning "prisoner of Christ" (cf. Rom. 7:23; 2 Cor. 10:5; Eph. 4:8; also see 2 Cor. 2:14). Both interpretations would seem possible.

The mention of **Mark the cousin of Barnabas** is enlightening. The kinship between Mark and Barnabas helps explain the complications underlying the "sharp contention" mentioned in Acts 15:39, which resulted in the separation of Paul and Barnabas. Moreover, the reference here shows that to some extent Barnabas' confidence in Mark was subsequently vindicated through his performance (cf. 1 Peter 5:13; 2 Tim. 4:11). Paul tells his readers to **receive** Mark, using a word connoting the most hospitable kind of reception (*dechomai;* see Acts 18:27; cf. Matt. 10:14; John 4:45; Gal. 4:14; Heb. 11:31). Paul reminds his readers of instructions regarding Mark unknown to us. The reference to **Barnabas** indicates that he was apparently well-known in the area, although the New Testament provides no indication of his travels there.

[11] **Jesus who is called Justus** is not mentioned elsewhere. **Jesus** is the Greek form of the common Hebrew name "Joshua" or "Jeshua" (cf. Act 7:45; Heb. 4:8). **Justus,** a popular Latin surname among Jews and proselytes, denotes obedience to the law. Paul states that Aristarchus, Mark and Jesus Justus are the only Jewish Christians, **men of the circumcision,** among those of his immediate circle of **fellow workers.** His statement that **they have been a comfort** to me may refer to some specific task they have performed on Paul's behalf (perhaps in line with the continuation of his ministry). Paul's word for **comfort** (*parēgoria*) carries medical connotations, although it may be used here in a general sense. This reference may reflect Paul's sensitivity and even bitterness to the tensions in the churches

[12] Epaphras, who is one of yourselves, a servant[9] of Christ Jesus, greets you, always remembering you earnestly in his prayers, that you may stand mature and fully assured in all the will of God.

[9] Or *slave*

---

between Jew and Gentile Christians (cf. Phil. 1:15, 16; Gal. 3:28; 5:6). Certainly he was also aware of the tragic separation between the Old Israel and the New Israel (see Rom. 9:3). This tension may explain Paul's use of **kingdom of God** in a letter where, due to the problems posed by the heresy, he had previously referred to the "kingdom of his beloved Son" (1:13). At any rate, Paul here uses the phrase in a general sense and not with specific futuristic connotations (see 1 Cor. 15: 24, 50; cf. comment on 1:13). He is here concerned to contrast the all-inclusive implications of the Kingdom of God with the petty elevation of racial distinctions which were being maintained by many Jewish Christians (cf. Phil. 1:15; 3:2ff.).

[12] Epaphras, founder of the churches at Colossae, Laodicea and Hierapolis (cf. 1:7; 4:13; Phile. 23) also sends his greetings, perhaps conveying personal messages through Tychicus and Onesimus. Paul calls him a **servant of Christ Jesus,** a designation used elsewhere only for himself and Timothy (Phil. 1:1). The use of this unique term regarding Epaphras indicates something of the esteem in which Paul holds him, reflecting exceptional services and dedication on Epaphras' part, if not also some special mission Paul has assigned him. In describing Epaphras' continuing intercessory prayer on behalf of his converts, Paul uses the word *agōnizomenos* (RSV, **remembering you earnestly**), elsewhere translated "strive" (2:1; cf. Luke 13:24) and "fight" (John 18:36; 1 Tim. 6:12; 2 Tim. 4:7). The KJV here seems to capture more of the weight of the word in rendering "laboring fervently." Some scholars have suggested that this echoes the Lord's "agonizing" prayer in the garden (Luke 22:44).

The substance of Epaphras' prayer brings the apostle again to the problems occasioning the letter (see 1:28). Paul's word *peplērophorēmenoi* (see 2:2; **fully assured**) may mean either "complete" (Rom. 4:21; 14:5) or "con-

¹³ For I bear him witness that he has worked hard for you and for those in Laodicea and in Hieropolis. ¹⁴ Luke the beloved physician and Demas greet you. ¹⁵ Give my greetings to the brethren at Laodicea, and to Nympha and the church in her house.

---

vinced" (2 Tim. 4:5, 17). Most scholars prefer "convinced," thus making the following in all the will of God describe either the object, abode, or the circumstance of the conviction.

[13] Paul further testifies to Epaphras' continuing concern for all the churches in the Lycus Valley (a further indication of his central role in evangelizing the area). Worked hard carries implications of a struggle in battle and may refer to Epaphras' fidelity to his converts as manifested through incessant prayer.

[14] This reference is important in identifying Luke (*Loukas:* elsewhere mentioned in Phile. 24; 2 Tim. 4:11) as a physician and Gentile (separated from Paul's Jewish "fellow workers" in verse 11). The identification of Luke with Lucius is doubtful and problematic, since Lucius is identified as Paul's kinsman in Romans 16:21 (cf. Acts 13:1). Further, Luke's designation as a Gentile casts strong doubt on a number of traditions regarding him, e.g., as author of Hebrews and as a member of the seventy. Demas, possibly short for Demetrius, is given sparse mention, conceivably in anticipation of his future defection (cf. Phile. 24; 2 Tim. 4:10).

[15] In spite of the customary assumption that Nympha is a woman of Laodicea, the text does not make such an interpretation necessary. Scholars are divided on whether or not the name is feminine. Also, textual variants read her, "his" and "their" house (i.e., "they" being the brethren at Laodicea). The verse does indicate the early church's practice of meeting in private homes (Phile. 2; Acts 12:12; Rom. 16:5; cf. 1 Cor. 1:11). Some scholars contend that there is no evidence of the church's meeting in a special building before the third century. Nympha's house may have been in Laodicea or in Colossae; the word church or "assembly" (*ekklēsia*) is an appropriate designation for gatherings of any size (see comments on 1:18).

¹⁶ And when this letter has been read among you, have it read also in the church of the Laodiceans; and see that you read also the letter from Laodicea. ¹⁷ And say to Archippus, "See that you fulfil the ministry which you have received in the Lord."

¹⁸ I, Paul, write this greeting with my own hand. Remember my fetters. Grace be with you.

---

[16] Here again one sees the close relationship between these neighboring churches. Paul's instruction to have the letter read also in the church of the Laodiceans (see 1 Thess. 1:1) may indicate that the same difficulties are besetting that church. This practice may also cast some light on the earliest impetus to collect the letters of the apostle (see 1 Thess. 5:27). Obviously, such exchanges may well have led to the circulating of the apostle's letters at an early date (cf. 2 Peter 3:15, 16).

Paul's reference to the letter from Laodicea has occasioned some uncertainty. Several solutions have been suggested: (a) a letter from Laodicea to Paul, Epaphras, or even the church at Colossae (possibly critical of the church at Colossae and seeking the apostle's censure of the heretical practices); (b) a letter written by Paul from Laodicea (possibly one of the canonical letters); (c) a letter from Paul to Laodicea, now lost; (d) a letter from Paul to Laodicea, possibly Ephesians or Philemon. None of these is certain.

[17] Concluding his greetings, almost as an afterthought, the apostle tells the church to exhort Archippus to remain steadfast in the completion of some specifically Christian charge that he has received. Archippus' designation as "fellow soldier" (Phile. 2) may indicate that he is acting in some leadership capacity for the absent Epaphras. It is unnecessary to infer that Paul is correcting Archippus for previous lassitude in performing his ministry (whatever the precise nature of his task).

[18] Paul concludes with a poignant reminder of his situation. Yet he is primarily concerned with emphasizing the authority that is his through the testimony of his suffering (cf. Gal. 6:17; Phile. 9, 10, 13; Eph. 3:1; 4:1; 2 Tim. 1:8). Paul's greeting in his own hand indicates that the

letter was written by an amanuensis (a practice not un-common with the apostle; see 1:1; Rom. 16:22; 2 Thess. 3:17; 1 Cor. 16:21), although it is unclear whether the apostle's own writing begins here or at some earlier point in the letter (e.g., 4:7). Paul's "signature" may be due in part to the fact that letters written by false teachers had circulated bearing his name (cf. 2 Thess. 2:2). Conjectures have linked this practice of the apostle with his infirmity, postulating that Paul's eyes were in some way connected to his "thorn in the flesh" (cf. Gal. 6:11).

The apostle also re-emphasizes his earlier request that his readers **remember** (*mnēmoneuete*) his situation in their prayers (see 4:2; Eph. 1:16; Phile. 4; 1 Thess. 1:3; 2 Tim. 1:3), using a word from the language of worship which may carry the connotation of intercessory prayer. **Grace be with you** marks a change in Paul's writing. All later letters use **grace** in the benediction without further definition, whereas previous letters have spoken of "the grace of our Lord Jesus Christ" (cf. 1 Thess. 5:28; 2 Thess. 3:18; 1 Cor. 16:23).

III

The Letter of Paul to the Ephesians

Introduction

AUTHORSHIP OF EPHESIANS

As EARLY AS Erasmus the unique style of Ephesians was noted, but it was not until 1792 that the letter was asserted to be an outright forgery. Since then numerous arguments have been leveled against the Pauline authorship based principally on (a) style and vocabulary, (b) literary relationships, (c) historical problems, and (d) theological points.

Style and Vocabulary

The sentences of Ephesians are much longer and more complicated than those of other Pauline letters (see especially 1:15-23 in KJV). Those rejecting Paul's authorship single out such things as the heavy use of synonyms and adjectives (as in 1:19, where four different words are used with approximately the same meaning: power, energy, might, and strength). The letter demonstrates Semitic syntax much more frequently than other Pauline letters, and it is also said that the style is highly liturgical, "artifically eloquent" and even "monotonous," distinguishing it from Paul's other letters. And the organization of the opening remarks differs from Paul's customary introductions.

Even more significant is the unique vocabulary of the letter. It contains approximately thirty-eight words not occurring elsewhere in the New Testament and approximately ninety others found only in Ephesians among the Pauline corpus. For example, in Ephesians one finds "devil" (*diabolos*) instead of Paul's more customary "satan" (*satanos*). Likewise, the expression "in the heavens" is found five times in Ephesians but not in the other undisputed letters of Paul.

The chief limitation of arguments such as these is essentially that they assume the existence of an adequate sample of Paul's writing (based on the accepted letters) to allow a fairly certain determination of the limits of his style and vocabulary. Such an assumption is questionable, for Paul, an intelligent and active person, would have had an ever-changing and increasing vocabulary. Colossians is an indication of the manner in which the apostle is capable of adopting terms even from his opponents.

It may be argued that the letter's purpose partially accounts for its linguistic difference from other letters where Paul attacks specific problems or writes specific churches. Ephesians is possibly a general letter to several churches (see Destination), written in a more reflective mood than many of the apostle's other writings and with a different intent. Paul is perhaps intentionally composing a "theological tract" or homily, consciously developing the letter in the form of an extended prayer. It must be admitted, too, that Paul elsewhere demonstrates a capacity for the unwieldy style found in Ephesians.

Additionally, those defending the Pauline authorship of the letter may cite the role of the amanuensis, or secretary, in the first century. General assumptions that the apostle's secretaries performed much as their modern counterparts, taking a passive role in receiving dictation, are questionable. Many scholars maintain that the first-century secretary was given considerable latitude in actually composing a letter, acting much in the sense of a collaborator (cf. Col. 1:1; 1 Thess. 1:1). The one in whose name a letter appeared would give a final approval and attach his personal greetings at the letter's end (cf. Col. 4:18; Gal. 6:11). So it may be argued that an alteration in Paul's situation of imprisonment placed greater responsibility on the secretary in writing Ephesians. Likewise, if Paul's secretary were a trusted companion (cf. Rom. 16:22), the apostle may have been inclined to allow more leeway in certain aspects of the letter's composition.

Thus arguments based on the apostle's style and vocabulary are inconclusive. It is next to impossible to make definitive assertions regarding what a writer could not have said, especially when conclusions are predicated on such limited samples of the writer's material as are available to the student of Paul's letters. This, coupled with the uncertain role of the secretary and the unusual purpose of the letter, may sufficiently account for its unique aspects without recourse to a denial of Pauline authorship.

Literary Arguments

In addition to difficulties of style and vocabulary, Ephesians presents certain literary peculiarities which reflect on the letter's authorship. The problem is twofold, centering on the relationship between Ephesians and Colossians. First, approximately one-third of the words in Colossians are also found in Ephesians, a higher percentage than is found in comparing Ephesians with any other of Paul's letters. Of the 155 verses in Ephesians it is estimated that 73 have verbal parallels in Colossians. For example:

EPHESIANS	COLOSSIANS
2:12	1:21
2:14	1:20
3:2	1:25
3:5, 6	1:26, 27
4:16	2:19
5:20	3:17
6:9	3:25

The degree of exactness of the parallels suggests that the writer of Ephesians may have had Colossians fresh on his mind and thus have naturally repeated many of the phrases of the recently composed letter; or perhaps he actually had a copy of Colossians before him as he composed Ephesians.

Second, the differences between the two letters are also considered substantial. Particularly significant are cases where certain words and phrases, though parallel, are used in Ephesians in what is felt to be a much different manner than the manner in which they are used in Colossians. Thus the question is not whether the apostle's vocabulary changed over a period of time, since the letters were apparently written about the same time (cf. Eph. 6:21, 22; Col. 4:7, 8). The question is whether such different uses of words could have occurred within such a short period of time as that which apparently separated the writing of Ephesians and Colossians if the former letter is Pauline.

Generally cited as examples of "Colossian" words used in Ephesians with new or different emphases are the three words "mystery," "stewardship," and "head." In Colossians Paul uses the term "mystery" (*mustērion*) to designate Christ himself, whereas in Ephesians the term is used in three other ways: in 1:9 it designates the unity of all in Christ; in 3:3 it specifies the uniting of the Jew and Gentile in Christ; and in 5:32 it designates the analogy of marriage to the relationship of Christ and the church. In Colossians 1:26 Paul's word "stewardship" (*oikonomia*) describes his commission to preach, whereas in Ephesians 3:2 the term designates God's plan of salvation or the "economy of salvation." Finally, it is argued that the Colossian description of Christ as the "head," a description of his relationship to all the cosmic powers (Col. 2:9, 10), is substantially different from the use of the appellation in Ephesians 4:15, 16, where Christ is referred to as the head of the church.

In addition to the literary problem of the relationship between Ephesians and Colossians, it is felt that Ephesians also demonstrates significant parallels with other Pauline letters, particularly with Philippians (e.g., Phil. 1:27b and Eph. 4:3; Phil. 2:9 and Eph. 1:21), which would be written about the same time as Ephesians if the letter is Pauline. The letter also draws on significant statements in other letters (e.g., compare Rom. 1:21-24 with Eph. 4:17-19), a characteristic some maintain would more likely be found in the work of a devoted disciple than in a letter written by the apostle himself.

With regard to the problems of parallelism between Ephesians and Colossians, it may be observed that the peculiar characteristics of close similarities and yet different emphases may as well be attributed to Paul as to an imitator. It may be argued that the letter shows the freedom more likely expected of a writer dealing with his own thought than that of an imitator. It is difficult to explain why an imitator, working with a copy of Colossians, would have varied so significantly from the apostle's work. Hypotheses explaining the imitator's divergences on grounds that he did not actually have access to a copy of Colossians but was dependent on memory encounter difficulty with the exceedingly close parallelism of the letters' references to Tychicus (cf. Eph. 6:21, 22; Col. 4:7, 8). It is difficult to explain why the copier would have carefully committed this passage to memory.

Further, the use of different nuances does not necessarily point to a different writer. *Mustērion* ("mystery"), used in Colossians to designate God's disclosure of himself in Christ, tends to have different meanings in Ephesians; but these are not necessarily incompatible with Paul's still earlier uses (such as in Rom. 16:25, 26). Likewise, allegedly different uses of the idea of Christ as "head" are not conclusive. Even in Colossians Christ is specifically designated as head of the church in 1:18 (as in Ephesians) in addition to implications that he is also head of the entire cosmos (cf. 2:19). And it should be noted that *oikonomia* ("stewardship") possessed several variant meanings in secular Greek of the period.

Judgments of non-Pauline authorship of Ephesians based on the fact that it contains literary parallels with other letters of Paul are questionable. For example, arguments that Ephesians contains impressive phrases and statements from Paul's earlier letters do not preclude the possibility that the apostle himself might have written a letter reflecting familiarity or even dependence on his earlier letters. Paul might naturally have shown an affinity for especially important or central phrases in his earlier writings. It must be concluded that such arguments, while perhaps plausible, in no wise constitute a compelling case for rejecting Pauline authorship.

Historical Considerations

Other objections have been raised to the Pauline authorship of Ephesians on grounds that many of its statements reflect concerns that did not develop until the post-apostolic

113

age. Generally cited in this regard is the fact that the letter suggests that the tension between Jewish and Gentile Christians, so strongly reflected in most of Paul's letters, has ceased. Further, it is argued that the letter portrays the church as essentially Gentile (2:11), the writer even identifying himself as a Gentile (2:3). Additional objections are made on the grounds that the letter tends to view the apostles as belonging to a past era, arguing in such passages as 2:20, 3:5 and 4:11 that the writer looks back on the early church with a reverent nostalgia uncharacteristic of the apostolic period. These objections, however, are far from being convincing. Tensions between Jewish and Gentile Christians would have lessened very gradually, probably varying from area to area. Although Ephesians represents a later standpoint in the Jewish-Christian controversy than Galatians, it by no means assumes all controversy has ceased or that the church is predominantly Gentile—the contents are explained if Gentile Christians are being addressed. Thus the assertion that the letter portrays a picture of the church after Paul's lifetime is predicated upon a questionable reconstruction of the history of the early church.

Arguments that the "dividing wall of hostility" refers to the Jerusalem temple and thus indicates that the letter was written after the destruction of Jerusalem are equally unconvincing. Even if the statement does refer to a wall in the Jerusalem temple (which is by no means certain), the conclusion that such a statement would only be possible after the destruction of Jerusalem does not necessarily follow. Nor is there evidence that the fall of Jerusalem was seen in such a symbolic manner by New Testament authors writing after the event occurred. Additionally, it may be argued that a writer alluding to the event would have more explicitly and forcefully developed his arguments instead of making such a passing reference as is found in the text.

It cannot be denied that the letter does ascribe to the apostles a prominent role in God's plan of salvation. Yet while perhaps offensive to modern sensibilities, this is hardly incompatible with Paul's views of his function as an apostle (see 1 Thess. 1:6; 2:4, 6; 2 Thess. 2:15; 3:8, 9; 1 Cor. 3:10; 12:28). And objections focusing on the use of "holy" (3:5) tend to be based on modern understandings of the word rather than on its original use as a designation of those chosen by God for the performance of special tasks. This meaning is hardly out of phase with the apostle's understanding of his role as apostle.

Doctrinal Arguments

Other arguments have been made against the Pauline authorship of Ephesians based on seeming differences in theology between it and the generally accepted Pauline letters. The first type of theological concern giving rise to questions is ecclesiastical. Whereas in Paul's other letters the term "church" designates both the local church and the church universal, in Ephesians the term refers solely to the universal church. Also, in the same regard, the apostles are included as part of the foundation of the church in Ephesians in contrast to 1 Corinthians 3:11 where the only foundation of the church is Christ.

Second, there are numerous Christological emphases presented in the letter that are singled out as differing substantially from those of Paul's other letters. For example, in Ephesians certain actions are attributed to Christ that Paul elsewhere ascribes to God. In 2:16 reconciliation is the work of Christ, in contrast to Colossians 1:20 and 2:14-16, where reconciliation seems to be attributed to God. Likewise, in 4:11 Christ appoints the officers of the church, a task performed by God in 1 Corinthians 12:28. Also, Christ's descent into the underworld (4:9) is not supported elsewhere in Paul's letters. And objections are made that Paul's frequent phrase "in Christ" is used in Ephesians not with the deeper sense of identification with Christ by incorporation that it has in Colossians but in an instrumental manner. It is felt to be important that Ephesians emphasizes the exalted Christ, not directly mentioning his death in the important statement on redemption found in 1:15–2:10. Nor, so it is argued, does the letter show any indication of expected consummation in the return of Christ, a significant departure from the emphases of 1 Corinthians 7 and the Thessalonian letters (or even Colossians with its emphasis on the present completion and reality of redemption). Finally, concentration on the unification of Jews and Gentiles as the primary work of Christ is felt to be unPauline.

Third, the social teachings of the letter are felt to be explicitly and implicitly different from those of Paul elsewhere. The view of marriage and the relationship between Christ and the church seems distinctly more positive than that of 1 Corinthians 7. And it is felt that the author envisions a more enduring concern for religious instruction of children than that elsewhere demonstrated (6:4).

In weighing such objections, it is important to re-emphasize that there is no question as to whether Ephesians differs from Paul's earlier correspondence. The letter does present ideas and emphases not explicitly found in the apostle's other letters. The decisive question is whether the differences that exist necessarily constitute innovations in Paul's views that cannot be accounted for as developments naturally growing out of his earlier thought.

Although the differences between the emphasis in Ephesians on the church and that of Paul's earlier letters cannot be denied, such differences are less substantial than is often indicated by those rejecting apostolic authorship of the letter. A comparison of the letter with the church literature from the period from which a non-Pauline Ephesians is supposed to come (e.g., *I Clement*) indicates that the letter is far more akin to Paul than to supposedly contemporary church literature of the late first century.

In part, Ephesians' emphasis on the church may be understood in light of the apostle's opposition to the Colossian heresy that threatened to fragment the church with individualism and intellectualism alien to the Christian message of universal redemption. The letter may have been written as a more general counter to such tendencies as those opposed specifically in the letter to Colossae; such an example is seen in the apostle's emphasis on the church in face of similar threats of divisiveness found in the Corinthian church (see 1 Cor. 11, 12). Thus viewed in conjunction with Colossians, Ephesians' ecclesiology may be seen as a development of the doctrine of the church and its present function in God's plan of redemption along lines suggested by the former letter's Christological assertions (cf. Eph. 3:10; Col. 2:3).

Allegedly un-Pauline emphases in the Ephesian Christology are often predicated on unnecessarily rigid views of

Doctrinal Arguments

Paul's earlier Christological statements. Objections arising from the fact that in Ephesians Paul attributes functions to Christ which are elsewhere attributed to God assume a systematization which is not Pauline. There are occasions even in the apostle's earlier letters when he varies in ascribing functions to various members of the Trinity (cf. Rom. 8:9-11; 2 Cor. 6:16). The descent of 4:9 may be to the earth, not to the underworld, but even so, such would not necessarily be incompatible with his previous thought. The statement of the descent may, for example, be taken as an extension of Paul's assertions in Colossians of Christ's superiority and reign over even the astral powers which were feared and worshiped by both pagans and Jews. In an environment permeated with belief in countless spiritual forces, the apostle may portray Christ's reign as extending over the frightfully hostile powers of the underworld (e.g., Pluto, god of the dead and the underworld in classical Greek mythology), a prominent point of concern in Paul's time. Thus, Christ's descent may be seen as consistent with previous concerns emphasizing Christ's reign over every sphere of the universe (cf. Col. 1:16; Phil. 2:10).

Whereas the phrase "in Christ" is used in Colossians and in other letters to designate incorporation into Christ's corporate body, in Ephesians it tends to be used in an instrumental manner, indicating Christ as the agency through which various things are brought about. But Ephesians 2:13 does definitely embody a meaning akin to that in Colossians. Additional uses in Ephesians may also reflect Paul's distinctive use of "in Christ," and the concepts represented by the "in Christ" formula are definitely present in the letter. The emphases on the universal church (1:21, 22; 4:4; 5:29f.) and the work of the Holy Spirit (4:4f., 30) are both integrally related to the Pauline understanding of Christ as a corporate personality into which one is incorporated by the Holy Spirit (1:13; 4:30; cf. Gal. 3:27).

Objections that Ephesians seriously minimizes Paul's earlier emphasis on the Lord's return (e.g., 1 Thess. 1:10; 2:19) often ignore the fact that the expectation is in fact present in the letter (e.g., 1:14; 4:30). And again the letter may be understood in light of Colossians, developing themes present in that letter. In Colossians the apostle stresses the present reality of Christian redemption against insinuations that it is incomplete or inadequate (cf. Col. 1:12, 13). Ephesians continues in much the same vein, asserting the central importance of the church in the present period of God's plan. It cannot be maintained, however, that either letter totally lacks mention of the as yet incomplete aspects of God's plan of redemption (cf. Eph. 1:14; 4:30; 5:26, 27; Col. 1:5; 3:4, 6).

Likewise, objections that Ephesians places an un-Pauline emphasis on the unification of Jews and Gentiles as the primary work of Christ are misleading. First, there is nothing in this emphasis that is essentially incompatible with Paul's earlier thought (cf. Rom. 3:22; 10:12; Gal. 3:28). Second, while Ephesians does focus on the unification of Jews and Gentiles, this function does not exhaust the work of Christ as presented in Ephesians. Third, the harmony established between Jews and Gentiles is representative for Paul of the restored harmony brought to fragmented mankind in Christ, which is anticipatory of the eventual culmination of God's plan when all things will be united in Christ (1:10; cf. Col. 1:20).

Objections raised against Pauline authorship on grounds that the letter portrays an un-Pauline view toward social relationships are not substantial. To be sure, Paul's earlier letters, influenced by an expectation of the Lord's imminent return, do not reflect as much interest in the home, marriage, and family relationships as is seen in Ephesians. However, the change in emphasis may be at least partially accounted for by the apostle's changing situation. Imprisonment and the realization that Christ's return might come after his death may have increased Paul's concerns for the seemingly more mundane affairs of life such as marriage, family, and household ethics. Additionally, it should not be overlooked that the letter's statements on marriage are closely interwoven with the concern to portray the mystery of Christ's relationship to the church, possibly with the latter concern actually paramount over teachings regarding marriage. Nor should it be ignored that, as a Jew, Paul possessed a rich heritage in which marriage was often used as a symbol for God's relationship with his people (cf. Isa. 54:4, 5; 61:10; 62:4, 5; Jer. 3:20; Hosea 2; Mark 2:19, 20).

For the most part, apparent doctrinal divergences from other Pauline letters may be accounted for as growing out of the thought of Paul's earlier letters. Different emphases that are presented may be due partially to the apostle's imprisonment and his opposition to heretical tendencies such as those opposed in the letter to Colossae.

DESTINATION, OCCASION, AND DATE

Acceptance of the Pauline authorship places the Ephesian letter in the same time and circumstances as Philemon and Colossians. Yet even among those accepting Paul as the author of Ephesians, there is widespread agreement that the letter was not originally addressed to the church at Ephesus. This judgment is based on several factors. First, the earliest Greek manuscripts of the letter lack the designation "in Ephesus" (1:1). Further, the heretic Marcion (*circa* A.D. 140) knew Ephesians as the epistle to the Laodiceans. While it may be maintained that Marcion preserved the original destination, more likely he was dependent on conjectures linking Ephesians with the letter to Laodicea mentioned in Colossians 4:16. Laodicea is questionable as the original destination inasmuch as the Laodicean letter apparently was written prior to Colossians, and Ephesians is generally believed to have been written after Colossians.

Many scholars also feel that the content of the letter is not what one would expect of the apostle in writing to the Ephesian church. In light of Paul's three-year residence in Ephesus during his evangelization of Asia (cf. Acts 19:10, 26; 20:31; 2 Tim. 1:16-18), it may be safely assumed that he would have many friends and acquaintances to address in an Ephesian letter (e.g., Rom. 16:3ff.). And even if the apostle chose to send personal greetings through the letter's bearer, the general tone of the letter does not reflect the longstanding relationship which Paul would have shared with Ephesian readers. Ephesians seems to indicate that the writer and his readers have only indirect knowledge of one another (see 1:15; 3:1f.). This would hardly be true of Paul's relationship with the Ephesian church. Accordingly, the designation "in Ephesus" possibly owes its origin to the prominence of the Ephesian church in Asia, likely one of the early centers of Christianity in which Paul's letters were collected.

For reasons such as the foregoing, it is widely believed that Ephesians was originally addressed to some church (or churches) other than Ephesus. Many efforts have been made to locate the original destination and explain how it came to be altered to Ephesus (e.g., that the letter was originally addressed to Laodicea but in light of Revelation 3:14f., later Christians changed the designation); but as early as Archbishop Ussher (1654), there have been those who maintained that the solution is to be found in the letter's unique purpose. Ussher and others since have held that the letter was intended for circulation among the several Asian churches established under the apostle's leadership. Such a view seems compatible with the letter's general tone, explaining the lack of personal references and the early uncertainty as to where it was originally sent. If such a view of the letter is accepted, its intent may be understood in light of the Colossian problem, the close similarities between Ephesians and Colossians being accounted for by their having been written at approximately the same time from the apostle's Roman imprisonment (see Introduction to Philemon regarding the location of Paul's imprisonment).

Ephesians may be viewed as a development of some of the central implications of the Colossian letter, as Paul elaborates the role and importance of the universal church coinciding with the "cosmic Christology" asserted in Colossians (cf. Col. 1:15ff.). Whereas the Colossian heresy gave occasion for the apostle to concentrate on the superiority of Christ, in Ephesians he expounds upon the nature and function of the church, the body of the exalted Christ, in God's plan to redeem all things (1:10). Likewise, the letter is concerned to nurture the church against tendencies such as those threatening the Colossian church. Gentile Christians are especially in view, and the letter stresses the unity of Jews and Gentiles in the one body, the church. All is placed within a history of salvation in which Christ and the church are the climax of God's eternal purposes. In Colossians the emphasis is on Christ and the cosmos; in Ephesians it is on Christ and history, in which the church becomes vitally important.

Outline

OUTLINE

SELECTED BIBLIOGRAPHY

BARTH, MARKUS. *The Broken Wall.* Valley Forge: The Judson Press, 1959.

BEARE, FRANCIS W. "The Epistle to the Ephesians," *The Interpreter's Bible,* edited by George A. Buttrick, *et al.* Vol. 10. New York: Abingdon Press, 1953.

BRUCE, F. F. *The Epistle to the Ephesians.* London: Pickering & Inglis, Ltd., 1961.

————. "St. Paul in Rome: The Epistle to the Ephesians," *Bulletin of the John Rylands Library.* Vol. 49, No. 2, 1967.

FULLER, R. H. *A Critical Introduction to the New Testament.* London: Gerald Duckworth & Company, Ltd., 1966.

GOODSPEED, EDGAR J. *The Meaning of Ephesians.* Chicago: University of Chicago Press, 1933.

GUTHRIE, DONALD. *New Testament Introduction.* London: The Tyndale Press, 1961.

MARXSEN, W. *Introduction to the New Testament.* Philadelphia: Fortress Press, 1968.

MITTON, C. L. *The Epistle to the Ephesians.* Oxford: The Clarendon Press, 1951.

ROBINSON, J. Armitage. *St. Paul's Epistle to the Ephesians.* London: Macmillan & Company, 1903.

See further the Bibliographies to Philemon and Colossians.

Commentary

GOD'S PLAN AT WORK IN THE CHURCH, 1:1—3:21

Salutation, 1:1, 2

[1] Much like his opening remarks in Colossians, Paul identifies himself as an **apostle** (see comment on Col. 1:1). The phrase **by the will of God** probably indicates the apostle's profound consciousness that he was called by God apart from his own merit (see 3:7, 8; 1 Cor. 15:8, 9; 2 Cor. 8:5; 1 Tim. 1:1). One notices that Timothy, co-author of Philemon and Colossians, is not mentioned. By **saints** (*hagiois*) Paul means "consecrated to God" (see comments on Col. 1:2). Echoing the Old Testament idea of Israel's consecration to God, Paul here indicates that the New Israel created in Christ is consecrated to God. The word **faithful** might also be translated "believe in," the object of belief being Christ. See the Introduction, pp. 119-120, for a discussion of the destination of the letter.

[2] Paul's salutation is a uniquely Christian greeting. The general Greek greeting was *chairein* (see Acts 15:23; 23:26), but the apostle uses *charis,* meaning divine grace or favor (Eph. 2:8; Rom. 3:24; 4:16). The word **peace** (*eirēnē*) echoes the rich Old Testament concept of peace (*shalom*), which is understood as a special gift of God with the broadest possible applications (see Judges 6:24; Job 25:2; 1 Kings 2:33; Ps. 85; Lev. 26:6). Paul frequently uses it at the beginning and end of his letters.

Doxology, 1:3-14

The Magnitude of God's Plan, 1:3-10. Verses 3-14 are dominated by and structured around God's action, which is all directed "to the praise of his glory" (vss. 6, 12, 14). This phrase culminates sections which center respectively on the activity of God, Christ, and the Holy Spirit.

[3, 4] Normally at this point in Paul's letters comes a

¹ Paul, an apostle of Christ Jesus by the will of God,
To the saints who are also faithful ᵃ in Christ Jesus:

² Grace to you and peace from God our Father and the
Lord Jesus Christ.

³ Blessed be the God and Father of our Lord Jesus
Christ, who has blessed us in Christ with every spiritual
blessing in the heavenly places, ⁴ even as he chose us in him
before the foundation of the world, that we should be holy
and blameless before him. ⁵ He destined us in love ᵇ to be
his sons through Jesus Christ, according to the purpose of
his will,

ᵃ Other ancient authorities read *who are at Ephesus and faithful*
ᵇ Or *before him in love, having destined us*

---

prayer on behalf of his readers (e.g., Col. 1:3ff.; Phile. 4).
That the prayer does not come until verse 15 in this letter
and that Paul has broken his form with this insertion shows
the importance of the following verses for the theme of the
letter. The phrase **blessed be** echoes a Hebrew liturgical
phrase (see 2 Cor. 1:3; 1 Peter 1:3). **Every spiritual blessing** indicates neither the special blessings given by the Holy
Spirit (Gal. 5: 22) nor those apprehended by the Spirit.
Rather, **spiritual** here probably designates the quality of
the blessings as eternal and imperishable. There is no question of a distinction between "spiritual" and "material" here.
In the heavenly places is used five times in the letter (1:20;
2:6; 3:10; 6:19), possibly being astrological terminology
Paul has borrowed in order to emphasize the scope of the
Christian's blessings. The Christians' blessings come not
just through Christ but come **in Christ**. That is, insofar as
they are incorporated into him, his body the church, they
partake of these eternal blessings.

Even as introduces the explanation of the spiritual blessings—God elected us. Christians were chosen before the
creation—**the foundation of the world**—indicating that
God's purpose in Christ has been his plan from the beginning (cf. 1 Peter 1:20). Paul now uses the sacrificial terminology of the Old Testament, stating that it is God's desire
to present the church to himself **holy and blameless before
him** (see 5:27; Col. 1:22; Phil. 2:15; Deut. 32:5).

[5] It is difficult to determine whether the words **in love**

⁶ to the praise of his glorious grace which he freely be-
stowed on us in the Beloved. ⁷ In him we have redemption
through his blood, the forgiveness of our trespasses, according to the riches of his grace ⁸ which he lavished
upon us.

---

should be read with this verse or with the one preceding
(NEB, KJV, Jerusalem Bible). Contrary to the majority of
modern translations, the RSV understands the words to
refer to the great love of God in which his purposes are
grounded (see 2:4). The alternative is to understand the
words as referring to the love of Christians uniting them to
God and to one another (see 4:2, 16; Col. 3:14). Paul states
that it was God's purpose that believers (us) be God's
adopted sons (see Jerusalem Bible) through Jesus Christ.
Significant for Paul is the manner of God's election of an
undeserving people, which reflects the greatness and mercy
of God. It is through Jesus Christ that Christians are empowered to call God "Father" (cf. Rom. 8:14, 15; Gal. 4:5,
6). The word purpose (*eudokian*) may also be rendered
"favor" or "good will," indicating that the ground of God's
purpose is not anything innate in man but is rather God's
own righteous character. That is, God's adoption of sons
through Jesus Christ points to his own merciful character
and not to commendable characteristics in those chosen (see
vs. 6; 2:7ff.).

[6] Paul specifically states what is implied in the previous verse. God's favor has been unmerited; he freely be-
stowed on us his grace (see 2:5; Rom. 3:24; 11:5). Further,
it is through Christ that God has done all that he has done.
It is the act of God in Christ that occasions Paul's reflections
both in these verses (3-14) and in the entire letter. Beloved
is not found elsewhere in the New Testament, although a
different form of the word does occur in Matthew 3:17 and
Mark 1:11 (cf. Ps. 2:7; Isa. 5:1; 42:1). It is for the purpose
of magnifying God's name and publishing the greatness of
his power that Christians are called (see vss. 12, 13; 1 Peter
2:9; Phil. 1:11; cf. Isa. 43:21; Matt. 5:16; 6:9).

[7, 8] The statement here closely parallels Colossians
1:13 and has been thought to embody an early Christian

125

⁹ **For he has made known to us in all wisdom and insight the mystery of his will, according to his purpose which he set forth in Christ** ¹⁰ **as a plan for the fulness of time, to unite all things in him, things in heaven and things on earth.**

---

confession (cf. Rom. 3:24, 25). The phrase **in him** is instrumental, indicating that God shows his grace (vs. 6) through Christ (Col. 1:14; Rom 3:24). Yet, the preposition **in** may also include the idea of incorporation into Christ which is so prominent in Colossians (cf. Col. 2:6, 7), signifying that redemption is by virtue of inclusion into the person or body of Christ and is sustained by that relationship (see 4:13-16). **Redemption** (*apolutrōsin;* see 1:14; 4:30) means "to set free" (sometimes implying "for a ransom") and is used regarding the release of military prisoners and condemned criminals (Heb. 11:35, "release"). Here, it is specifically the death of Christ (**through his blood**) that is noted as the "ransom price" (see Col. 1:20; Rom. 3:24f.; 1 Peter 1:18, 19). This emphasis may be in opposition to tendencies at work in certain heresies which refused to see Christ as actually existing in a human body and dying on the cross (1 John 1:7; 5:6, 7). Likewise, as in Colossians (cf. Col. 1:13, 14), Paul's specification of redemption as forgiveness of our **trespasses** (*paraptōmatōn;* literally "false step"; see 2:1, 5; cf. Gal. 6:1) may be taken in opposition to heretical tendencies (see comment on Col. 1:14).

[9, 10] In addition to the experience of forgiveness, the believer also receives other gifts from Christ (cf. 4:8), namely in him the Christian receives **wisdom** and **insight** (see 3:10; comments on Col. 1:9; 2:3) by virtue of knowing the all-encompassing plan of God, now revealed in Christ. **Mystery** here refers to God's plan to unite all things in Christ (cf. 3:3, 4; 5:32; 6:19). God's purposes of reconciliation, revealed to Paul by special revelation (3:3), are made known to all Christians through the preached message. More precisely, what God has **set forth in Christ** is his plan for the redemption of the universe, a plan now unfolding in history. **Fulness** is a difficult word, which here probably refers to the completion (cf. use of *plērōmatos* in Gal. 4:4) of the successive stages or periods of redemptive history

¹¹ In him, according to the purpose of him who accomplishes all things according to the counsel of his will, ¹² we who first hoped in Christ have been destined and appointed to live for the praise of his glory.

(cf. 1 Peter 1:20). The scope of God's plan is all-embracing, being nothing less than the ultimate conclusion of all things in subjection to Christ. Paul's word unite (*anakephalaiōsasthai*) is an unusual word, meaning "to bring to a conclusion" or "to sum up" (possibly "reunite"). Here it is to be understood in light of the occurrence of the related word "head" (*kephalēn*) in verse 22 below. **In heaven** and **on earth,** while emphasizing the inclusive scope of God's redemptive plan in Christ, also opposes certain heretical tendencies which diminished the significance of Jesus' role in God's plan (see comment on vs. 21 below).

The Unification of Jew and Gentile, 1:11-14. [11] In him now doubtlessly refers to Christ, the sole agent through whom God's predetermined purpose of redemption—now revealed as unfolding in history—is achieved. Essentially, the writer affirms the fact that God's **counsel** (*boulēn,* "resolve") rules over history (Acts 2:23; 13:36). Now, in the Christian message, God's controlling and immutable purpose for history is revealed (cf. Acts 20:27; Heb. 6:17).

[12] Paul's expression **we who first hoped** designates the Jews (now Jewish Christians) who for centuries had awaited the Messiah. Paul asserts that Judaism's expectations and hopes are now fulfilled in Christ (cf. Luke 2:28ff.) and that the Jews were **destined and appointed** for the **praise of his glory.** His word **destined** (*prooristhentes,* "set apart before hand" or "marked out," see vs. 5 above; cf. Acts 4:28; Rom. 8:29, 30; 1 Cor. 2:7, "decreed") probably refers to God's choice of a people as his own. **Appointed** obscures the full meaning of the term *eklērōthēmen* (cf. ASV, NEB, Jerusalem Bible) which describes God's having "appointed" or "determined" a special goal to those he called as an "inheritance" or "portion" for himself through Christ (see vss. 5, 14; cf. Deut. 32:9, 10). The movement of God's purpose in history occasions exaltation of his glorious power through which his predetermined purposes are achieved (see Col. 1:11; see comments on vss. 19f.).

[13] In him you also, who have heard the word of truth, the gospel of your salvation, and have believed in him, were sealed with the promised Holy Spirit, [14] which is the guarantee of our inheritance until we acquire possession of it, to the praise of his glory.

---

[13] Turning from Jewish Christians, Paul now specifically addresses Gentiles who have come to know of God's redemptive plan through missionary preaching of **the word of truth** (cf. Col. 1:5), **the gospel of your salvation** (see 6:17; Rom. 1:16, 17). Although **believed in him** may be interpreted to refer to acceptance of the gospel (cf. Jerusalem Bible "believed it"), the pronoun (*hō*) probably continues the "in Christ" concluding the preceding verse and opening the present verse. Yet, the pronoun is to be taken not only with **believed**, but also with the verb **sealed.** That is, the believers were sealed in Christ with the **Holy Spirit** concurrent with their reception of the Christian message (see ASV). The reference to the readers, mostly Gentiles, having been **sealed** (see 4:30; cf. 2 Cor. 1:22) connects the Spirit received in baptism (Acts 2:38) with circumcision (see Col. 2:11-13), the term having been used in that connection in Judaism (cf. Rom. 4:11). **Sealed** was also familiar to Paul's Gentile hearers who had participated in pagan religious rites in which emblems and tatoos were cut on the body as a "seal" of a divinity's ownership. Paul's designation of the Holy Spirit as **promised** refers to the centuries of anticipation which Jews had endured (Ezek. 36:22-31; Isa. 59:20f.). The Spirit received in the believer's acceptance of the gospel (cf. Acts 2:38f.; Gal. 3:14) is seen as the fulfilment of former promises of God as the plan of salvation unfolds in history. As the fulfilment of God's promises, the presence of the Holy Spirit is an indication of God's faithfulness (cf. 2 Cor. 1:18-22).

[14] The presence of the Holy Spirit in the church and in the life of the individual believer, empowering him to meet the tasks of discipleship (see 1:19; 3:16, 20; cf. 2 Thess. 1:11), is the source of the believer's confidence. Paul's word **guarantee** (*arrabōn;* see 2 Cor. 1:22; 5:5) is a Semitic commercial term (cf. Gen. 38:17) designating a partial payment ("deposit" or "pledge") which binds both

¹⁵ For this reason, because I have heard of your faith in
the Lord Jesus and your love ° toward all the saints, ¹⁶ I do
not cease to give thanks for you, remembering you in my
prayers,
° Other ancient authorities omit *your love*

---

seller and purchaser. The presence of God's Spirit in the
believer is the **guarantee** of his **inheritance** (NEB, "heritage"; see comments on Col. 1:12; 3:24) to be received in
the future (cf. 1 Cor. 2:9; 1 Pet. 1:4f.). The last part of
the verse becomes somewhat obscure (see KJV). Several
translations refer the words **acquire possession** to God's
final possessing of a people purchased by him as his own
(ASV, NEB, Jerusalem Bible; see 1 Peter 2:9; Acts 20:28;
Titus 2:14; cf. Ex. 19:5; Deut. 14:2; Ps. 74:2; 135:4; Mal.
3:17). Although the train of thought would seem more
naturally to follow the RSV's interpretation, the abruptness
of the shift to God may only be apparent, the major theme
underlying the entire section being God's glorious plan of
salvation (vss. 4-6, 10-12). This is brought out in the concluding phrase **to the praise of his glory** which echoes the
conclusion of verse 12.

Prayer for the Readers, 1:15—2:10

Prayer for Enlightenment, 1:15-18. [15, 16] **For this
reason** marks a transition (2 Cor. 4:1; Col. 1:9; Rom. 5:12).
Paul now introduces a prayer for his readers because of
their having received the gospel. It expresses some of the
central concerns of the letter. For the formulas linking
thanksgiving and petition, compare Romans 1:9f.; Philippians 1:3; Colossians 1:3. **Remembering** carries implications
of intercession (cf. comments on Col. 4:18; Phile. 4). The
reference to having **heard** of the readers' faith has been
taken as evidence that the letter cannot be to Ephesus
where Paul had spent many months (cf. Acts 19). The
RSV footnote indicates an early variant omitting **your love,**
making the text read "faith in the Lord Jesus and toward all
the saints." Thus the variant closely links Christ and the
church, an emphasis which would be in keeping with the
letter's ecclesiological concern and would mean loyalty to
Christ and his people. **Faith in the Lord and love toward**

129

¹⁷ that the God of our Lord Jesus Christ, the Father of
glory, may give you a spirit of wisdom and of revelation
in the knowledge of him, ¹⁸ having the eyes of your hearts
enlightened, that you may know what is the hope to which
he has called you, what are the riches of his glorious inheritance in the saints,

---

all the saints should be taken to indicate the essential trust
in Christ which is outwardly manifested and exercised
through love among the members of his body (cf. Col. 3:14;
1 John 4:9-11). One may note that faith, love, and hope
(vs. 18) form a common triad in Paul's prayers at the beginning of his letters (1 Thess. 1:3f.; Col. 1:3-5).

[17] Paul's address insures that the prayer is to the
God revealed through Jesus Christ (cf. Col. 1:15). The expression **Father of glory** is not found elsewhere in the New
Testament and has occasioned some uncertainty regarding
the writer's intent. **Glory** indicates God's uniqueness and
majesty, and the phrase could be translated "glorious
Father" (cf. translation of 1:18). The term perhaps is liturgical or rhetorical without more specific intent, being used
somewhat in the manner of "God of glory" (Acts 7:2) and
"Lord of glory" (James 2:1).

Paul's prayer makes two specific petitions on behalf of
his readers. First, he prays that they might have a disposition
(spirit here does not mean Holy Spirit) of wisdom (*sophia*),
which in Colossians 1:9, 10 is the discernment to choose
between good and evil in the ordering of conduct. Here
wisdom seems more related to the divine plan for man (cf.
1 Cor. 2:5ff.). Second, the apostle also prays that his readers
might have more specific **knowledge** of God which is revealed through his revelation of himself as Father and his
plan of salvation in Jesus Christ through the preaching of
the church (1 Peter 2:9).

[18] **Having the eyes of your hearts enlightened** advances on the previous verse, describing the manner of the
readers' reception of discernment and knowledge. Although
enlightenment at times is used in reference to Christian
baptism (see comment on 5:14), the term probably does
not have this specific content here. The expression **eyes of
your hearts** refers to the inner man; the term "heart" is used

[19] and what is the immeasurable greatness of his power in us who believe, according to the working of his great might [20] which he accomplished in Christ when he raised him from the dead and made him sit at his right hand in the heavenly places,

---

in Hebrew thought to designate the seat of intellect, will, and emotion (cf. for eyes Matt. 6:22; and for hearts Ps. 119:2, 11; Matt. 5:8; Rom. 1:21, 24; 10:10). The purpose of the enlightenment is that the readers may know three things. (1) Hope (*elpis*) refers not merely to the emotion but also the content of that hoped for. The readers, many of whom as Gentiles were previously without hope (2:12), await the future culmination of God's redemptive plan (cf. 4:4; Col. 1:5). (2) The riches of his glorious inheritance in the saints further elaborates the hope. Inheritance (*klēronomias;* see 1:14; 5:5; comment on Col. 1:12) here refers to the redeemed as a possession which God claims for himself (while the parallel statement in Col. 1:12 refers to the believer's future possession; cf. Acts 20:32).

God's Power Now at Work, 1:19, 20. [19] Still elaborating the significance of verse 17, the apostle prays for (3) his readers to have both the knowledge and the experience of the power of God (see vss. 21; 3:7, 16, 18, 20; cf. 2 Cor. 13:4) which works in those who receive the Christian message (in us who believe; see vss. 13, 14 above). Paul uses the term immeasurable (*huperballon,* found only in Paul in the New Testament; see 2:7; 3:19; 2 Cor. 3:10; 9:14) and almost redundant synonyms for power (*dunamis*): working (*energeia*), might (*kratos*), and strength (*ischuus*). These are not all present in the RSV translation, the Greek reading literally "the working of the might of his strength." These almost repetitious terms accent the scope and majesty of God's recreative power, which is at work in the believers, as the same power that raised Christ from the dead (Col. 1:11; 2:12).

[20] God's creative and redemptive power has been displayed and released in specific historical events in the recent past: the death, resurrection, and exaltation of Jesus of Nazareth. Christian preaching does not cite vague pre-

131

²¹ far above all rule and authority and power and dominion, and above every name that is named, not only in this age but also in that which is to come;

---

historical myths or espouse abstract philosophical principles. Nor is the preaching of the church focused on the believers' own private religion (cf. 2 Cor. 4:7); it is centered in the transcendent power of God **accomplished in Christ.** It should also be noted that Paul here uses the article with **Christ,** that is, *the* Christ (as in verses 10 and 12 above), suggesting the use of the term as the title of the Jewish Messiah. God's transcendent power has been demonstrated in Christ's resurrection and exaltation to God's **right hand** (figuratively emphasizing the bestowal of divine power on Christ; cf. Matt. 26:64; 28:18; Col. 3:1; Heb. 1:3, 13; 8:1; 10:12). These events are the core of Christian preaching (Acts 2:22ff.; 17:31f.; Rom. 10:9; 1 Cor. 15:3f.; 1 Thess. 1:10; 4:14) and are the ground of the believer's hope (cf. 1 Peter 1:3, 4).

Exaltation of Christ, 1:21—2:10. [21] The exaltation of Christ to God's right hand (vs. 20) indicates his superiority over all other powers throughout every sphere of the universe (see Matt. 28:18f.). The terms **rule, authority, power,** and **dominion** are designations for members of a hierarchy of celestial beings or angels which played a prominent part in contemporary Jewish and Hellenistic religious speculations. These powers were conceptualized as both good and evil and variously identified with the celestial bodies. They were believed to control the changes of the seasons and, ultimately, the fate and destiny of man, naturally giving rise to much superstition, awe, and reverence (see 3:10; 6:12 and comments on Col. 1:16; 2:8, 15, 20; cf. Rom. 8:38, 39; 1 Cor. 15:24; Heb. 2:5; 1 Peter 3:22). Paul specifically speaks in opposition to popular beliefs in which the names of various supernatural beings were regarded as treasured possessions (often guarded secrets) enabling their possessor to have special powers (exorcism or conjuring being possibly connoted by Paul's verb "naming"; see Acts 8:9f.; 19:13ff.). It is in this context and against the threat of such views influencing believers that Paul asserts that Christ, and consequently his name, is exalted

²² and he has put all things under his feet and has made
him the head over all things for the church, ²³ which is his
body, the fulness of him who fills all in all.

---

above every name that is named (see Phil. 2:9). Christ
now rules above all powers inhabiting the heavens (note
the emphasis on the "heavenly places" in the letter: vss.
3, 20 above; 2:6; 3:10; 4:10; 6:9). Paul further asserts that
Christ is exalted not only in this age but also in that which
is to come. Thus Christ is the whole of God's redemptive
plan—its beginning, its mid-point, and its final goal (cf.
Col. 1:16).

[22, 23] Paul continues to affirm God's exaltation of
Christ (cf. 1 Cor. 15:25-27), here echoing Psalm 8:5 (which
had apparently come to be associated with the expected
Messiah; see Heb. 2:6-9; 1 Peter 3:22). As in Colossians,
the concern is to emphasize the centrality of Christ in God's
redemptive plan. Here, and throughout the letter, the argument centers on the subsequent significance of the church.
The church here is the universal church and not, as is more
usual for Paul, the local congregation. The church is understood to occupy a unique relationship to the sovereign Lord
of the universe. The understanding here, and throughout
the letter, is influenced by the Christology of Colossians.
As body (*sōma*) the church is subject to the head (*kephalē;*
see comments on Col. 1:18; 2:19), the metaphor probably
implying the body's dependence on the head as the source
of its life (cf. Col. 2:19). Also, the words indicate the closeness between Christ and the church—namely, that of the
head to the body. The two are inseparable.

Paul's description of the church as the fulness of him
who fills all in all is possibly to be understood against the
background of the Colossian letter's identification of Christ
with God's creative Wisdom. Fulness (*plērōma;* see comments on Col. 1:19; 2:10) may be taken to mean that Christ
"fills" the church with himself. Some have had difficulty
with this interpretation, assuming that it abandons the metaphor of head and body, the head not "filling" the body.
Such criticism, however, presses the metaphor too far and
assumes too much. It is possible to interpret the meaning
of *plērōma* as "completion," here indicating that the church

¹ And you he made alive, when you were dead through
the trespasses and sins ² in which you once walked, following the course of this world, following the prince of the
power of the air, the spirit that is now at work in the sons
of disobedience.

---

is the "completion of Christ." Thus it has been suggested
that the church "completes" Christ in the sense that it is in
the church and through the church that Christ's Lordship
is visibly actualized ("completed") in the world. That is,
although Christ's sovereignty is a reality, it is not recognized
throughout the universe. The church is a visible pronounce-
ment of Christ as Lord. And through the proclamation of
the gospel, the church is the instrument through which God
announces Christ's Lordship and furthers its realization in
the universe (see 4:13, 15, 16). Further, it should be noted
that the verb fills may be either middle voice (KJV, ASV,
RSV) or passive voice ("who is being completed" or "fulfilled"; cf. NEB). Regardless, the general meaning of the
phrase points to the close connection between Christ and
the church and the universal scope of God's plan of redemption brought about through Christ and his church.

[1, 2] Continuing the same line of thought, namely,
the power of God demonstrated in the resurrection of
Christ, Paul shifts more specifically to the readers' experience of that power in their acceptance of the Christian
message. He has in mind both individual and corporate
aspects of that experience (see the similar shift from Col.
1:15-20 to vss. 21-23). As Christ was raised from the grave,
the readers have been delivered from being dead, a fact of
which Paul reminds them.

The time sequence in this chapter is important: verses
1-3, the unredeemed period—"once" (vs. 2; cf. vss. 11f.);
verses 4-10, God's action; verses 13ff., the present Christian
existence—"now." By this sequence Paul places his readers
in the divine history of salvation.

The terms trespasses (see 1:7; 2:5 below) and sins
are probably to be taken as synonymous (see Rom. 4:25 and
1 Cor. 15:3). The phrase in which you once walked (see
Col. 4:5) further emphasizes that the apostle is describing
the former life style of the Gentiles (see Col. 1:21; 2:13).

³ Among these we all once lived in the passions of our flesh, following the desires of body and mind, and so we were by nature children of wrath, like the rest of mankind.

Following the course of this world is more literally translated "according to the age of this world" or even "this age." The expression may echo the Jewish concept of the two ages, a present age under the forces of evil and a coming age of divine intervention and the subjection of evil forces (see Gal. 1:4; 1 Cor. 2:6; 3:18). The term **world** is also frequently used to designate the realm of evil or alienation from God (see 6:12; Rom. 12:2; 1 Cor. 1:21; 3:19; John 12:31). Believers' lives, empowered by the redemptive power of God, are contrasted with the lives lived under the influence of **the prince of the power of the air,** Satan (see 6:11, 16; 2 Cor. 4:4). This expression may owe its origin to Jewish intertestamental speculation or may be derived from contemporary Hellenistic religions encountered by Paul. Possibly it is related to rampant astrological speculations locating the sphere of astral powers in the earthly atmosphere. The meaning, however, is clear: the force controlling the present age and shaping the conduct of men is evil and separates man from God. **Sons of disobedience** (5:6) is a Hebraism, further describing the course of conduct which the Gentile readers formerly followed (cf. 1 Peter 1:14).

[3] Now shifting to include Jewish Christians as well (**we all**), Paul says that it is not only the Gentiles who have been enslaved by evil and alienated from God (see Rom. 3:9). The description of this state as one **lived in the passions of our flesh** indicates that men lived wholly at the mercy of their uncontrollable **desires of body and mind.** The word **flesh** does not designate the physical body but rather the whole carnal disposition which enslaves man. **Mind** here translates *dianoiōn,* literally "understandings," possibly using the plural to indicate vacillation or multiple attitudes and conflicting purposes incapacitating man (cf. 1 Peter 1:13). The reference is not specifically to immoral passions and desires per se but rather to the ungoverned and irrational influences that self-will has on one's actions. The expression **we were by nature** (*phusei;* cf. Gal. 4:8;

⁴ But God, who is rich in mercy, out of the great love with which he loved us, ⁵ even when we were dead through our trespasses, made us alive together with Christ (by grace you have been saved),

---

Rom. 2:14; 1 Cor. 11:14) may mean Jews and Gentiles are "naturally," in light of their sins, the objects of God's **wrath** (*orgē;* see comments on Col. 3:6, 8). The expression **children of wrath** is another of the writer's Hebraisms.

[4, 5] This tragically helpless situation of alienated mankind sets the stage for a demonstration of God's greatness, his abundant **mercy** (cf. Rom. 9:23; 11:31, 32; 15:9ff.; 1 Peter 1:3; Titus 3:3-7) and **great love** (see 1:5; 3:17, 19; 5:2; cf. Rom. 8:39; John 3:16). Never are God's love and power more clearly demonstrated than in the repeated deliverances of his people in times of crisis (cf. Ps. 136:10ff.), culminating in the final act of deliverance wrought in the death and resurrection of Christ (see 1:19, 20). Paul returns to emphasize the circumstances and inclusion of the Jews in the plight of mankind in general (**we were dead**). **Through our trespasses** (cf. 1:7; 2:1) emphasizes man's culpability for his situation of alienation from God and God's rightful wrath toward mankind. Yet Paul also stresses that the act of deliverance is totally God's doing, proclaiming his might in **mercy** and **love. God made us alive** clearly indicates God as the source of deliverance, also specifying that believers are already delivered (Col. 1:13; cf. 1 Peter 1:3). More specifically, the apostle refers to the readers' baptism as the point at which they were incorporated into Christ and empowered by God (see 5:14; Col. 2:12, 20; 3:1ff.). The phrase, **made us alive together with Christ** employs the first of three compound verbs prefixed with the preposition "with" (*sun*) emphasizing the believers' union "with Christ," inaugurated at baptism (cf. Gal. 3:27; Col. 2:12). **By grace you have been saved** (see verse 8) interrupts the flow of the argument and punctuates the fact that life is God's free gift, not based on man's goodness or ability. **Have been saved,** the perfect participle (*sesōs-menoi*), might better be rendered "are saved," emphasizing salvation as a continuing reality in the believers' lives (cf. NEB).

⁶ and raised us up with him, and made us sit with him in
the heavenly places in Christ Jesus, ⁷ that in the coming
ages he might show the immeasurable riches of his grace
in kindness toward us in Christ Jesus. ⁸ For by grace you
have been saved through faith; and this is not your own
doing, it is the gift of God—⁹ not because of works, lest
any man should boast.

---

[6] Continuing to expound the implications of the readers' union with Christ, Paul uses two verbs from 1:20 (prefixed with *sun*) to emphasize the readers' participation with
Christ in his resurrection and exaltation. Again, weight is
given the present reality of incorporation in and with Christ
and is not limited to the readers' baptism.

[7] Whereas in 1:19 **immeasurable** (*huperballon*) describes God's power demonstrated and released in the resurrection, it here describes God's **grace** toward believers who
were raised with him (vs. 6). That is, the death, resurrection and exaltation of Christ is more than a past demonstration of God's power. It is the source of the empowerment
and vivification of the church. Through the Christian proclamation, continuing generations encounter the power and
grace of God in Christ. The expression **in the coming ages**
emphasizes the future goal of God's act in Christ and also
suggests that its duration extends beyond human history
(cf. Ps. 103:17; Jude 25; 1 Tim. 1:17). It should be noted
that Paul's word **kindness** (*chrēstotēti*) points to the manner
in which God's grace is manifested in Christ (cf. Rom. 2:4;
Titus 3:4). This same word is used elsewhere to denote an
element of the Christian's character (cf. Col. 3:12; Gal.
5:22).

[8, 9] Paul now returns to the subject of the parenthesis
of verse 5 and one of his main theses: **by grace you have
been saved** (cf. Rom. 1-5). Salvation is worked by God's
grace (1:6, 7) and is made available to the believers
through acceptance of the Christian message, itself the
source of **faith** (or trust, cf. 1:15; Rom. 5:1; 1 Cor. 1:18).
It (*touto*) may refer back to faith (*pisteōs*), indicating
that faith is itself a gift from God not to be misconstrued as
a human achievement (cf. Rom. 10:17; 1 Cor. 12:9; Phil.
2:13). Yet, the word **faith** is feminine while **it** is neuter,

¹⁰ For we are his workmanship, created in Christ Jesus for good works, which God prepared beforehand, that we should walk in them.

---

probably referring to the more general concept of "salvation." Grace is called a gift in Romans 3:24, but it too is feminine. Again the use of the perfect tense should be noted; the RSV's **you have been saved** is perhaps better translated "you are saved" (see NEB; see verse 5 above; for future salvation cf. Phil. 3:20; 1 Peter 1:5). Salvation is a present reality, a gift of God which is not predicated on meritorious efforts (**works** here is probably intended inclusively, contravening tendencies toward pride and exclusivism among both Jews and Gentiles) **lest any man should boast** (Jerusalem Bible "so that nobody can claim the credit"; see 1 Cor. 1:29-31; Rom. 3:24-27; 9:16; Gal. 6:14). The word **boast** (*kauchēsētai*) is an everyday Greek word designating an excessive or undue valuation of one's self or one's accomplishments. It is used in the Septuagint to denote the basic attitude of the ungodly man—trust and confidence in himself rather than God. As such, the boastful attitude is the opposite of faith. Paradoxically, the believer "boasts" in his own weakness (2 Cor. 11:30) and suffering (Rom. 5:3, Jerusalem Bible) and in God, through whose power he is saved (2 Cor. 10:17, 18).

[10] The believer, contrary to presuppositions of boastful pride, is God's **workmanship** (*poiēma*, perhaps better rendered "product" or "making"). Yet, as elsewhere, it is asserted that salvation by grace does not mean moral indifference (e.g., Rom. 6:15ff.). The believer's conduct is a matter of utmost importance, a point distinguishing Christianity from much of Hellenistic religion (and heretical tendencies within the church) which had little or no connection with morality (see comment on walk in Col. 4:5). **Good works** (Col. 1:10; Titus 2:14) are a goal rather than a condition of salvation (cf. Matt. 7:16-20). God's power, through Christ (cf. 1:19f.; 3:20), expresses itself in a transformed life which itself communicates God's purposes to those outside of Christ (see Col. 4:5; 1 Thess. 4:12; 1 Peter 2:12; 3:1, 2). Paul's expression **created** (*ktisthentes;* cf. vs. 15; 4:24) coupled with **workmanship** (elsewhere only in

¹¹ Therefore remember that at one time you Gentiles in the flesh, called the uncircumcision by what is called the circumcision, which is made in the flesh by hands—¹² remember that you were at that time separated from Christ, alienated from the commonwealth of Israel, and strangers to the covenants of promise, having no hope and without God in the world.

Rom. 1:20; referring to the creation of the world) suggests that the believer is a "new creation" (2 Cor. 5:17; Gal. 6:15). **Prepared beforehand** indicates that the new life style and behavior of the believer is also an essential part of God's plan, purposed "before the foundation of the world" (1:4f.), and also further emphasizes that good works are not the believer's own doing.

Gentiles' Present Exaltation in Christ, 2:11-22

Paul now turns from the theme of reconciliation with God to a discussion of one of the main themes of the entire letter: unity among all believers. It is particularly the incorporation of Gentiles into the spiritual Israel which Paul has in mind here. This unity of Jew and Gentile in the "one new man" (2:15) is the culmination of the history of salvation which has been developed from the beginning of the letter. The section 2:11-22 is the doctrinal heart of the letter.

Gentiles' Lack of Hope in the Past, 2:11, 12. [11] Paul now calls to mind the Gentiles' situation prior to their deliverance in Christ. **Gentiles** is accompanied by the article and probably should be read as designating the class "the Gentiles." The phrase **in the flesh** may be intended to signify the temporariness of the Gentiles' former condition of alienation. Likewise, **called** may emphasize the superficiality of the distinctions made or that the distinctions are wrongly employed (cf. Gal. 5:6; Phil. 3:2f.). **Uncircumcision** (*akrobustia;* literally "foreskin"; cf. Lev. 26:41; Jer. 6:10) is a derogatory term used by Jews for Gentiles (Acts 11:3). **Circumcision . . . in the flesh by hands** is probably to be understood as emphasizing the outward, external and superficial nature of these distinctions, counteracting Jewish tendencies to overemphasize their value.

[12] Nonetheless, the Gentiles' former situation was

¹³ But now in Christ Jesus you who once were far off have been brought near in the blood of Christ.

---

severe and the Jews did have an advantage of sorts (cf. Rom. 3:1ff.). The Gentiles were **separated** from the Jewish Messiah (RSV's **Christ** is probably "the Christ" as the Jewish Messiah) by virtue of being alienated from God (see comment on Col. 1:21). They had no part in Israel (**commonwealth**, *politeias,* may here mean "citizenship") and actually were hostile to Israel. Thus separated, the Gentiles were **strangers** (*xenoi;* see vs. 19 below; cf. Heb. 11:13) to the **covenants of promise.** Here implied are God's various covenants with the patriarchs and Moses (cf. Gen. 12:2f.; 26:2f.; 28:13f.) all unfolding and finding fulfilment in the promise of the Messiah. Paul describes the Gentiles as **having no hope.** Although **hope** may be used with regard to specific "hopes" (cf. 1 Thess. 4:13; 1 Peter 1:3) and may here refer to the hope of the Messiah, the absence of the article suggests a more general reference: relief from their dire situation in the world. **Without God** (*atheos*) likely indicates the practical atheism of immoral and purposeless lives (see 4:17ff.; Rom. 1:30; Ps. 10:4; 14:1ff.) rather than an abstract or intellectual denial of God's existence. The Gentiles, without knowledge of God and the power of his presence (cut off from the community wherein he had made himself known), were vulnerable to the onslaughts of hostile spiritual powers **in the world** (cf. NEB, "Your world was a world without hope and without God"; 2:2, 3; 6:12ff.; cf. John 1:10).

The Gentiles' Reconciliation, 2:13-22. [13] **But now** (see comments on Col. 1:24) this situation has been radically altered by the cross. A new stage has now been revealed in the unfolding of God's redemptive plan. **Now, by the Messiah's blood** (taking **Christ** as the title "Messiah"), the breech between Jew and Gentile has been overcome (cf. Mark 14:24). **In the blood** (see 1:7; Col. 1:20) is probably instrumental, though some would interpret the phrase to suggest incorporation into Christ (cf. Heb. 9:22, 25). The Jewish Messiah is now specifically identified as Jesus, the historical man through whom God's plan has been demonstrated in all its power (see 1:10, 19, 20; 3:11).

¹⁴ For he is our peace, who has made us both one, and has broken down the dividing wall of hostility,

---

The designation of the Gentiles as **you who once were far off** indicates the influence of the aforementioned promises (vs. 12 above), echoing Isaiah 57:18, 19 (vs. 17 below) where the reference is to Jews of the dispersion (cf. Acts 2:39). Readers are again reminded of the fact that God's plan has reached a new stage: Gentiles are **brought near.**

[14] The new stage of redemption history is characterized by **peace,** a term having many facets (1:2; 6:23; Col. 1:20; cf. Luke 1:79; 2:14). Peace is frequently found in the prophets and comes to have an eschatological association with the anticipated acts of God (see Isa. 9:2-7; 11:1ff.; 48:18; 52:7; 57:19; 60:17; Micah 5:2-5; Zech. 9:10). In the New Testament it is closely linked with the presence of Jesus (see Luke 1:79; 2:14; 19:38b) and his disciples (Luke 10:5; John 14:27), emphasizing that the long-awaited "peace of God" has finally broken into human history. Thus the Christian message is called the "gospel of peace" (6:15; cf. Acts 10:36) and God is known as "the God of peace" (Rom. 15:33; 16:20; Phil. 4:9; 1 Thess. 5:23; Heb. 13:20). The word is comprehensive, describing a relationship toward God in which the Christian is placed (Col. 1:20; Rom. 5:1) that also qualifies his relationship with his fellows, especially other believers (see 2:14; 4:3; 6:23; 1 Cor. 7:15; Col. 3:15; Heb. 12:14). The word also designates the inner harmony that individual Christians possess by virtue of being in Christ (see Rom. 15:13; cf. Phil. 4:11-13).

The new relationship between Jew and Gentile is indicative of the eventual unifying of all things in Christ (see 1:10; cf. Col. 1:20). **He is our peace** moves beyond simply identifying Christ as the agent of peace, indicating that by their mutual incorporation into his person, both Jew and Gentile are made one (cf. Gal. 3:28, 29; Col. 3:11). The expression that Christ has **broken down the dividing wall** may refer to the actual wall in the Jerusalem Temple which restricted Gentiles to the Court of the Gentiles (under penalty of death), separating them from the inner courts which were accessible only to Jews.

¹⁵ by abolishing in his flesh the law of commandments and ordinances, that he might create in himself one new man in place of the two, so making peace, ¹⁶ and might reconcile us both to God in one body through the cross, thereby bringing the hostility to an end.

---

[15] Christ has brought peace to the division between Jew and Gentile in his flesh. That is, it is through Jesus' life and death (vs. 16) that the abolishing (*katargēsas;* literally "nullifying" or "invalidating") of the hostility between Jew and Gentile has been accomplished (cf. Col. 2:14). The phrase **in his flesh** probably carries an implicit refutation of the heretical view that denied Jesus had a physical body (cf. Col. 1:21, 22; 2:9, 14; John 1:14; 2 John 7). The implication is that the enmity between Jews and Gentiles is destroyed through the invalidating of the law (Rom. 10:4; 2 Cor. 3:14). The reference to **the law of commandments and ordinances** (cf. Col. 2:14, 20, 21) is probably inclusive, extending beyond the Torah or first five books of the Old Testament and encompassing the entire legal system of laws and ordinances under which the Jews lived. Both Jews and Gentiles are now incorporated into an entirely new creation (cf. 2 Cor. 5:17; Gal. 6:15) as they are both brought into Christ's body (**in himself;** cf. 1 Cor. 12) wherein all the fractures of humanity are healed corporately in **one new man** (cf. 1:10; Col. 1:20). **Making peace** (*poiōn eirēnēn*) employs the present participle, suggesting the ongoing of reconciliation in Christ (cf. 4:1ff.; Matt. 5:9).

[16] In contrast to the universal implications of the cross elaborated in Colossians, Paul now reiterates that the goal of the cross is to **reconcile** (*apokatallaxē;* see Col. 1:20) both Jew and Gentile to God (cf. Col. 1:21, 22). **In one body** designates the new body into which believers are incorporated through baptism and the operation of the Spirit (see 4:4f.; Gal. 3:28; Col. 2:10f.). It is the cross that is the agency of the reconciliation and the cause of the cessation of hostility (cf. 1 Cor. 1:17, 18). **Bringing to an end** (*apokteinas*) is better translated "killing" (NEB, "killed"; cf. Rom. 7:11 RSV, "killed"). Ironically, the cross is the agency

[17] And he came and preached peace to you who were far
off and peace to those who were near; [18] for through him
we both have access in one Spirit to the Father.

---

not of Jesus' defeat but of his victory (cf. John 19:30). This
new harmony in Christ is indicative of the great magnitude
of God's unfolding plan of redemption, foreshadowing the
ultimate reunification of all things (1:10).

[17] Paul now more fully echoes Old Testament anticipation of God's coming peace (cf. Isa. 52:7; 57:19; Zech.
9:10). This anticipation is understood as now actualized in
Christ's person wherein the breach between Gentiles (**you
who were far off**) and Jews (**those who were near;** see vs.
13 above) is annulled, a definite sign that the believer is
living in the "last days," the new age, part of the new creation. **He came** refers to the Incarnation in general (cf.
Luke 2:14) and not specifically to the return of the resurrected Lord. The special, long-awaited time has now come,
and the Christian proclamation is one of peace (see 6:15;
Rom. 10:15) by virtue of what God has accomplished in
Christ. The reference to Christ's "preaching" is probably a
figure of speech for the preaching of the apostles and early
Christian evangelists rather than Jesus' preaching (cf. Mark
1:14, 15), which was primarily to Jews.

[18] Peace between Jew and Gentile has still further
implications. There is here a conscious contrast between
both and **one;** all believers, former Jews and Gentiles, are
now incorporated together into one new reality **through**
Christ (cf. John 14:6), and together are presented before
God. **Access** (*prosagōgēn;* see comment on 3:12; cf. Rom.
5:2) literally means "brought before" and suggests the pres-
entation of an emissary before a king (cf. Matt. 18:24). The
reference to **one Spirit** may refer to the common disposition
now characterizing the formerly separate groups. Or, the
reference may be to the Holy Spirit (as the RSV indicates)
which nurtures and empowers the new unity (see 4:4; cf.
1 Cor. 12:4f.; 2 Cor. 13:14). To those having access to God
through Christ, God is known as **Father,** a relationship particularly stressed throughout the letter (see 1:17; 3:12, 14,
15).

[19] So then you are no longer strangers and sojourners, but you are fellow citizens with the saints and members of the household of God, [20] built upon the foundation of the apostles and prophets, Christ Jesus himself being the cornerstone,

---

[19] Gentile Christians are now informed of further implications of their new position before God and man. Strangers (*xenoi*) refers to their former status as "strangers to the covenants of promise" (vs. 12). Sojourners (*paroikoi*, "foreigner," "alien"), which is sometimes used to describe Jews of the Diaspora (1 Peter 2:11) and even the patriarchs (Heb. 11:13; cf. Gen. 23:4), was also used by Jews to designate Gentiles living within Israel. Here the word is consciously contrasted with **fellow citizens** and carries the implication of those who reside in a community but do not share full civic rights (like the God-fearers attached to the synagogues). Thus, in contrast to their former condition (see 2:1f., 12f.), Gentile believers are now **fellow citizens** (*sumpolitai*) and share full status with all of God's called people (3:6). **Saints** (*hagiōn*, see 1:18; 3:8; 4:12; 5:3; 6:18; cf. Col. 1:26) refers specifically neither to Jews nor to Jewish Christians but to the new people of God called through Christ into a new creation. In addition to having "citizenship" and commensurate rights, Gentile believers are further described as **members of the household of God** (cf. Gal. 6:10; 1 Tim. 3:15; Heb. 3:6; 1 Peter 4:17) suggesting that their new relationship is that of "kinsmen."

[20] Paul's statement here may have been suggested by Colossians 2:7 but flows naturally from the previous allusion to believers as the "household of God." Believers are now portrayed as having been **built** (probably a reference to the time of conversion) into a building; this metaphor embodies the vision of the corporate body of believers as a spiritual temple (vs. 21 below). Whereas the apostle elsewhere designates Christ as the sole **foundation** (cf. 1 Cor. 3:11), here **the apostles and prophets** (cf. 1 Cor. 12:28) of the early Christian movement are included. Although **foundation** (*themelios*) is used elsewhere referring to the teachings of the early church (see Heb. 6:1), here the term refers primarily to the men themselves and their unique role in God's

²¹ in whom the whole structure is joined together and grows into a holy temple in the Lord; ²² in whom you also are built into it for a dwelling place of God in the Spirit.

---

redemptive scheme unfolding in history (see 3:5; 4:11; cf. Rev. 21:14). However, the central role of Christ in the new creation is the main concern of the statement. Christ is here described as the **cornerstone** (*akrogōniaiou;* cf. 1 Peter 2:6; Matt. 21:42; Mark 12:10; Rom. 9:33; Isa. 28:16), referring to the final stone completing a structure or a significant stone like the center stone in an arch.

[21] Continuing to portray believers as a spiritual building, Paul further describes Christ as the source of both the church's life and its cohesion and harmony. **Whole structure** may refer to several separate buildings (cf. ASV, Jerusalem Bible, "every structure"), suggesting that individual congregations (or individual Christians) are being built into one universal church. However, the idea of a universal church made up of individual congregations finds little warrant in the New Testament. Customarily Paul indicates that each local church is a complete manifestation of the body of Christ in itself. **Joined together** (*sunarmologoumenē;* see 4:16; NEB, "being bonded"), a present participle, indicates a continual process of unification existing in the church. **Grows** (*auxei;* see 4:16; Col. 1:6, 10; 2:19) is a word generally indicative of bodily growth and conveys the idea of the church as a living organism (cf. Col. 1:24; 2:19). The goal of this process of growth and unification is that believers might become **a holy temple in the Lord** (cf. 1 Cor. 3:16, 17; 6:19; 2 Cor. 6:16f.; 1 Peter 2:5). **Temple** (*naos*), derived from a word meaning "to dwell" or "to inhabit" (*naiō*), designates the "sanctuary" rather than the temple in general. The entire statement pictures a process working toward a goal that is as yet only partially fulfilled, God's presence among his people (cf. Rev. 21:22). **In the Lord** identifies Christ, the cornerstone of the spiritual temple, as the agent through whom the divine redemptive process is being brought to completion.

[22] **You also** again refers specifically to the Gentiles as the apostle indicates their role and place in the redemptive

¹ For this reason I, Paul, a prisoner for Christ Jesus on behalf of you Gentiles—² assuming that you have heard of the stewardship of God's grace that was given to me for you,

---

process; dwelling place here refers to the whole corporate body of believers and not to individuals. Gentiles, too, are being built (present tense) into the spiritual sanctuary wherein God dwells (1 Peter 2:5; cf. Acts 7:48). In the Spirit (cf. Rom. 8:1ff.; John 4:23, 24) may refer either to the agency of the building process, the Holy Spirit which is at work in baptism and is the source of the cohesion in the church; or it may designate the mode of God's dwelling in the body of believers as "spiritual" (so NEB, "spiritual dwelling"; cf. 4:3, 4), or "by the Spirit." The former is to be preferred.

The Christian Ministry, 3:1-13

God's Plan in Christ, 3:1-6. [1] Paul now, as so often elsewhere (Rom. 15:15ff.; 2 Cor. 3:4—6:10; Gal. 1:15f.; 2:7f.; 1 Tim. 2:7), discusses his unique role as the apostle to the Gentiles in the revelation of God's will to them. As is characteristic of Ephesians, the discussion here is placed in relation to the working out of the divine purposes in the whole history of salvation (cf. Col. 1:24ff.). The opening words of the verse, **for this reason,** again take up the prayer which began in 1:15 but was interrupted by the remarks of 2:11-22. Yet the apostle immediately digresses again, not supplying a verb for the sentence beginning in verse 1 until verse 14, where he again resumes by repeating **for this reason.**

[2] **Assuming that you have heard** has been taken as an indication that Paul could not be writing to Ephesus, where he had lived for three years (Acts 20:31). The RSV is probably to be preferred in translating **assuming** rather than the KJV's "if." The statement may be rhetorical, assuming familiarity with the following (see 4:21; Col. 1:23; Gal. 3:4 where the same expression is used). The expression **stewardship of God's grace** has occasioned some difficulty. **Stewardship** (*oikonomian;* cf. 1:10) may be used to designate an

146

³ how the mystery was made known to me by revelation, as I have written briefly. ⁴ When you read this you can perceive my insight into the mystery of Christ,

---

administrative office (e.g., the office of an apostle; see 1 Cor. 9:17 and RSV of Col. 1:25) or the administration of that office (see 1:10; 3:9). In this latter sense it is used in reference to the plan of redemption (see 1 Tim. 1:4, where the text is ambiguous). Thus the **stewardship** or dispensation of God's grace which is given the apostle may indicate the apostle's office or his work in the bringing of **God's grace** (the gospel) to the Gentiles (probably the primary designate of Paul's **for you**). **Given to me for you** refers to Paul's being entrusted with the gospel (Gal. 2:9) for the Gentiles (see Rom. 1:5) as well as to the grace personally received by the apostle in God's special election of him as an agent of reconciliation.

[3] Paul again speaks of the **mystery** which he has received. He has previously used the term in contexts where it was possibly borrowed from heretical opponents (see comments on Col. 1:26, 27) and was used regarding the whole spectrum of God's redemptive plan for the universe (e.g., 1:9). Here he has in mind a more particular aspect of that all-inclusive mystery, namely the incorporation of the Gentiles into God's elect people (see comments on 1:9 above). It is not illogical to find the apostle thinking of his special call in this particular context. He is not necessarily validating his authority, but when speaking of the inclusion of the Gentiles his mind naturally thinks of the role alloted him by God in the unfolding plan (see Gal. 1:1, 12, 16). Although Paul's statement as **I have written briefly** has been understood to refer to a previous letter, it probably refers to the previous remarks of the same letter (cf. Jerusalem Bible, "as I have just described it").

[4] To some this statement has seemed incompatible with the apostle's humility and indicative of a later author here lauding the apostle. Yet the statement seems not to be irreconcilable with other similar statements which are incontestably Pauline (e.g., 2 Cor. 11:6). Nor does it appear that a disciple trying to praise his former instructor would have penned the statement found in verse 8 below. The spe-

⁵ which was not made known to the sons of men in other generations as it has now been revealed to his holy apostles and prophets by the Spirit; ⁶ that is, how the Gentiles are fellow heirs, members of the same body, and partakers of the promise in Christ Jesus through the gospel.

---

cific insight (*sunesin,* "understanding"; see comment on Col. 1:9; 2:2; Mark 12:33) alluded to is the following elaboration of the Gentiles' place in God's plan of salvation unfolding in history.

[5] As is the case with other statements in the letter, this statement has also been interpreted as a later writer looking back on the work of the apostles (cf. 2:20), but this is unnecessary. Paul's word **holy** may be taken as substantive, thus rendering "saints, apostles and prophets"; but it is better taken as an adjective modifying both **apostles and prophets.** Other uses of **holy** by Paul are consistent with its application to the apostles. **Sons of men** is a Hebraism meaning simply "men" (see Mark 3:28). Although the term has been understood to apply to Gentiles alone, Paul probably has in mind both Gentiles and Jews prior to the Incarnation (see Col. 1:26; Rom. 16:25). Paul again indicates that what has been revealed has come **by the Spirit** of God, not by human attainment.

[6] Paul now defines the contents of the mystery of which he has been speaking. In particular, he has in mind the present unity between Jews and Gentiles, a state brought about through the agency of the proclaimed message about Christ (**through the gospel**), itself a vital part of God's astounding plan of redemption now becoming visible to all men through the church (see 3:10 below; cf. Rom. 1:16; 1 Cor. 1:18ff.; 1 Thess. 1:5; Col. 1:5, 6). Three words express this sharing and opening of previously closed avenues of fellowship. First, the Gentiles are now **fellow heirs** (*sugklēronoma;* see Heb. 11:9; cf. Rom. 8:17; Gal. 3:29), a term used to demonstrate the closeness between the heirs and the lack of superiority on the part of either Jews or Gentiles (see 2:19). Second, believers are presently (not "should be" as in KJV, ASV, but "are" already by virtue of God's act in Christ; see Col. 3:1-5) also fellow **members of the**

⁷ Of this gospel I was made a minister according to the gift of God's grace which was given me by the working of his power. ⁸ To me, though I am the very least of all the saints, this grace was given, to preach to the Gentiles the unsearchable riches of Christ,

---

same body, the church. Third, the Gentiles are also joint partakers of the promise in Christ (see 2:12; Heb. 11:9), the fulfilment of God's covenant with Abraham.

Paul's Mission to the Gentiles, 3:7-9. [7] Of this gospel refers to the good news of what God has done in Christ but more particularly in this context to the inclusion of the Gentiles into God's plan (vs. 6 above; cf. Col. 1:25). It is of this message of reconciliation that Paul has been **made a minister** (*diakonos*, "servant"; see comment on Col. 4:7; cf. 1 Cor. 3:10; 4:1; 2 Cor. 5:19), not according to his own efforts but by **the gift of God's grace** (see Gal. 1:1). Further, the apostle states his intense conviction that God's **power** is guiding his mission and empowering him to perform the task God has assigned him (see 1:19; 3:20; Col. 1:29; cf. 2 Cor. 3:4ff.; 12:9, 10).

[8] Paul now describes himself in contrast to the greatness of God's power: he is **the very least of all the saints** (cf. 1 Cor. 15:9; 2 Cor. 12:11; 1 Tim. 1:15). It should be noted that this expression poses difficulty for those denying the Pauline authorship of the letter in that it is doubtful whether a Pauline disciple would so describe his venerated teacher. Additionally, it has been suggested that the term **the very least** (NEB, "least of the least") carries a play on the apostle's own name, the Latin *paulus* meaning "little." Nonetheless, the apostle's purpose is not primarily to play down himself but to magnify the power of God working through him and his proclamation of the gospel (see 1:19; 2 Cor. 4:7). The apostle's specific ministry or assigned task just alluded to is that of proclaiming **to the Gentiles** the **riches** of God's plan (Gal. 1:16; 2:7) now revealed through the proclamation about the Messiah (the Christ). For Paul, nowhere have the riches of the gospel been more clearly demonstrated than in the inclusion of the long excluded Gentiles (see 2:11, 12) into God's redemptive plan (cf. Rom. 11). This event exhibits the **unsearchable riches** of

⁹ and to make all men see what is the plan of the mystery hidden for ages in ᵈ God who created all things; ¹⁰ that through the church the manifold wisdom of God might now be made known to the principalities and powers in the heavenly places.

ᵈ Or *by*

---

the Messiah. The term **unsearchable** (literally, "not to be tracked" or "indetectable"; cf. Rom. 11:33; Job. 5:9; 34:24) may further imply that the apostle's insight into the long-hidden mystery has been imparted by God and is not something he discovered or discerned on his own (cf. 1 Cor. 2). Paul had a high view of his unique place in the history of salvation (cf. 2 Cor. 2:17—6:10). The present section of the letter has a close parallel in 2 Timothy 1:8-12.

[9] Paul again specifies his own ministry as the proclamation of the gospel: **to make all men see** (*phōtisai;* literally "to give light" or "bring to light"; see 1:18; cf. 2 Cor. 4:6). The purpose of apostolic preaching is to reveal God's redemptive plan **to all men,** not some exclusive few (see comments on Col. 1:28). That which he preached is that which has been **hidden for ages** (cf. Col. 1:26, 27; Rom. 16:25; 1 Cor. 2:7) until its recent disclosure in Christ (2 Cor. 3:14). It is through the Christian proclamation of the death, burial, and resurrection of Christ that the plan of the mystery is revealed to all hearing the gospel (Col. 1:27, 28; 1 Cor. 4:1; Rom. 16:25f.). Paul's word **plan** (*oikonomia;* NEB, "put into effect"; Jerusalem Bible, "dispersed"; see 1:10; 3:2 and comments on Col. 1:25) indicates the manner in which God's redemptive purpose, designed before the creation (1:4), unfolds in history as it moves into various ages or stages of completion (cf. comments on 1:10), all of which is now revealed in Christ (cf. 1:9, 10) and the church (see vs. 10 below). Some have understood Paul's designation, **God who created all things,** to indicate the church as the new creation. Yet the point emphasizes the fact that the entire creation has been from the very first directed toward a specific goal, now revealed in Christ (cf. 1:4).

God's Purposes Through the Church, 3:10-13. [10] Paul now makes the astounding assertion of the greatness

¹¹ **This was according to the eternal purpose which he real-**

of the church's role in the divine plan of redemption. It is **through the church** that God's plan continues to develop and unfold; its very existence is a visible exhibit of God's unifying purpose at work in history. The continual growth of the church points forward to the yet unrealized future goal of God's plan, the ultimate unification of all things through Christ (see 1:10). The church's message, an announcement of God's plan and of the Incarnation which calls the church into existence, is continually published by the church (cf. Col. 1:26; 1 Peter 1:12).

Manifold indicates a variety (NEB, "wisdom of God in all its varied forms"), possibly in reference to the diversity of ways in which God has previously manifested himself but more probably signifying as a superlative the richness of God's grace (cf. 1 Peter 4:10). Undergirding the entire statement, however, is the cosmic scope of redemption as expressed in Colossians (see 1:10 and comments on Col. 1:15f.). Whereas in Colossians the emphasis is on Christ's superiority, here Paul proclaims the central role of the church as making God's plan known to the supernatural powers inhabiting the heavens. Though **principalities and powers** has been taken as designating earthly rulers, the terms are probably to be understood as technical terms for celestial beings feared and worshiped by many Hellenists, Jews, and even some Christians (see comments on Col. 1:16; 2:15). The astounding claim is made that through the church God has chosen to instruct and unify all things in heaven and on earth (see 1:10; cf. 1 Cor. 11:10; 1 Tim. 3:16).

[11] The apostle repeats the fact that the visible purpose of God which is exhibited in the church is no capricious development but the result of God's plan, laid prior to the creation of the universe (see 1:4, 11). In Christ is focused all of God's redemptive activity which has been at work throughout the unfolding of history; the full purpose is only now made visible, revealed, in the Incarnation and the subsequent creation of the church. It is this purpose to which all previous ages of history have pointed and which subsequent ages of history work to fulfil. Paul's expression **eternal purpose** is literally rendered "purpose of the ages,"

ized in Christ Jesus our Lord, [12] in whom we have boldness
and confidence of access through our faith in him. [13] So
I ask you not to * lose heart over what I am suffering for
you, which is your glory.
* Or *I ask that I may not*

---

suggesting the various epochs of redemptive history moving
toward this the final goal. Yet the expression more probably
indicates the purpose from all time or eternity. The center
or focus of this entire cosmic-embracing purpose is **Christ
Jesus** (John 14:6) and is revealed through the church (vs.
10 above).

[12] Attention now shifts to the direct implications of
the previous statements for the lives and experience of the
believers (the entire statement being reminiscent of Romans
8:38, 39). **In whom** does not indicate incorporation into the
body of Christ as in Colossians but is instrumental, designating Christ as the agent of the Christian's **access** (*prosagōgēn;* 2:18; cf. Rom. 5:2) to God. This relationship, in
contrast to that of many of the Hellenistic religions involving multiple mediators, is one of direct access before
God, the adequacy of which is emphasized by the believers'
stance of **boldness and confidence.** The word **boldness** (*par-
rēsian,* 2 Cor. 3:12; Heb. 4:16; RSV "confidence," cf. Acts
4:29) designates the freedom of a citizen in a Greek democ-
racy, with emphasis on his right to speak openly and partici-
pate in the governing procedures and his entire life style
(cf. Lev. 26:13). This experience the Christian has through
Christ involves not subordination to various mediators but
direct access to God (cf. 2:18, 6:19). **Faith in him** indicates the enduring relationship of trust in Christ through
which the believers' access to God is maintained.

[13] Attention now returns to the apostle's condition as
a prisoner. As in the Colossian letter, the concern is that
Paul's imprisonment not lead to discouragement among
Christians. Readers are urged **not to lose heart** (see 2 Cor.
4:1, 16), a phrase possibly carrying the connotation of flag-
ging in the fulfilment of their Christian obligations (see Gal.
6:9; 2 Thess. 3:13). The apostle's situation is not to be construed as in any fashion deterring the readers from the full
realization of the previously mentioned relationship of bold-

¹⁴ For this reason I bow my knees before the Father, ¹⁵ from whom every family in heaven and on earth is named, ¹⁶ that according to the riches of his glory he may grant you to be strengthened with might through his Spirit in the inner man,

---

ness and confidence which they have with God through Christ (vs. 12). Contrary to what might be thought, **suffering** is not an occasion for discouragement but actually performs a vital role in God's continually unfolding redemptive plan (see comment on Col. 1:24; cf. Phil. 1:29; 1 Peter 4:1f., 13).

Prayer for the Readers' Completion in Christ, 3:14-21

Prayer for Strength, 3:14-19. [14] The prayer which was interrupted in verse 2 now resumes. **For this reason** repeats the opening words of verse 1 but refers to the immediately preceding affirmation of the apostle's own suffering as a vital part in God's redemptive plan. This knowledge serves in part to strengthen and encourage the apostle in meeting the various vicissitudes of his ministry (cf. 2 Cor. 4:17, 18). Although **I bow my knees** may be rhetorical, it may also be indicative of the early Christian manner of praying which was derived from the practice of Jesus himself (cf. Luke 22:41; Acts 7:60; 20:36; 21:5). The contemporary Jewish practice was praying while standing (cf. Mark 11:25; Luke 18:11). As throughout the letter, God is addressed as **the Father** (see 1:2, 3, 17; 2:18; 4:6; 5:20; 6:23), reflecting Jesus' mode of address in prayer (cf. Matt. 6:9; 7:11; Luke 11:13) and the nature of the Christian's access to God through Christ (see vs. 12 above).

[15] Verse 15 forms a parenthesis further punctuating God's Fatherhood by pointing to his role as creator of all things, a role which anticipates the ultimate redemption of all that he has created (see 1:10; Col. 1:20; Phil. 2:10). **In heaven and on earth** repeats another of the letter's themes (see vs. 10 above; 1:10, 21; 4:9, 10). The phrase emphasizes the fact that there is no sphere of the universe (visible or invisible, in heaven, on earth, or "under the earth," 4:9) toward which God does not stand as Creator and Father.

[16] The apostle now makes three petitions for his read-

¹⁷ and that Christ may dwell in your hearts through faith; that you, being rooted and grounded in love,

---

ers. The first of the requests is that the readers **be strengthened** by God (cf. 6:10). Thinking of his own experiences of God's sustaining power (see 3:7 above; 2 Cor. 1:8-10; Phil. 4:13; 1 Tim. 1:12; 2 Tim. 4:17), Paul prays that his readers might become strong (cf. 1 Cor. 16:13) **with might** (*dunamei;* cf. 3:7, 20) which can only come from God. This redemptive power, displayed in the resurrection of Christ and encountered in the proclamation of the gospel (see comment on 1:19, 20; Rom. 1:16; 1 Thess. 1:5; 2:13), is the source of the strength and cohesion of the Christian community and is that power which undergirds all Christians in the tasks of discipleship. The agent of God's strengthening activity is here identified as **his Spirit** (see Luke 11:13; Rom. 15:13), the same agent through which the church is created and is held together (see 4:4; 1 Cor. 12:1ff.). The expression **inner man** (*esō anthrōpon*, Jerusalem Bible "hidden self") is not to be equated with the "new man" created in Christ (see 4:24; Col. 3:9, 10) but designates that aspect of all men which is the essential being in which God's transforming redemptive power works (cf. Rom. 7:22; 2 Cor. 4:16; 1 Peter 3:4).

[17] This verse may be considered as the prayer's second petition although it may be intended as an advance upon the first request, stating much the same thing in a different manner. The reference to the readers' **hearts** may here be taken as synonymous with the "inner man" of the preceding verse. **Through faith** in the Christian message (cf. Col. 3:16) the believer experiences the operation of God's redemptive power transforming his "inner man" into the "new man" after the likeness of Christ (see 4:15; Gal. 2:20; Col. 3:4; Phil. 1:21; 2:5). Faith is not the manner but the means of Christ's indwelling. It should be noted that Paul's manner of speaking of both Christ and the Holy Spirit does not yield to modern concerns in regard to the precise distinctions of functions among the members of the Trinity. (For the indwelling Christ, cf. Col. 1:27; John 14:23; 2 Cor. 6:16; Rev. 3:20; Matt. 18:20; 28:20.) **Rooted** (*errizōmenoi*, "fix firmly," "planted," see Col. 2:7) **and**

[18] may have power to comprehend with all the saints what is the breadth and length and height and depth, [19] and to know the love of Christ which surpasses knowledge, that you may be filled with all the fulness of God.

[20] Now to him who by the power at work within us is able to do far more abundantly than all that we ask or think, [21] to him be glory in the church and in Christ Jesus to all generations, for ever and ever. Amen.

---

grounded (*tethemeliōmenoi*, "established," "built," see Col. 1:23; 2:7; cf. Matt. 7:24-27; 1 Cor. 3:10, 11; 1 Peter 5:10) **in love** indicates the Christian's participation in the divine love which undergirds the entire plan of God (see 1:5) and of which the life of the individual Christian and the community of believers is an expression (see 4:2; 5:2; Col. 3:14).

[18, 19] The third request has been called the zenith of the prayer, indeed of the entire letter. It is expressed in the form of a paradox that the readers might have the ability **to comprehend** (*katalabesthai*, "grasp," "fathom" or "perceive fully"; cf. Acts 10:34) that which **surpasses knowledge,** namely the love of Christ (see Col. 2:2). Full comprehension of the greatness of God's love as expressed in his redemptive plan is only possible within the Christian community (**with all the saints**). The prayer emphasizes that Christian knowledge is integrally related to and rooted in **the love of Christ** (see 1 Cor. 8:1-3; cf. 1 Cor. 13).

The ultimate goal of the prayer and the result of the Christian's knowing the love of Christ is **that you may be filled with all the fulness of God.** Fulness (*plērōma;* see 1:10, 23; 4:13; comments on Col. 1:19; 2:9) is an expression used in the vocabulary of contemporary religious groups and is of some importance in later Gnosticism. Here the meaning is probably akin to "completion" or "finality" in religious experience. It is a reference to the maturity that in Christ is totally complete (4:13).

Doxology, 3:20, 21. [20, 21] As is the case with transitions elsewhere in Paul's letters, the first half of Ephesians is concluded with a prayer (1 Thess. 3:11ff.; 2 Thess. 2:16f.) and a doxology (cf. Rom. 11:33f.). The focus of the doxology is the recognition of God's power which exceeds human imagination and expectation (see 1:19; 3:16; cf. 2

¹ I therefore, a prisoner for the Lord, beg you to lead a life worthy of the calling to which you have been called,

---

Cor. 13:4). God's power is presently upholding and undergirding the church and the life of the individual Christian (at work within us; see 1:10; Col. 1:29; Phil. 2:13). The second half of the doxology reiterates a main theme of the entire letter: the all-encompassing scope of God's redemptive plan unfolding in history. The phrase **all generations for ever and ever** is probably a combination of two formulas (see Col. 1:26; cf. 1 Tim. 1:17; Gal. 1:5; Phil. 4:20), indicating that the scope of God's redemptive plan is limitless and all-embracing. **Glory to God in Christ** is common (for elaborate doxologies, see Rom. 16:25-27; 1 Tim. 1:17; Jude 24, 25, and for simpler ones, Gal. 1:5; Phil. 4:20; 1 Peter 4:11; Rev. 1:6). What is unique in this doxology is the addition **in the church.** The church, as the body of Christ, is the source of knowledge of God's purpose in Christ (see comments on 3:10 above).

CHURCH LIFE IN GOD'S REDEMPTIVE PLAN, 4:1—6:24

Unity and Diversity in the Church, 4:1-16

Appeal for Unity, 4:1-6. [1] **Therefore** marks a shift to the ethical implications of not only the immediately preceding remarks but the first half of the entire letter (cf. Rom. 12:1; 1 Thess. 4:1). In effect, it asserts that the following injunctions are based on the foregoing elaborations of God's plan of salvation. The writer is described as **a prisoner,** but in contrast to the previous reference to his imprisonment (3:1), the statement is made in order to ground his appeals in the relationship which he shares with the readers in the body of Christ (the RSV's **for the Lord** is misleading and should be rendered "in the Lord"; see Jerusalem Bible). The word **beg** (*parakalō*) has a variety of meanings (summon, invite, implore, urge), but compliance with the plea is mandatory, not optional, for the readers (see Rom. 12:1).

Paul's admonition is that his readers **lead a life worthy of their calling** (1 Thess. 2:12; Col. 1:10). Literally, he uses

² with all lowliness and meekness, with patience, forbearing
one another in love, ³ eager to maintain the unity of the
Spirit in the bond of peace.

---

the expression "walk" (*peripatēsai;* see Col. 4:5), a common
metaphor for conduct. His term **worthy** (*axiōs;* see Phil.
1:27; cf. 3 John 6) should not be construed as expressing a
legalistic concept (see 2:9). Rather, though unworthy when
called (see 2:5, 8; cf. 1 Cor. 6:11), believers are made
"worthy" by the power of God (see 2:1, 5, 8; 3:7, 20; 5:27;
cf. 2 Thess. 1:5; 1 Peter 5:10). The exhortation here is that
members of the body of Christ live in harmony with God's
redemptive purpose. Thus being worthy is closely linked
with harmony in the church (cf. Phil. 1:27; 1 Cor. 11:27).
The Christian call finds its background in the Old Testament concept of God's call closely linked with both deliverance of his people (e.g., Hos. 11:1; Isa. 43:1) and their
consequent submission to a divinely assigned task (e.g., Isa.
45:3, 4; Jer. 1:15). The Christian's call, then, is deliverance
and also submission to a special task or role in God's redemptive plan (Col. 3:15; 1 Cor. 1:9; 7:15; 1 Tim. 6:12).

[2] The characteristics of the Christian life are now
presented through the use of terms of Christian virtue:
lowliness, meekness, patience, and forbearance (found in
the same order in Col. 3:12). It should be noted that all these
characteristics are necessary for the maintenance of the new
community and for its exhibition of unity to the surrounding world. The church's unity (peace of God) foreshadows
the future encompassing of the entire cosmos in God's purpose. **In love** may be taken not only as descriptive of the
manner of Christian forbearance (cf. 1 Cor. 12:26) but also
as a manner of life which is the essential ingredient for the
cohesion of the entire Christian community and the individual Christian life (see 3:17, 19 above; Col. 3:14; Phile. 9;
Phil. 2:1-3).

[3] The unity of the Christian community, which exhibits God's purposes for all the cosmos, is to be the constant
concern of the readers. They are to "spare no effort" (NEB;
cf. 1 Thess. 2:17; Gal. 2:10; Tit. 3:12) **to maintain** (cf. Matt.
27:36, 54; 1 Thess. 5:23) the presently existing unity of the

⁴ There is one body and one Spirit, just as you were called
to the one hope that belongs to your call, ⁵ one Lord, one
faith, one baptism,

---

community. The unity of which Paul speaks is God-given,
not man-made. **The unity of the Spirit** may be understood as
either the unity which is derived from the Holy Spirit (RSV,
NEB) or the attitude or disposition of harmony and sameness of purpose which characterizes the church (cf. Phil.
1:27; 2:2). The phrase **in the bond of peace** may be taken
as the agent of maintaining the unity ("by maintaining
peace," Jerusalem Bible and NEB) or may be further descriptive of the unity of the Spirit, simply identifying it with
the bond of peace.

[4] Paul now shifts abruptly back to the motive for the
exhortation, a reminder of knowledge already given the
readers. Here the apostle introduces a sevenfold confession
which is reminiscent of 1 Corinthians 12:12, 13 and is possibly a conscious parallel to the *shema* which was recited
daily by Jews (cf. Deut. 6:4; Zech. 14:9). With an eye to
the tendency toward division between Jew and Gentile
Christians, Paul asserts that Christians are **one body** (see
1:23; 2:16; 3:6; vs. 25 below; cf. Rom. 12:5; 1 Cor. 12; Col.
3:15), not divided into several groups (or more precisely,
between Jew and Gentile). Likewise, there is **one Spirit**
(see 2:18) or life-giving force sustaining both Jew and Gentile in the one body (cf. 1 Cor. 12:13; Acts 11:15ff.). It is to
this common unity of body, Spirit, and purpose that the
readers have been **called** (cf. 1:18 and 4:1). **Hope** is the
consequence of the believers' common **call** and not the
source of the unity.

[5] The **one Lord** is Jesus, exalted at the resurrection
(cf. 1:20, 21) and now Lord of all the universe. This affirmation of Jesus' Lordship, probably the earliest baptismal
confession (1 Cor. 8:6; 12:3; Rom. 10:9; Col. 3:17), log-
ically leads to the terms **faith** and **baptism. One faith** is
probably to be taken as objective, indicating the specific
content of Christian teaching (4:13; Col. 2:7; Rom. 10:8).
The **one baptism** indicates that there is neither two rites
(i.e., water and spirit) nor a series of initiatory rites (as

⁶ one God and Father of us all, who is above all and through all and in all. ⁷ But grace was given to each of us according to the measure of Christ's gift. ⁸ Therefore it is said,

"When he ascended on high he led a host of captives,
and he gave gifts to men."

---

asserted by some groups) through which initiates are advanced toward increased spiritual maturity. Baptism is the sole rite in which one is incorporated into the one body which is sustained by the one Lord (1 Cor. 12:13).

[6] This statement culminates in pointing to the ultimate source of unity, God—the Father, creator and sustainer of the entire universe (cf. Rom. 9:5; 1 Cor. 8:6). He is also the source of the life of the new creation, the church, where the all-inclusive sweep of redemptive history, as yet incomplete, is now manifested. The RSV's us should be omitted (so KJV, ASV, NEB, Jerusalem Bible), the point here being that the universal fatherhood of God encompasses the entire created universe.

Diverse Gifts, 4:7-16. [7] Attention now turns to the individual Christian, **each of us,** not only called into the body but called to perform a special function within the body (see 3:7; 4:11). Each believer has received strength (cf. 1:19; 3:7, 16f.; Col. 1:29) to perform his proper function in the body. Here, in contrast to other references where the Holy Spirit is the source of the gifts of the community (e.g., 1 Cor. 12:4ff.; Rom. 12:4-6), these gifts are viewed as from Christ (who gives the Holy Spirit; John 15:26). If the church is viewed as an organism, it follows that all functions are vital. The very diversity of modes of service assures the health and completeness of the body (see 1 Cor. 12:14f.). Christian "maturity" (vs. 13 below) is thus not "sameness" or "uniformity" but the performing of one's function within the context of the life of the organism, the church which is the body of Christ (vs. 16 below; cf. 1 Cor. 12:19).

[8] The preceding reference to gifts inspires a quotation from Psalm 68:18 as a reference to Jesus' exaltation and the defeat of his enemies (cf. Col. 2:15; John 17:4f.; Acts 1:9). There are indications that the synagogue calendar used this psalm at the time of Pentecost (cf. Acts 1:4, 5; 2:33). The

⁹ (In saying, "He ascended," what does it mean but that he had also descended into the lower parts of the earth? ¹⁰ He who descended is he who also ascended far above all the heavens, that he might fill all things.)

---

reading of the text differs from both Greek and Hebrew Old Testaments, reading gave instead of "received." This difference has occasioned several speculations, but the most probable interpretation is that Paul here follows his rabbinical background (cf. Gal. 1:14; Phil. 3:4ff.; Acts 22:3) and quotes from a rabbinical commentary on Psalm 68:18 which referred the verse to Moses' receipt of the law on behalf of the Israelites (cf. Ex. 19). The Psalm is cited not as a proof text of any argument but rather as an illustration. The host of captives should be distinguished from the men receiving gifts (Christians). The expression may be understood as designating the enemies defeated at the cross and eventually to be totally subjugated (cf. 1 Cor. 15:25).

[9, 10] These difficult verses are to be understood in light of the complicated background of Jewish speculations, current religious mythology, rabbinical methods of argumentation, and speculative questions about such things as Jesus' three days in the tomb and the state of the dead residing in Sheol. The apostle's overall purpose is to apply the preceding quotation from the Psalms to Jesus and affirm the fact that God's plan of reconciliation in Christ is all-inclusive; there are no areas outside the scope of what is accomplished in him. Thus it is necessary for Paul to demonstrate the inadequacies of Jewish speculations applying Psalm 68:18 to Moses' ascent of Sinai to receive the Torah (vs. 8 above). Paul's argument is that the Psalm must refer to one who first descended, i.e., it is necessary for one to descend before ascending (cf. John 3:13). Moses is excluded and the prior descent posited is better identified with Jesus' Incarnation (cf. John 1:14). Thus it is by his descending and ascending that Jesus fills all things. The phrase fill all things may indicate that Jesus' presence actually permeates the entire universe, an implication of Paul's identification of Jesus with God's divine Wisdom (see 1:20, 23; see comments of Col. 1:15ff.; 2:9).

¹¹ And his gifts were that some should be apostles, some prophets, some evangelists, some pastors and teachers,

Lower parts of the earth is also somewhat ambiguous. Paul may be opposing a tendency like that countered in the Colossian letter, in which case the statement would refer to the earth itself (NEB "the very earth"; cf. Isa. 44:23) and specifically to the Incarnation (cf. John 3:13). In an environment where many conceived of the earth as a realm of darkness alienated from God and under the domination of various spiritual forces (cf. 2:2; 6:12; cf. Col. 1:16; 2:8, 15; John 1:5), the Incarnation may have been envisioned as the breaking of the wall between God and the alienated earth. On the other hand, the reference may be taken to designate the underworld, the abode of the dead and the realm of evil spirits (see Ps. 16:10; 1 Peter 3:19f.), which played a significant part in contemporary Jewish (see *Enoch* 6:1f.; 10:12) and pagan religious thought (e.g., Pluto, god of the underworld and the dead in classical Greek mythology). Such a meaning may also be understood as a logical advance on the assertions of Christ's universal lordship in the Colossian letter. Here, Paul would be stating that Christ's redemption and reign penetrate even the realm of death (cf. Ps. 71:20; Matt. 27:52; Rom. 10:7; 1 Cor. 15:54f.; 2 Tim. 1:10; Heb. 2:14; Rev. 1:18) and the powers of the underworld. The repeated emphasis on **the heavens** throughout the letter (1:10, 20; 2:6; 3:10; 4:10; 6:12; cf. Heb. 4:14; 7:26) again indicates that all realms of the universe are subordinated to Christ's lordship and God's redemption at work in and through him.

[11] Having justified the application of Psalm 68:18 to Christ, Paul identifies the gifts Christ gives to the church as specific ministries performed in the body. Christ's gifts are now defined as specific functions within the church, and their goal of **building up the body of Christ** is stressed (see 1 Cor. 12:7, 28-31). This goal includes not only numerical increase but the nurturing of the body which enables it to fully embody God's redemptive purposes. The first two gifts of **apostles** and **prophets** (see comment on 2:20 and 3:5) belong to the first generation of Christians and form the foundation on which the church is built. **Evangelists** are

¹² for the equipment of the saints, for the work of ministry, for building up the body of Christ, ¹³ until we all attain to the unity of the faith and of the knowledge of the Son of God, to mature manhood, to the measure of the stature of the fulness of Christ;

---

those preaching the gospel, a function of Christians in every generation (Acts 21:8; 2 Tim. 4:5). Finally, **pastors and teachers** share the same definite article in the Greek and are probably not two separate functions but two aspects of the same work, i.e., "teaching pastors" or "pastoring teachers." **Pastors** (*poimenas*, literally "shepherds"; cf. Acts 20:17, 28) describes the leaders of local congregations, probably modeled after the governing bodies of Jewish communities. The term most likely refers to the same function as "elder" (Acts 14:23; 1 Tim. 5:17) or "bishop" (Phil. 1:1). **Teachers** (cf. Acts 13:1) thus probably designates leaders involved in teaching the Christian message and giving ethical instructions (cf. 1 Tim. 3:2).

[12] While not intended as an all-inclusive list of the gifts of Christ, those functions mentioned in the previous verse are all specifically for the edification of the saints (cf. 1:15, 18; 2:19; 3:8, 18; Col. 1:26). The three clauses of the verse may be taken either as coordinate or with the last two defining the first and more general statement. **Equipment** (*katartismon*, found only here in the New Testament) refers to the placing of someone or something in proper working order. This word often carries a connotation of restoration (cf. Mark 1:19; 2 Cor. 13:9; Gal. 6:1) and indicates that all gifts are directed toward the proper function of the saints. **Ministry** (*diakonia*) here designates all activity for the strengthening of the church (cf. 1 Cor. 16:15), though it is elsewhere used to designate specific Christian tasks (Col. 4:17; Eph. 6:21) or even an "office" (cf. 1 Tim. 3:8ff.). **Building** (*oikodomēn*, "constructing"; see the verb in vss. 16, 29 below; cf. 1 Cor. 8:10; 1 Thess. 5:11) **up the body** mixes metaphors but is clear; the purpose of all the gifts mentioned is the nourishment of the totality of the church (cf. 1 Peter 2:5).

[13] The concern of this statement is that the church, the corporate **all** (literally "the all," *hoi pantes;* cf. 1 Cor.

¹⁴ so that we may no longer be children, tossed to and fro and carried about with every wind of doctrine, by the cunning of men, by their craftiness in deceitful wiles.

10:17) might achieve its appropriate degree of unity (previously referred to as something to be "kept," here "attained"). Though Paul's **mature manhood** uses the singular, referring to the whole church, the statement suggests that individual Christian maturity is not achieved separately from the corporate body (cf. vs. 16 below; also Col. 1:28). **Son of God,** an unusual expression for Paul, is the object of both **faith** and **knowledge.** The term is probably used to emphasize the importance of the one whom the believer trusts and in whose body the believer has access to a comprehension or knowledge which "exceeds knowledge" (cf. 3:18, 19). **Unity** is that harmony which characterizes those sharing the common trust and belief in Christ and knowledge of God's redemptive purposes. It should be noted that **unity** is here spoken of as being not yet actual, whereas in verse 3 it is evidently regarded as a present God-given reality. The contradiction, however, is only apparent; the church receives its character from God but must progressively realize and actualize the true nature of its role and function in God's plan. **To the measure of the stature of the fulness of Christ** further punctuates the emphasis on the unity of the body, indicating the complete embodiment of Christ in the church (note 3:19 speaks of "the fulness of God"). The image here is of the church as a corporate personality whose various parts when working properly contribute to its completeness (cf. 1 Cor. 12:12).

[14] For the individual, properly equipped and functioning in the body, one of the significant results of growth and maturity is the ability to discriminate between truth and error. **Children** (cf. 1 Cor. 3:1; 13:11; 14:20; Heb. 5:13) probably designates an immature state in which one is vulnerable to the appeal of the strange, different, and new. The metaphor of a rudderless ship in a storm is used to portray this vulnerability to **every wind of doctrine.** The misleading forces of false teaching implied here are probably similar to those refuted in the letter to the Colossians (Col. 2:8), though Paul's day knew of many philosophies

163

[15] Rather, speaking the truth in love, we are to grow up in every way into him who is the head, into Christ, [16] from whom the whole body, joined and knit together by every joint with which it is supplied, when each part is working properly, makes bodily growth and upbuilds itself in love.

---

and teachings through which unscrupulous teachers preyed on the ignorant (cf. 2 Cor. 2:17). As elsewhere, the warning is against those practicing intentional deceit (cf. 6:11; Gal. 1:6, 7; Rom. 16:17; 2 Cor. 4:2).

[15] Christian growth and maturity is to be found in Christ and not in the chasing of strange and different notions. **Speaking the truth** somewhat limits the term used (*alētheuontes,* cf. vss. 21, 24; 5:9), which is probably better rendered more comprehensively as "truthing" or "dealing truthfully" (cf. Jerusalem Bible, "live by the truth"). **In love** may be taken to amplify the breadth of living truthfully, implicitly refuting any unloving adherence to "truth" as abstract intellectualism divorced from the appropriate character of life. Note the recurrence of **in love** in this epistle (1:5; 3:17; 4:2; 5:2). Virtually all aspects of growth are to be found in Christ (**in every way**). **Into him who is the head, into Christ** emphasizes the centrality of Christ and the church as the source of maturity, growth, strength and power (cf. Col. 2:19; 1 Cor. 11:3). "The fulness of Christ" may be the implication here, the proper embodiment of Christ (vs. 13 above). Or the metaphor may refer to the proper conformity of the body with the impulses and directions of the head.

[16] Though Paul here uses language quite similar to that of Colossians 2:19, the point is somewhat different. Whereas in Colossians he emphasized the necessary link with the head, the emphasis here is on the interdependence of the diverse members. This interrelationship is as vital for each separate part as it is for the whole organism. **Joined** and **knit** are both present participles, indicating the process now going on. **Every joint** might well be translated "every contact," conveying the idea of each individual Christian forming a vital link between the parts through which the whole organism is nourished (**supplied**). **Each part work-**

¹⁷ Now this I affirm and testify in the Lord, that you
must no longer live as the Gentiles do, in the futility of

---

ing properly ("according to its separate function," cf. Jerusalem Bible) again emphasizes the vital aspect of unity
which is derived from Christians in their diversity operating
harmoniously within the body. It is in this manner that the
body upbuilds itself, the whole process characterized by
the manner and climate of love.

Ethical Injunctions, 4:17—5:20

Contrast of the Old Life With the New, 4:17-24. The
readers, largely former Gentiles (see 2:11; 3:1), are now
reminded of the contrast between their new manner of life
in Christ and their former manner of life (the statements
here are quite similar to those of Rom. 1:21-32 and Col. 3:1-
17). The plight of the Gentiles is a result of their willful
separation from God, the source of life (see vs. 18). The
terminology of this section is drawn from Jewish and Christian preaching to Gentiles. "Futility" (*mataiotēs*) is associated with idolatry (Acts 14:15, "vain things"). "The life of
God" recalls the common designation in preaching to Gentiles of "the living God" (Acts 14:15; 1 Thess. 1:9f.). "Darkened in their understanding" occurs in similar words in the
description of the Gentiles' condition in Romans 1:21. "Ignorance" (*agnoia*) is one of the themes of Paul's sermon in
Athens (Acts 17:23, 30). Because of the Gentiles' "hardness of heart," they are handed over to immorality (cf.
Rom. 1:24). "Licentiousness" (*aselgeia*) and "greediness"
(*pleonexia*) fit into this picture as associated with idolatry
(5:5; Col. 3:5; 1 Cor. 5:10; 6:9f.; Gal. 5:19; 1 Peter 4:3).

What follows this description of the Gentile life drawn
from the language of missionary preaching is an ethical
exhortation utilizing baptismal language (vss. 22ff.). It is
interesting that a similar pattern is followed here as in 1
Timothy: (1) the doctrine of the church, particularly the
structure of the church (1 Tim. 3:1-13; Eph. 4:7-16); (2)
the church's proclamation or confession (1 Tim. 3:14-16;
Eph. 4:17-21); (3) exhortation to live according to the
church's life (1 Tim. 4:1ff.; Eph. 4:22ff.).

[17] I affirm and testify in the Lord gives the statement

their minds; [18] they are darkened in their understanding,
alienated from the life of God because of the ignorance
that is in them, due to their hardness of heart;

---

emphasis and may be an appeal either to apostolic authority
(cf. 1 Thess. 2:4) or to the writer's common participation
in the Lord (cf. Phile. 16, 17). Futility (*mataiotēti*) indicates "illusion" or "deception" (cf. 1 Cor. 15:17; Ezek. 13:6)
and is elsewhere used by Paul to describe the condition of
the whole creation (Rom. 8:20). The **mind** (*nous*) is significant as the seat of man's reasoning powers, but here the
connotation is probably more broadly the "disposition" (see
vs. 23 below; cf. Col. 2:18). The "futile mind" (1 Peter 1:18;
Rom. 1:21) indicates the mind distorted, possibly "purposeless" or even "worthless" (NEB, "good for nothing notions"). The construction of verses 17 and 18 should probably be seen as stating **ignorance** to be the cause of living
in futility and as paralleling being **darkened** and being
alienated.

[18] The Gentiles are further described as **darkened in
their understanding.** In contrast to the "mind" of the previous verse, **understanding** (*dianoia*; see 2:3; comments on
Col. 1:21; 2 Peter 3:1) refers specifically to the intellectual
powers (Jerusalem Bible, "intellectually they are in the
dark"). This statement is a conscious contrast to that of
1:18. The expression **alienated** ("estranged" or "excluded")
from the life of God (see Col. 1:21) points to the underlying explanation for the state of the Gentiles.

It is hardly surprising that those in such a condition are
called ignorant. However, whereas at times the concept of
ignorance is seen as excusable (e.g., Acts 17:30), it is here
thought of as the ignorance of the perverted mind (cf. 2:12;
1 Peter 1:14). Cut off from God, the source of life, the Gentiles are ignorant of the very purposes and goals of life;
they are ignorant of God's redemptive purpose in Christ.
The whole state of affairs is attributed to **their hardness of
heart** (Jerusalem Bible, "having shut their hearts"), an Old
Testament figure indicating a conscious insensitivity to God
(see Rom. 11:25; cf. 2 Chron. 36:13). **Heart** in this sense
refers to the total man—his intellect, his emotions, and the
will which guides his ultimate direction.

[19] they have become callous and have given themselves up
to licentiousness, greedy to practice every kind of uncleanness. [20] You did not so learn Christ!— [21] assuming that you
have heard about him and were taught in him, as the
truth is in Jesus.

---

[19] It follows that the moral lives of the Gentiles reflect their perverted wills (cf. Col. 1:21; 1 Peter 4:3). They
have become callous (*apēlgēkotes*) employs a medical expression indicating a deadness to pain in describing the
Gentiles' loss of moral sensitivity. The degenerate state of
those described is envisioned as one for which they are
themselves responsible (have given themselves up; cf. Rom.
1:24, 26, 28). Greedy (*pleonexia*; 5:3 below; see Col. 3:5)
describes the general stance of those alienated and is usually
rendered "covetous." Though capable of a specific connotation of adultery (cf. Col. 3:5; 1 Thess. 4:6), here the word
probably indicates a more general selfishness, manifesting
itself in licentiousness and uncleanness. Licentiousness
(*aselgeia*) carries the general sense of "debauchery" with
connotations of sexual excess (cf. Mark 7:22; 2 Peter 2:2, 7,
18; Gal. 5:19; Rom. 13:13; 2 Cor. 12:21). Uncleanness (5:3
below; see Col. 3:5), the opposite of righteousness, is the
state which characterizes the Gentile world subject to the
natural passions, cut off from God.

[20] You did not so learn Christ refers to the acceptance
of the gospel, the content of which may be called Christ
(see Col. 1:28; 2:6; Gal. 1:16; 1 Cor. 1:23; 2 Cor. 1:19; Phil.
1:15). The manner of life just described as characterizing
the Gentiles is incompatible with receiving Christ, an event
involving a relationship with Christ and an empowerment
to live a new life style, not just an intellectual assent to
propositions about Christ. Here again, Paul binds faith in
Christ with the shape of the moral life (see comments on
Col. 3:1ff.).

[21] Assuming that you have heard about him is for
emphasis, not expressing doubt (see Col. 3:1). Again the
reference is to the preaching which the readers previously
received. Taught in him (not "by him," KJV) indicates the
sphere of fellowship with Christ in which Christians continue to be instructed. The reference to Jesus, unusual in

²² Put off your old nature which belongs to your former manner of life and is corrupt through deceitful lusts, ²³ and be renewed in the spirit of your minds, ²⁴ and put on the new nature, created after the likeness of God in true righteousness and holiness.

Paul's letters, probably indicates the historical person whose words are given in instruction to new converts (cf. Col. 1:22; 1 Cor. 7:10; 9:14).

[22] **Put off** is elsewhere used to connect the Christian's ethical life with the symbolism of baptism (1 Peter 2:1; James 1:21; cf. the imagery of removing clothing before baptism, Col. 3:9 and vs. 24 below). Here the stress is on the Christian's continual renouncing of his old **manner of life** (cf. Heb. 12:1 and vs. 25 below). Nothing less than the death of the **old nature** (literally, "the old man") is required, not merely a denouncement of external characteristics of alienation. The word **corrupt** (*phtheiromenon*; see Gal. 6:8; 2 Peter 1:4) is used in the present participle to indicate a process of corruption or decaying (NEB, "sinking toward death"; cf. Rom. 6:21, 23; 8:13). Again, the apostle is punctuating the fact that the life style of the individual believer must correspond to his beliefs.

[23, 24] **Be renewed** is best taken as passive, indicating that the renewal here urged is not "self-renewal" but that which is worked in the believer by God's renewing power. Nothing short of a total transformation of the core of man's existence is called for: he must have a new mind (see Rom. 12:2; 8:7). Though **spirit** (*pneumati*) possibly bears some meaning different from **mind** (cf. 1 Cor. 14:14), here it probably indicates the inner life of the human personality or one's total disposition. Yet there is a part required of man: **put on** the new garment (cf. 6:11, 14). The expression is best understood as a technical term used in Christian ethical instruction, probably originally based on the symbolism of unclothing and reclothing at baptism, an occasion where ethical instruction was imparted (see Gal. 3:27 and comments on Col. 3:5, 8, 10, 12). **The new nature** (literally "the new man") is Christ, the true image of God (see Rom. 13:14; Gal. 3:27; Col. 1:15; 3:10). **True righteousness and holiness** (Luke 1:75) should not be too closely pressed for

²⁵ Therefore, putting away falsehood, let every one speak the truth with his neighbor, for we are members one of another. ²⁶ Be angry but do not sin; do not let the sun go down on your anger, ²⁷ and give no opportunity to the devil.

---

separate meanings. Though the terms are specially significant for Paul (e.g., Titus 3:5; Phil. 3:9) and have rich Old Testament connotations, their use here is possibly influenced by the general Greek linking of the two terms to express a summary of true human virtue ("right before God and man," cf. 1 Thess. 2:10).

Specific Commands, 4:25—5:14. [25] Specific instructions are now elaborated regarding the Christian life in light of the previous emphasis on the community of Christians as a single organism. It is on this basis that the whole argument rests. Readers are urged to "put off" (see comments on vss. 22, 24 above) **falsehood,** a general characteristic of the Gentile life (cf. Rom. 1:25, Col. 3:8f.; Rev. 22:15), which is a life built on illusion (cf. vs. 18 above). **Let every one speak the truth with his neighbor** echoes Zechariah 8:16, but the main line of appeal is the fact of the incorporation of the believer into the corporate body of Christ, a "social organism." As members of the same body, Christians share the closest of relationships with one another—**we are members one of another** (Rom. 12:5; 1 Cor. 12:12). **Falsehood,** deceit and the like are incompatible with the true character of this mutual interrelationship with Christ and one's neighbor (see Col. 3:9, 15).

[26, 27] **Be angry but do not sin** quotes the opening words of Psalm 4:4. Essentially this is a warning that one who is angry should be especially careful not to sin. Though anger itself is not necessarily sin, it may provide the occasion for temptation and sin (see vs. 31 below; cf. James 1:19; Matt. 5:22; Rom. 12:19). The point is reinforced by the use of a familiar quotation of a popular Greek axiom: **do not let the sun go down on your anger.** That is, the day of anger should be the same as the day of reconciliation, as brooding over anger only gives occasion for evil or "gives the devil a foothold" (Jerusalem Bible). The word **devil**

²⁸ Let the thief no longer steal, but rather let him labor, doing honest work with his hands, so that he may be able to give to those in need. ²⁹ Let no evil talk come out of your mouths, but only such as is good for edifying, as fits the occasion, that it may impart grace to those who hear. ³⁰ And do not grieve the Holy Spirit of God, in whom you were sealed for the day of redemption.

---

is used only here and in the Pastorals in Paul (cf. Acts 13:10).

[28] The thief (*ho kleptōn;* cf. John 12:6) may refer to those in the Christian community who are or have been thieves by profession. The designation is intended rather broadly, including the casual misdemeanors of slaves or simply the misdeeds of all those living at the expense of others. The motive of the exhortation is, as before, the priority of the Christian community: so that he may be able to give to those in need (cf. Rom. 12:13; Tit. 3:14).

[29] Evil talk means "rotten," "diseased," or "worthless" talk (cf. 5:4 below; Matt. 15:11; James 3:10). Such speech is rebuked on a level with lying and stealing, the context showing that Paul's primary concern is that kind of speech which works harm in the life of the community of faith which is to be harmonious and mutually edifying. That is, again the motive for the ethical exhortation is the primacy of the unity and harmony of the church corporate. Paul's word edifying (*oikodomēn,* "building up"; cf. Rom. 15:2; 1 Cor. 14:12) must be understood in light of its previous use in verses 12 and 16 above, where it designates the nurturing and upbuilding of the whole body. Here the apostle asserts that Christian speech should be toward the goal of nurturing the body of Christ (cf. 2 Cor. 12:19; Rom. 1:11, 12; Col. 3:16f.). Thus the believer's speech should be as is fitting or demanded by the need or occasion (*chreias;* cf. Phil. 2:25, "need," RSV), imparting benefit or grace (*charis*) to those who hear (cf. Col. 4:4-6).

[30] The admonition not to grieve the Holy Spirit is taken from Isaiah 63:10. Again, the context indicates that the previously listed actions of stealing, lying, and using unedifying language are grievous to the Holy Spirit, not

³¹ Let all bitterness and wrath and anger and clamor **and** slander be put away from you, with all malice, ³² and be kind to one another, tenderhearted, forgiving one another, as God in Christ forgave you.

---

simply as isolated individual sins but precisely because **of** the threat that they pose for the harmony of the church. Peace is the work of the **Spirit of God** which constitutes **the** church as a single, unified body empowered with divine strength (1:19; 2:22; 4:3). **Were sealed** (see 1:13) points to the time of the readers' baptism when they received **the** Spirit and were joined to the community of believers (cf. 1 Cor. 12:13; 2 Cor. 1:21, 22). It is the present experience of God's Spirit that is the basis of the Christian's future hope in the day of redemption (see 5:27; cf. 1 Thess. 4:17).

[31] Now a more comprehensive listing of things jeopardizing the unity of the church is presented (reminiscent of Col. 3:8). These vices are set forth for the specific purpose of setting the following Christian virtues in stronger contrast. **Bitterness** (*pikria;* NEB, "spite") probably is more inclusive than just harsh speech (cf. Rom. 3:14; James 3:14). **Wrath** and **anger** (see Col. 3:8) may possibly be distinguished by duration, **wrath** being a spontaneous outburst of passion and **anger** being a more sustained state **or** disposition. **Clamor** (*kraugē*) may mean any emotional outcry (cf. Luke 1:42), but here more likely indicates a disruptive "angry shouting" (NEB; cf. Acts 23:9). **Slander** is literally "blasphemy" (*blasphēmia*), but means slanderous speech against anyone (see comments on Col. 3:8). **All malice** (*pasē kakia*) is intended as comprehensive ("bad feeling of every kind," NEB), thus including all forms of thought, word, and action which fracture or disrupt the vital harmony of the body.

[32] Readers are exhorted to reflect the character of God's act in Christ in their attitudes toward their fellows (**as God in Christ forgave you;** see comments on 5:2 and cf. Col. 3:12f.). The church reflects God's redemptive purposes and is itself an instrument of his reconciliation of all things. **Kind** (*chrēstoi,* NEB "generous") may be understood as "loving" or "benevolent" (see comment on Col.

171

¹ Therefore be imitators of God, as beloved children.
² And walk in love, as Christ loved us and gave himself up
for us, a fragrant offering and sacrifice to God.

³ But immorality and all impurity or covetousness must
not even be named among you, as is fitting among saints.

3:12). **Tenderhearted** (*eusplagchnoi*) means "compassion-
ate" but possibly also "courageous" (cf. 1 Peter 3:8).

[1] Christian behavior is not based on or modeled after
human initiative. Christians are to be the imitators of God
(cf. 1 Cor. 4:16; 11:1; 1 Thess. 1:6; 2:14; 2 Thess. 3:7, 9;
Gal. 4:12), who is known as Father (cf. 1:17, 2:18). The
statement recalls the Lord's words: "You, therefore, must be
perfect as your heavenly Father is perfect" (Matt. 5:48).
The imitation of God the Father is natural for Christians
as **beloved children** (cf. 1:5). The context indicates that the
specific focus of the statement is the divine forgiveness that
the believer has experienced and is in turn called on to
manifest in his life style (cf. 1:15; Rom. 14:3; Col. 3:13;
1 John 4:7).

[2] The previous verses are summed up with the exhortation that the readers allow **love** to be the ruling factor in
their lives (see 4:15; Col. 3:14; cf. John 13:34). The motivation for love is God's love, which has been fully manifested in the selfless life and death of the Christ who **gave
himself up for us** (1:5; 2:4; 3:17-19; 5:25; Rom. 5:8; 8:32;
Gal. 1:4; 2:20; 1 John 4:10). The life of Jesus is clearly il-
lustrative of the limitless and sacrificial nature of the divine
love. For this as the basis of exhortation, compare 2 Corinthians 8:9. The reference to Christ's death as an **offering**
and a **sacrifice** is somewhat unusual for Paul and probably
should not be pressed regarding his "theory of atonement"
(Phil. 4:18; cf. Heb. 10:10). The two terms are used interchangeably as in Psalm 40:6, here indicating the totally
selfless nature of Christ's life and, by implication, the style
of life enjoined on the readers (cf. 2 Cor. 5:15).

[3] Whereas the preceding section was concerned primarily with the sins violating the harmony of the community, the attention is now shifted to those sins which are
totally incommensurate with the character of the individual

⁴ Let there be no filthiness, nor silly talk, nor levity, which are not fitting; but instead let there be thanksgiving. ⁵ Be sure of this, that no immoral or impure man, or one who is covetous (that is, an idolater), has any inheritance in the kingdom of Christ and of God.

Christian's place among God's elect (saints). Immorality, impurity and covetousness (see 4:19) are unworthy of the Christian calling and belong to the non-Christian life (see comment on Col. 3:5). As God's elect are his instruments in reconciling the world, these characteristics and qualities are incompatible with the very nature of what it means to be saints (see comments on Col. 1:2). Paul's directive that such vices are not even to be named among his readers indicates not only are such things not to be done but that they should not even be discussed (NEB, "mentioned") as if there could possibly be some question about them. They are always incompatible with God's will for his elect.

[4] It has been stated (vs. 2 above) that the believer's life style should reflect the character of God's call and purposes in Christ. Now more specific focus is made on the believer's speech (cf. James 1:19-21; 3:5ff.). Filthiness (*aischrotēs,* NEB, "coarseness"; cf. Col. 3:8) and silly talk (*mōrologia*) both occur only here in the New Testament. Silly talk might be rendered "pointless" or "stupid talk" (NEB). Levity (*eutrapelia*) may be used in a good sense as "wittiness" but here probably refers to "base" or even "sacrilegious speech" (NEB, "flippant"). Probably there is intended a play on words between *eutrapelia* (levity) and *eucharistia* (thanksgiving) to heighten the contrast between the mentioned vices which are not fitting and the recommended speech which is appropriate for the Christian (compare the contrast in vs. 18 below). Thanksgiving is the general response which should permeate the entirety of the believer's manner of life (cf. Col. 2:7; 3:16, 17; 4:2).

[5] Be sure of this is a Hebraism (cf. 1 Sam. 20:3) and may be taken as either indicative or imperative. It is unclear whether the one now described is intended as an immoral Christian or a pagan (cf. 1 Cor. 6:9). The expression the kingdom of Christ and of God is unique in the New Testament (cf. 1 Cor. 15:24; Col. 1:13; Rev. 11:15). The article

⁶ Let no one deceive you with empty words, for it is because of these things that the wrath of God comes upon the sons of disobedience. ⁷ Therefore do not associate with them, ⁸ for once you were darkness, but now you are light in the Lord; walk as children of light

---

is missing before **God,** making it possible to interpret here an unusual reference to **Christ** as God. Yet it is not unusual for the article to be omitted in a series (cf. 2:20). Probably no distinction between the kingdoms is intended, with the emphasis rather being that the kingdom of Christ is in fact the kingdom of God (both now and in the future).

[6, 7] As elsewhere, the readers are warned against being **deceived** (cf. Rom. 7:11; 16:18; 1 Cor. 3:18; 2 Thess. 2:3) by **empty words** (NEB, "shallow arguments"; cf. Rom. 16:18; see comments on Col. 2:4, 8). Though it is uncertain whether those against whom the readers are warned are heretical Christians or non-Christians, it is suggested that their clever arguments may be misleading believers to think that offenses of the flesh are insignificant for the true man of the spirit, an argument perhaps based on a misunderstanding of "Christian freedom" (see vs. 9 below; cf. 1 Cor 6:12ff. and Gal. 5:13ff. where an apparently similar view is opposed). Such antinomianism is known to have been a way of misunderstanding Paul (cf. Rom. 6:1) and to have characterized later systems of Gnosticism. Readers are warned that it is precisely because of such actions that the dreaded **wrath of God** (cf. 2:2, 3; see comments on Col. 3:6) comes on man. The expression **sons of disobedience** is a Hebraism probably indicating immoral Christians and pagans (cf. 1 Cor. 5:11; 6:16ff.; 2 Cor. 6:14). Readers are urged not to share or **associate** (see 3:6) with such ones. Although **associate** may specifically refer to table fellowship (1 Cor. 10:21, 30), probably the general concerns of fellowship are intended (cf. 2 Cor. 6:14).

[8] In contrast to the view, prominent in much Hellenistic religion, that religion and morality are unrelated, Paul continues to stress the importance of the sober, moral life that should result from one's being a Christian. As elsewhere for Paul, the imperative **walk** (see comment on Col.

⁹ (for the fruit of light is found in all that is good and right and true), ¹⁰ and try to learn what is pleasing to the Lord. ¹¹ Take no part in the unfruitful works of darkness, but instead expose them. ¹² For it is a shame even to speak of the things that they do in secret; ¹³ but when anything is exposed by the light it becomes visible, for anything that becomes visible is light.

4:5) is grounded in the indicative **you are.** The readers are exhorted to become what they are (see comment on Col. 3:1; cf. Gal. 5:25). The contrast between the pagan and the Christian is frequently shown as a contrast of **darkness** and **light** (see comments on Col. 1:12, 13; cf. 1 Thess. 5:4, 5; John 3:20; James 1:17; 1 Peter 2:9). The statement suggests that **in the Lord** an essential change in the nature of the individual is brought about (Rom. 12:2; cf. 2 Cor. 5:17). Pagans were not just "in" the darkness, they **were darkness.** Likewise, **now,** in light of what God has done in Christ, Christians **are light.** Believers are part of the new age (light being a frequent eschatological symbol in the Dead Sea Scrolls and the New Testament; cf. 1 Thess. 5:5), a fact that should be visible in their behavior.

[9] Paul continues to emphasize the moral significance of the concept of the Christian as **light.** The term **fruit** may have been used by Hellenistic religions in reference to ecstatic experience (cf. Col. 1:10), actually devoid of moral implications. If this is so, Paul's remarks would be in stark contrast to such views, emphasizing that the true **fruit of light** (eschatological fruit) is to be found in the altered moral conduct, namely, **all that is good and right and true** (cf. Hosea 10:12; Gal. 5:22; John 3:19-21; 1 John 1:5-7; 2:8-11).

[10] All the Christian's actions should be governed by his relationship with the Lord. **Try to learn** (*dokimazontes;* cf. vs. 17 below) might be translated "put to the test" or "prove" (NEB, "make sure what would have the Lord's approval"; Rom. 2:18; 12:2; Phil. 1:10; cf. John 7:17). **Pleasing** (*euareston*) is frequently a sacrificial term (Rom. 12:2; Phil. 4:18; Heb. 13:16; cf. Col. 3:20), perhaps here suggesting that the believer's life is an offering to God.

[11-13] Echoing verse 7 above, Paul urges his readers

[14] Therefore it is said,
   "Awake, O sleeper, and arise from the dead,
   and Christ shall give you light."
   [15] Look carefully then how you walk, not as unwise men
but as wise, [16] making the most of the time, because the
days are evil.

---

to have no part (*sugkoinōneite*, cf. Rev. 18:4) with those
practicing the unfruitful (*akarpos*, "meaningless" or "without purpose") works of darkness (cf. Rom. 13:12). Though
this expression may refer to acts of immorality, it is also
possible that it may refer to specific iniquities practiced in
the secret gatherings of the devotees of various pagan cults
and perhaps even groups of Christians meeting in secret.
Christians are urged to expose ("bring to light") such practices. The exposure suggested is that brought about by the
penetrating redemptive effect of the Christian life which
reveals or illumines evil practices just as light silently pene-
trates the darkness. Verse 13 continues the thought, creating
some difficulty in the statement that anything that becomes
visible is light. The statement cannot mean that darkness is
light. Perhaps a more subtle suggestion is made here. The
statement may refer to the process of transformation by
which evil is exposed and recognized as evil: that which is
illumined becomes or is made light.

[14] Although Paul's expression it is said customarily
introduces Old Testament quotations (cf. 4:8), such is not
the case here. Some suppose that the quotation is taken
from the Apocrypha or from a combination of verses in
Isaiah (9:2; 26:19; 60:1; 62:1), but more likely the quotation is from an early Christian baptismal hymn which
was partially inspired by Isaiah 60:1. Not only are the words
of the hymn appropriate for the occasion of baptism, when
the candidate's ascent from the water symbolizes his being
raised with Christ (see comments on Col. 3:1ff.), but the
concept of "enlightenment" is also known to have been used
to describe Christian baptism quite early (cf. Heb. 6:4).

Summary, 5:15-20. [15, 16] These words now resume
the advice of verses 8-10, though they possibly derive their
content from verse 14. The verse shifts from the words
"darkness" and "light" to wise and unwise. Christians are

¹⁷ Therefore do not be foolish, but understand what the
will of the Lord is. ¹⁸ And do not get drunk with wine, for
that is debauchery; but be filled with the Spirit, ¹⁹ addressing one another in psalms and hymns and spiritual songs,
singing and making melody to the Lord with all your heart,

---

urged to examine their conduct (**walk**; see comment on
Col. 4:5), making sure that it is **wise** (cf. Rom. 16:19; Matt.
10:16; Jerusalem Bible, "intelligent") or that it is in harmony with the will of the Lord (see vs. 17 below). Wise
conduct is also that which is **making the most of the time**
(see comment on Col. 4:5), as Christians seek every fleeting
opportunity for good. There is urgency in the statement,
for the days are evil (cf. Gal. 1:4; Acts 2:40; 1 John
5:19).

[17] Paul now reiterates the exhortation of verse 10
above. The Christian life is one of thoughtfulness (Jerusalem Bible, "don't be thoughtless"). The word **understand**
(*suniete;* see 3:4 "insight"; cf. Col. 1:9; 2:2; Mark 12:33)
points to the fact that the Christian possesses a new mind
(4:23) with which he is enjoined to judge and determine
his proper course of conduct in any given situation.

[18] The admonition **do not get drunk with wine** (cf.
Prov. 23:31; Gal. 5:21; 1 Cor. 6:10) is not the abrupt change
of subject that it might at first appear to be. Many ancient
religions (e.g., the cult of Dionysius) used wine, dancing,
and music in wild rites designed to produce a frenzied
intoxication which was believed to facilitate escape from
the limitations of mortality, enabling communication with
deity. Readers are here informed that such efforts are
merely **debauchery** (*asōtia;* see Titus 1:6; 1 Peter 4:4; Jerusalem Bible, "debasement") and are not the way to discern the true will of God (vs. 17 above). As elsewhere (see
vs. 9 above), Paul is concerned to emphasize that the Spirit-
filled life is given a definite structure and shape.

[19] **Psalms and hymns and spiritual songs** (see comment on Col. 3:16) stresses the manner in which the Christian gatherings should display their exuberance in the Spirit.
Although there is evidence that by A.D. 110 the church
probably engaged in responsive hymn singing or alternate

²⁰ always and for everything giving thanks in the name of our Lord Jesus Christ to God the Father.

²¹ Be subject to one another out of reverence for Christ.

---

chanting (Pliny's Letter to Trajan, A.D. 110), it is difficult to derive a reference of this practice from the expression **addressing one another**. More probably the meaning is simply that of mutual edification (see 4:12, 16, 29). **Making melody with all your heart** (NEB, Jerusalem Bible, "making music") stresses the total involvement of the Christian in the thanksgiving offered through worship (cf. 1 Cor. 14:15; James 5:13). Paul's language may be influenced by Psalm 33:2, 3.

[20] The context is now broadened beyond that of the corporate worship, indicating that the continual attitude of the Christian is one of thanksgiving to God (cf. Col. 3:16, 17; 4:2; 1 Thess. 5:18). **In the name of our Lord** indicates the one in whom the believer has redemption and through whom he addresses God (Eph. 3:12; see comments on Col. 3:17). It should be noted that the role of God as Father is a matter of particular emphasis. Paul uses this mode of address several times in the letter (e.g., 1:2, 3, 17; 2:18; 6:23).

Christian Household Ethics, 5:21—6:9

The familar table of household instruction (see comments on Col. 3:18f.; cf. 1 Peter 2:18—3:7) is now employed not only to communicate ethical instruction but also as a vehicle further to stress the central significance of the mystery of Christ and the church (vs. 32).

Husbands and Wives, 5:21-33. [21] Some translators take these words as the conclusion of the preceding statement (KJV) while others set them apart as a bridge between verses 20 and 22ff. (NEB makes a separate paragraph out of the verse.) It is probably best to take the statement as opening the following ethical exhortations regarding the Christian household. **Be subject** (see comment on Col. 3:18) **to one another** expresses the general rule of Christian society, that of liability and concern for one's fellows. Underlying the exhortation is the principle of harmony that should be manifest in the church, the instrument of God's reconciliation (see comments on Eph. 2:16; 3:6; 4:3ff., 16).

²² Wives, be subject to your husbands, as to the Lord. ²³ For
the husband is the head of the wife as Christ is the head of
the church, his body, and is himself its Savior. ²⁴ As the

Reverence (literally "fear") **for Christ** points the readers
to the example of Jesus, a common basis for Christian ethical exhortation (see vs. 25 below; cf. John 13:4; Phil. 2:5;
1 Peter 2:21f.).

[22] The concept of submission is focused more specifically on the wife-husband relationship (the verb is actually
supplied by the previous verse; cf. Col. 3:18). The appeal
is possibly grounded in a view of the natural order which
is to be preserved (cf. 1 Cor. 7:17; 11:3; 14:34; Gal. 3:28).
There is no indication that women are inferior; rather, they
have a divinely ordained place in the structure of society
which should be preserved. **As to the Lord** points to the
Lord's sanction of the wife's submission to her husband;
the meaning is not that the wife should show her husband
the same degree of submission shown to Christ (cf. 1 Cor.
7:12ff.; 1 Peter 3:1, 2).

[23] As is often the case (cf. Isa. 54:4, 5; 61:10; 62:4, 5;
Jer. 3:20; Hos. 2; Mark 2:19f.), the marriage relationship
is symbolic of a theological truth—here the relationship between Christ and the church (cf. 2 Cor. 11:2, 3). The prevailing concern of the letter, that of the church in relation to
Christ, comes to control even the treatment of household
duties, so that the Christ-church relationship is the standard
for the husband-wife relationship. That he is the **head of the
church** (see 1:22; cf. comments on Col. 1:18; 2:19) emphasizes not only the authority but also the closeness between
Christ and the church, comparable to the ideal relationship
between man and wife. **Savior** (*sōtēr;* cf. Phil. 3:20; John
4:42; Luke 2:11) may be taken as continuing the analogy,
hence better rendered as "preserver." Or it may be a departure from the analogy, stressing the differences.

[24] Continuing the analogy, Paul indicates that the
wife should **be subject to the husband as the church is to
Christ.** As the will of the church is at one with that of
Christ, its Savior (vs. 23), the will of the wife should coin-
cide with that of her husband.

church is subject to Christ, so let wives also be subject in everything to their husband. [25] Husbands, love your wives, as Christ loved the church and gave himself up for her, [26] that he might sanctify her, having cleansed her by the washing of water with the word, [27] that he might present the church to himself in splendor, without spot or wrinkle or any such thing, that she might be holy and without blemish.

---

[25] Now attention is shifted to the husband. As in Colossians (see comment on Col. 3:19f.; 1 Peter 3:7), Paul stresses the fact that the husband has duties as well as rights. Again, the analogy of the relationship between Christ and the church is used, perhaps not so much to express an argument about the role of the husband as to introduce another emphasis on the vital relationship between the church and Christ. Thus, it may be argued that Paul here stresses two points. First, the husband has an obligation to self-giving love which is modeled after the example of Christ. Second, the apostle is equally concerned to remind readers of the loving act of the cross, in which God's love (see 1:5; 2:4; Rom. 5:8) is fully manifest.

[26, 27] It is this second point that is continued now, momentarily interrupting the ethical instruction to the husband. Now the goal of Christ's sacrificial love is contemplated. Sanctify indicates the actual bestowing of holiness on the church; cleansed is in the aorist tense, here indicating the specific act of baptism rather than the continual growth of the Christian. Washing (*loutron*) is literally "bath" (cf. Titus 3:5), so baptism is further likened to the ceremonial bath of the bride prior to the wedding ceremony. Reference to the word (*rhēma*) may indicate a caution against separating the rite from its purpose (cf. 1 Peter 3:21) and has been taken variously as the gospel preached prior to baptism (cf. Rom. 10:17; 1 Peter 1:23-25), the pronounced formula over the one baptized (cf. Matt. 28:19), the confession of the one baptized (see Col. 3:17; cf. 1 Cor. 1:2; Rom. 10:9), or God's word of promise attached to baptism (1 Peter 1:25). One of the latter two is to be preferred, for they could correspond to the vows and so fit the marriage imagery. Additionally, it should be noted

²⁸ Even so husbands should love their wives as their own bodies. He who loves his wife loves himself. ²⁹ For no man ever hates his own flesh, but nourishes and cherishes it, as Christ does the church, ³⁰ because we are members of his body.

---

that the symbolism here represents the corporate church rather than the individual Christian as being baptized, an emphasis in keeping with the entire letter's concern for the whole church (cf. 1 Cor. 6:11; Heb. 10:22).

That he might present the church is one of the few statements in the letter looking forward to the ultimate glorification of the church (cf. 4:30). The imagery here pictures Christ as both presenting the bride and receiving her, anticipating the reception of the bride by the bridegroom (cf. Rev. 19:7, 8). Christ is the sole source of the church's glory and moral perfection. Though the term **present** (*paristēmi;* see Col. 1:22) is often a sacrificial term (e.g., 1 Cor. 8:7), the term may not have that meaning here (cf. 2 Cor. 11:2). Likewise, the terms **holy and without blemish** call to mind sacrificial language (cf. Ex. 12:5; Col. 1:22). Here, however, the emphasis is on the separateness of the church from the world and the characteristics which Christ is able to achieve for his bride, clothing her in divine **splendor** (or "glory"; see comment on Col. 1:11).

[28-30] The discussion now briefly shifts to the husband's responsibility to love his wife before returning to the relationship of Christ to the church. At first impression, the argument seems to be an appeal to self-love; loving the wife, the husband **loves himself.** Yet the argument is probably intended to stress further the close union between Christ and the church he loves **because we are members of his body** (cf. 1:23; 4:4, 11-16). The expression **his own flesh** draws on Old Testament concepts, anticipating the quotation in the following verses (Gen. 2:23, 24) and at the same time emphasizing the closeness between husband and wife and the closeness between Christ and the church. The husband **nourishes** (cf. 6:4) **and cherishes** (*thalpei,* literally, "keeps warm"; cf. 1 Thess. 2:7) the wife as Christ sustains the church, his body.

[31] "For this reason a man shall leave his father and mother and be joined to his wife, and the two shall become one." [32] This is a great mystery, and I take it to mean Christ and the church; [33] however, let each one of you love his wife as himself, and let the wife see that she respects her husband.

[1] Children, obey your parents in the Lord, for this is right. [2] "Honor your father and mother" (this is the first commandment with a promise), [3] "that it may be well with you and that you may live long on the earth."

---

[31] Paul now introduces a quotation from Genesis, one used by Jesus to stress the permanence of marriage (see Mark 10:6ff.), arguing that the marriage relationship was from the first a type of foreshadowing of the relationship of Christ and the church.

[32] The expression **this is a great mystery** should probably be read "this mystery is great" (Jerusalem Bible). Mystery (*mustērion;* see 1:9; 3:3, 4, 9; 6:19; and comments on Col. 1:26) indicates something once hidden but now divinely revealed. Precisely what is intended to be described as a mystery is uncertain. It could refer to a deeper allegorical meaning of the scripture.

[33] **However,** that is, aside from such considerations about the "mystery," the practical implications of the preceding quotations are urged on each individual reader (**each one of you**), shifting attention back to wives as well as husbands. Wives are now urged to have **respect** (literally "fear" or "reverence" as in vs. 21 above; cf. 1 Peter 3:6) for their husbands' ordained authority, which is symbolic of the authority of Christ in the church.

Fathers and Children, 6:1-4. [1-3] Attention now moves from the husband-wife relationship to that between parents and children (see comments on Col. 3:20, 21). The admonition for children to **obey your parents** is grounded in the fact that this relationship, like that of husbands and wives, is also ordained by God (**for this is right**). For Paul, disobedience to parents is one of several signs of alienation from God and the consequent fragmentation of society (cf. Rom. 1:30; 2 Tim. 3:2). **In the Lord** (see comments on

⁴ Fathers, do not provoke your children to anger, but bring them up in the discipline and instruction of the Lord.

Col. 3:18) indicates the manner, not the limits of Christian obedience to parents. The instruction here is not that Christian children are to obey only Christian parents nor even that children are to obey their parents only insofar as parental wishes are commensurate with Christian action. The writer is here addressing families assumed to be Christian, showing that parental obedience, ordained by God, is heightened rather than weakened by one's relationship to Christ. Nonetheless, the injunction is reinforced with Old Testament quotations (cf. Ex. 20:12; Deut. 5:16) familiar to Jewish readers, promising longevity and well-being to those who comply with the divine will.

[4] Fathers, or parents (the plural *pateres* may better be rendered "parents" as in the Jerusalem Bible), have duties as well as rights (cf. comments on Col. 3:18, 21). Parents have a responsibility to aid the growth and development of their children. But parental authority is to be exercised with care not to create resentment on the part of the child. Extending the warning, Paul tells parents to bring children up **in the discipline and instruction of the Lord.** It is uncertain whether the phrase primarily refers to the manner of parental instruction or more precisely has in mind religious instruction given in the home after the fashion of the Jews.

Masters and Slaves, 6:5-9. Attention is now given to another vital relationship for believers of the first century, that of slaves and masters (see comment on parallel verses in Col. 3:22—4:1 and Introduction to Philemon; cf. 1 Tim. 6:1f.; Titus 2:9f.; 1 Peter 2:18). Such sections of instruction in New Testament letters may indicate that a significant number of Christians in the first century were slaves. Further, there may have been strong tendencies for slaves to misunderstand the "gospel of freedom" (Gal. 5:1) as a sanction for rebellious tendencies or at least as a lessening of their obligations to their masters (1 Cor. 7:22), especially those who were Christians (1 Tim. 6:2).

⁵ Slaves, be obedient to those who are your earthly masters, with fear and trembling, in singleness of heart, as to Christ; ⁶ not in the way of eyeservice, as men-pleasers, but as servants ᶠ of Christ, doing the will of God from the heart, ⁷ rendering service with a good will as to the Lord and not to men, ⁸ knowing that whatever good any one does, he will receive the same again from the Lord, whether he is a slave or free.

ᶠ Or *slaves*

[5, 6] Slaves are urged to **be obedient** to their masters. The term **earthly** sets the limits to the master's authority, indicating that superior social status has no special significance. The term should not be understood to contrast with Christ in the sense that he is not also master on earth. **Fear and trembling** is not meant to indicate either the harshness of service or future punishment by Christ. It rather indicates an anxiousness to do right in the master's service (cf. 1 Cor. 2:3; 2 Cor. 7:15; Phil. 2:12). **Singleness of heart** ("without divided loyalties," cf. Col. 3:22; Rom. 12:8) is elaborated by **as to Christ**. Slaves are not to compartmentalize their activities into "religious" and "secular" spheres; they are urged to serve their masters with the fidelity with which they serve Christ. The service they render to their masters is not merely "as if" it were to Christ but is actually their Christian vocation. Thus the slave finds his role in society elevated to a new level as it is given purpose and dignity in the apostolic phrase "slave of Christ" (Rom. 1:1; 1 Cor. 7:22; Phil. 1:1; Titus 1:1; Gal. 1:10). Fidelity to the earthly master actually constitutes **doing the will of God** and should not be performed with superficiality or with ulterior motives (see Col. 3:22 on **eyeservice** and **men-pleasers**). The phrase **from the heart** further punctuates this point.

[7, 8] The slave's attitude is further defined: **good will** probably indicating readiness or willingness to perform daily tasks (NEB, "cheerful service"). Such a stance by the slave is grounded in performing his efforts **as to the Lord and not to men**. The idea here developed is that the slave should neither seek recognition from the master nor be

⁹ Masters, do the same to them, and forbear threatening, knowing that he who is both their Master and yours is in heaven, and that there is no partiality with him.

¹⁰ Finally, be strong in the Lord and in the strength of his might.

---

discouraged by a callous or ungrateful master. Thus worthy service, though seemingly unrecognized, is not in vain. The attitude of the slave is ultimately to be based on the conviction that his proper recognition and recompense (see Col. 3:25; 2 Cor. 5:10; Matt. 5:12; 25:21, 23) will be received from the Lord. The same suggests that the slave will receive the "equivalent in return."

[9] Now, contrary to prevailing law and custom, **masters** ("employers" in the Jerusalem Bible), like parents, are said to have obligations as well as rights. They are urged to show consideration for their slaves in line with the fidelity previously enjoined on the slaves. Specifically, masters are warned against **threatening** (*apeilēn;* cf. Acts 4:17, 29; 9:1; 1 Peter 2:23) their slaves; but the motivation is more significant than the command itself. Masters also have a **Master;** furthermore, slaves and masters have the same Master in heaven, one who is impartial (see comment on Col. 4:1).

The Armor of Christian Warfare, 6:10-17

Now the Christian life is portrayed in terms suggestive of a great cosmic struggle. The imagery is that of Jewish eschatological thought, frequently employed in descriptions of the final conflict between the forces of good and evil (cf. 1 Thess. 5:4, 5, 8; 2 Thess. 1:6-9; 2:3-12; 1 Tim. 6:12; 2 Tim. 2:3; Rom. 13:12; Rev. 2:10, 16; 12:7ff.) and often using symbols of light and darkness (see 5:8f.; 1 Thess. 5:4ff.). The picture is that of Roman legionaries readying for martial combat.

[10] The overall point here is that Christians are to depend not upon themselves but on the power of God (see comments on 1:19; 3:16, 18, 20; cf. 2 Cor. 6:7; 10:4; Phil. 4:13; 2 Tim. 2:1), the power seen in the death and resurrection of Christ (1:19, 20; 2:6). **Be strong** (cf. 3:16) is passive, probably better rendered "be made strong" (cf.

[11] Put on the whole armor of God, that you may be able to stand against the wiles of the devil. [12] For we are not contending against flesh and blood, but against the principalities, against the powers, against the world rulers of this present darkness, against the spiritual hosts of wickedness in the heavenly places. [13] Therefore take the whole armor of God, that you may be able to withstand in the evil day, and having done all, to stand.

Rom. 4:20). In the Lord refers to the readers' incorporation into the church, the body of Christ, infused and sustained by his power (see 1:21, 22; 2:10, 15, 21, 22; 4:15, 16; see comment on Col. 1:15f.).

[11, 12] The thought of the previous verse is further elaborated, emphasizing both the divine nature of the Christian's weaponry (2 Cor. 10:4) and the threatening power of the opposition. The whole armor of God possibly suggests that the believer, having put on Christ, is armed with the armor of God (not merely armed by God), and picks up the Old Testament imagery of God as a warrior (cf. Isa. 42:13; 59:17; Ps. 7:12; 35:1ff.). Such armor is necessary to oppose the wiles (*methodeias*, "strategems, tactics, devices"; see 4:14; cf. Gen. 3:1; 2 Cor. 2:11; 1 Peter 2:11; 5:8) of the devil (*diabolos;* elsewhere in Paul only in 4:27 and the Pastoral Letters), identifying the nature of the conflict as essentially religious and moral. The term world rulers (*kosmokratoras*) is a rare word appearing neither in the Septuagint, Philo, nor anywhere else in the New Testament. Along with principalities and powers (see comments on Col. 1:16; 2:15) the word should be taken as an astrological term designating spiritual forces. The Christian fights against not human foes but spiritual hosts of wickedness in the heavenly places (cf. 1:3, 10, 20; 2:6; 3:10; 4:10).

[13] Again Paul urges his readers to be armed with the armor of God (vs. 11), here introducing the description of that armor. The evil day at first sight suggests the future day of judgment (e.g., 1 Thess. 1:10; 5:2; Heb. 12:26; Rev. 16:12-16; 20:7ff.); however, it probably refers to the present age (see 5:16; NEB, "when things are at their worst"; cf.

¹⁴ Stand therefore, having girded your loins with truth, and having put on the breastplate of righteousness, ¹⁵ and having shod your feet with the equipment of the gospel of peace; ¹⁶ above all taking the shield of faith, with which you can quench all the flaming darts of the evil one.

Jerusalem Bible). **Withstand** (*antistēnai,* "resist" or "oppose"; cf. James 4:7; Gal. 2:11) and **stand** (Ps. 36:12; Rev. 6:17) are both terms used with military overtones, encouraging readers to hold position or ground as in battle. **Having done all** (*katergasamenoi*) indicates the accomplishment of a difficult task. Here it probably describes more than preparation for battle, indicating the readers' proper discharge of duty in the periodic conflicts brought by this **evil day.**

[14] In specifically describing the Christian weaponry, Paul is probably dependent on the imagery of such Old Testament passages as Isaiah 11:5 and 59:17. The metaphor should not be pressed into allegory. Each item of equipment is the objective quality supplied by God. **Truth** is the belt, and **righteousness** is the **breastplate,** and so forth. **Truth** (*alētheia*) probably indicates the attitude of faithfulness (as in Isa. 11:5) rather than the specific content of Christian revelation. **Righteousness** (*dikaiosunē;* NEB, "integrity") may be understood as referring to the righteousness of Christ, now the Christian's own armor (Phil. 3:9, 10). The idea, however, involves the individual's participation in this righteousness and, consequently, his own personal conduct (see 4:24; 5:9; cf. Phil. 1:11).

[15, 16] Paradoxically, the Christian warrior stands for combat shod with the gospel of peace (cf. Rom. 10:15; Isa. 52:7), the eschatological peace (see comments on 1:2; 2:14, 15, 17; cf. John 16:33) which is now actualized in the church and will eventually embrace all the universe (see 1:10; Col. 1:20). The Christian warrior stands protected against the **flaming darts** of temptations (literally "burning arrows," a technical military term), launched by the attacking **evil one** (see 6:11; 2:2), by his trust and confidence in God, or alternatively the Christian faith itself.

¹⁷ And take the helmet of salvation, and the sword of the
Spirit, which is the word of God. ¹⁸ Pray at all times in the
Spirit, with all prayer and supplication. To that end keep
alert with all perseverance, making supplication for all
the saints,

---

[17] **Take** (*dexasthe*) may be translated "receive" or
"accept" (Jerusalem Bible), as the helmet and sword were
given to the armed combatant by an aide. Appropriately,
both **salvation** and **the word of God** are also given the
Christian. **Helmet of salvation** (Isa. 59:17; 1 Thess. 5:8)
emphasizes salvation as a source of safety, a symbol of
protection rather than a totally future goal. **The word of
God** represented as a **sword** is a concept of Judaism (cf.
Isa. 11:4; Hos. 6:5) found elsewhere in the New Testament
(cf. 2 Thess. 2:8; Heb. 4:12; Rev. 1:16; 19:13, 15). The
expression **word of God** (*rhēma theou*) is never used regarding scripture in the New Testament and may here
indicate the Spirit's guidance of the combatant's speech in
special times of crisis or temptation (see Matt. 4:1-10;
10:19f.; 1 Cor. 12:3; Acts 1:8; John 16:23; 17:8; see comments on Col. 4:5, 6). More probably, the word intended
is the gospel, God's redemptive plan now revealed in
Christ's life, death, and resurrection (see 1:13; 3:7f.; Col.
1:5f.; cf. Rom. 10:17).

Concluding Remarks, 6:18-24

Prayer Requests, 6:18-20. [18] **Prayer** is a vital part
of the Christian's armor, indicating his continual dependence on God's power (vs. 11) and the guidance of the Holy
Spirit. **In the Spirit,** although actually lacking the article
in Greek, should probably be taken as a reference to the
Holy Spirit (see 2:22 and cf. Jude 20). The exhortation to
prayer, alertness, and **perseverance** (*proskarterēsei*, "to hold
fast" or "to be persistent"; cf. Mark 3:9; Acts 2:42) calls to
mind Jesus' words to his disciples in Gethsemane: "watch
and pray" (Mark 13:33; 14:38; 1 Cor. 16:13; cf. Col. 4:2).
Obviously, the terms are also appropriate for the military
metaphor. **Supplication** (*deēsis;* literally "request" as in
Acts 21:39 but in the New Testament also designating

[19] and also for me, that utterance may be given me in opening my mouth boldly to proclaim the mystery of the gospel, [20] for which I am an ambassador in chains; that I may declare it boldly, as I ought to speak.

[21] Now that you also may know how I am and what I am doing, Tychicus the beloved brother and faithful minister in the Lord will tell you everything. [22] I have sent him to you for this very purpose, that you may know how we are, and that he may encourage your hearts.

---

specific prayers of a given situation; e.g., Rom. 1:10; 1 Thess. 3:10) here emphasizes the fact that the Christian does not stand alone but, by the Spirit, is united with the corporate body of Christ (see 2:22), making supplication for all the saints (cf. Phile. 25).

[19, 20] As is frequently his custom, Paul asks for a place in the readers' prayers for the saints (see comment on Col. 4:3; cf. Rom. 15:30; Phil. 1:19; 2 Cor. 1:11). More specifically, he desires that in his imprisonment he may have the wisdom and necessary guidance to speak the mystery of the gospel in an effective manner. The word boldly (*parrēsia;* see 3:12; cf. 2 Cor. 3:12; 1 Tim. 3:13; Phil. 1:20; "confidence") is elsewhere used to describe the manner of Christian preaching and is particularly apt in the apostle's situation where freedom may have been obtainable on the condition that he cease to preach (see Acts 4:29-31). He identifies himself as an ambassador (*presbeuō;* see comments on Phile. 9; 2 Cor. 5:20) in chains, referring to his paradoxical situation as the representative of Christ, incarcerated in a Roman prison. Again, the expression as I ought to speak indicates his desire for strength to speak in a manner commensurate with his apostolic office and his role as special ambassador for Christ.

Commendation and Benediction, 6:21-24. [21, 22] Closely paralleling Colossians 4:7, 8 (on which see comments), Paul now commends the letter's bearer, **Tychicus.** **Brother** (see comment on Phile. 16; Col. 4:7) and **minister** (*diakonos;* NEB, "helper"; see comment on Col. 1:7, 8) are not indicative of special offices. The terms are intended to convey Paul's trust and esteem for Tychicus and to secure a favorable reception for him. **How we are** broadens the news

²³ Peace be to the brethren, and love with faith, from God the Father and the Lord Jesus Christ. ²⁴ Grace be with all who love our Lord Jesus Christ with love undying.

---

to include Paul's associates who were engaging in an extensive mission under the apostle's direction.

[23, 24] The benediction is unusual for Paul in that it is in the third person. This fact, together with the lack of specific names of the apostle's many friends in Ephesus (cf. Rom. 16) may be taken as indicative of the encyclical intent of the letter rather than non-Pauline authorship. **Peace** is one of the main concepts of the letter and is substituted for hope in the customary triad of faith, hope and love. The peace referred to here is that between Jew and Gentile (see 2:14-18; 4:3; 6:15; cf. Col. 1:20; 3:14, 15) actualized in the church and anticipatory of the eventual cosmic redemption and reunification of all things (cf. 1:10). **Love** and **faith** are gifts of God which characterize the new community created in the body of Christ. The apostle requests **grace** (see 1:2) for the church. **Undying** (*aphtharsia*) is used by Hellenistic writers to designate that which resists decay, hence "incorruptible," "immortal" (cf. Rom. 2:7) or "imperishable" (1 Cor. 15:42). Thus the word may be taken with the entire statement (NEB and Jerusalem Bible) as a wish for immortality rather than as a modifier for **love.**